POPULATION AND DEVELOPMENT PLANNING

Edited by Warren C. Robinson

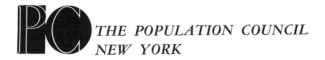

THE POPULATION COUNCIL
NEW YORK

The Population Council
245 Park Avenue
New York, New York 10017

The Population Council is an organization established
in 1952 for scientific training and study in the field
of population. It endeavors to advance knowledge in
the broad field of population by fostering research,
training, and technical consultation and assistance in
the social and biomedical sciences.

The Council acknowledges, with thanks, the funds
received from the Agency for International Development,
the Ford Foundation, the United Nations Fund for Population
Activities, the World Bank, and other donors
for the publication program of the Population Council.

Funds for this project have been provided
by the Robert Sterling Clark Foundation.

Library of Congress Cataloging in Publication Data

Robinson, Warren C
    Population and development planning.

    Includes bibliographical references and index.
    1. Demography—Addresses, essays, lectures.
2. Population policy—Addresses, essays, lectures.
3. Economic development—Addresses, essays, lectures.
I. Population Council, New York. II. Title.
HB855.R566   1975   301.32   74-84573
ISBN 0-87834-024-6

Contents

Preface

In the summer of 1971, the President of the Population Council, Bernard Berelson, remarked that development planners, even very sophisticated ones, seemed largely ignorant still on the topic of population. He wondered whether something might be done about this by publication of a "manual" on population and development under sponsorship of the Population Council. This idea was explored by a group of interested economists and demographers at a two-day meeting held at the Council in November 1971. The meeting endorsed the idea of a volume of essays, each to explore one facet of demographic-economic interrelations, particularly as they affect the planning process. A tentative outline was prepared, and the present writer was given the task of identifying authors and coordinating the various individual efforts. Since all the prospective authors were (and are) exceedingly busy people, further meetings would have been difficult, and frequent consultations by mail and telephone were substituted. Most of the authors were able, however, to confer around a single table at the 1972 meeting of the Population Association of America in Montreal. All the essays have been read by the entire group as well as many other reviewers. All have gone through revision and rewriting.

As the essays have developed, they do not in fact constitute a "manual" if that term is understood to imply a "how-to-do-it" approach. For most of the areas and topics covered, too little is known about the real nature of the demographic-economic inter-connections for us to be able to spell out precisely how the population variable should be treated in development planning. Instead, most of the essays summarize the present state of knowledge, leaning heavily in some instances on particular case studies or examples, and suggest approaches and a general set of probable interrelations to be explored in any given planning situation.

The essays differ in level of sophistication and degree of detail. This is, in large measure, simply because we know more about some areas than others. Some of the authors had to break new ground, while others had to summarize briefly a vast amount of material. Planners who are used to working with what is available will, we feel, be a sympathetic audience.

All in all, we hope these essays will be informative and useful to economic planners and other officials in the developing world. We trust that, by revealing the inadequacies of our present knowledge, they will also stimulate scholars to begin more definitive research work on these topics.

The many persons who assisted in this project include: Lee L. Bean, Philippe de Bourcier-Carbon, Lester R. Brown, Thomas Burch, Ta Ngoc Châu, Paul Demeny, John Durand, Richard Easterlin, Edgar O. Edwards, Sultan S. Hashmi, Carl Hemmer, John Herzog, John F. Kantner, James E. Kocher, Shigemi Kono, Harvey Leibenstein, W. Parker Mauldin, Jacob Mincer, James N. Morgan, Dorothy Nortman, Goran Ohlin, Harry Oshima, Lyle Saunders, Theodore W. Schultz, David L. Sills, Vincent H. Whitney, and Joe D. Wray.

Warren C. Robinson

Bangkok, Thailand
December 1974

The Authors

ROBERTO CUCA is an economist and demographer in the Population and Human Resources Division, International Bank for Reconstruction and Development, Washington, D. C.

PIERRE R. CROSSON is director of the Latin American Program at Resources for the Future, Washington, D. C.

GHAZI M. FAROOQ is a Population Council advisor and senior visiting research fellow at the Institute of Population and Manpower Studies, University of Ife, Ile-Ife, Nigeria.

TOMAS FREJKA is a staff associate in the Demographic Division of the Population Council, New York.

EDWARD K. HAWKINS is a fellow at the Center for International Affairs, Harvard University, where he is on leave from his position as senior advisor in the Development Economics Department, International Bank for Reconstruction and Development, Washington, D. C.

GAVIN W. JONES is a Population Council advisor on assignment at the Demographic Institute of the University of Indonesia, Jakarta.

BENJAMIN N. MOK is senior statistician in the Census and Statistics Department, Government of Hong Kong.

RONALD G. RIDKER is program director of population studies at Resources for the Future, Washington, D. C.

WARREN C. ROBINSON is a Population Council advisor on assignment with the Manpower Planning Division of the National Economic and Social Development Board, Bangkok, Thailand.

ISMAIL A. SIRAGELDIN is associate professor of population dynamics and political economy at Johns Hopkins University, Baltimore, Maryland.

Introduction

Although "development planning" is a widely-used term, no precise definition of it exists. Nearly all textbooks and country case studies make attempts, and we do not propose to add to this confusion. Instead, we will content ourselves with making one or two general observations that will help us to relate development planning to population and population planning.

Development planning can be viewed as a special subset of economic planning in general, different from but overlapping with such other subsets as counter-cyclical planning, regional planning, and manpower planning. Most definitions of "development" stress that it means increasing the rate of economic growth over what it otherwise would have been. Other objectives could be added, including structural change in the economic and social institutions, and perhaps changes in the distribution of income. The distinction between economic growth and economic development is a useful one, but it is also possible for "development" to mean planning for growth—that is, a scalar increase in output with composition and distribution remaining the same and with no effort at institutional change. By the same token, development that stresses institutional reform and structural change might not lead to increase in overall output or income for some time to come.

This difference in objective and emphasis is not always clearly stated, but it clearly influences one's judgment of the success or failure of a planning effort. Pakistan's planning effort in the 1960s promoted increases in output and was on this score judged successful; however, it did not promote structural change and thus, it could be argued, did not constitute real economic development. Alternatively, it might be argued that Burma and Cuba have been successful in achieving structural change, although no startling increases have occurred in their overall indexes of economic activity.

In any event, development planning is essentially an effort to focus on the key problems, both structural and dynamic, facing a country and to mobilize resources—public and private, domestic and foreign—to deal with these problems. The solutions proceed via policies and plans but, in the end, through projects and programs. Thus, a development plan assigns a priority to, let us say, transport and communications; draws up programs and projects to meet the chosen goal; accumulates resources to finance the projects; and then sees the projects undertaken and completed. Overall planning is the road-map to development, but specific projects and programs are the paved roads leading there.

The concepts of "population policy" and "population planning" are new. Traditionally, immigration has been the only major demographic process over which policy was consciously debated and fixed. Immigration remains an important process in some areas but, as the essays in this book point out, other demographic processes are now more dominant.

By some, "population policy" is understood to mean an organized effort by government to affect population size, growth, distribution, or structure. This may be called a "narrow" definition in that it includes only those actions taken with conscious demographic intent. Others believe a broader definition is more appropriate because the narrower definition ignores the fact that government actions taken for nondemographic reasons may have major demographic consequences. The broader definition, then, would include all government policies and actions that affect, either directly or indirectly, demographic processes. Although the broader definition runs the danger of being all-inclusive to the point of meaninglessness, it has the virtue of making policy-makers aware of the need to consider the demographic consequences of all decisions.[1]

By the end of 1973, 33 developing countries had an official policy to reduce the population growth or birth rate and supported family planning for economic reasons, as well as on health and humanitarian grounds. An additional 30 developing countries support family planning for nondemographic reasons. As of 1973, 44 developing countries had national family planning programs.[2] Yet, when one examines their economic development plans, a curious fact emerges very clearly: a disjuncture exists between economic planning and population planning. Population policy is most often seen in its narrowest sense, as fertility reduction, and population planning consists of little more than a family planning program. The typical development plan notes somewhere in the introductory chapter the deleterious effect of excessive population growth on economic goals and perhaps in the chapter on health and social welfare presents details of the family planning program. Most often, consideration of the demographic processes are missing from all other chapters or sections. In short, population planning is not an integral part of socioeconomic planning.

In a study of 70 national development plans, almost all of which cover a five-year period between 1965 and 1972, Stamper found only 27 that recognized population problems[1] in their development plans.[3] The following table lists the eleven general types of problems that were recognized in the order of the frequency with which they were mentioned:

Type of population problem mentioned	Total number of countries (of 70 studied)
Economic growth reduced by population growth	19
High rate of population growth (in and of itself)	18
Unemployment	18
Increasing school-age population	16
High dependency ratio	16
Population pressure on health services	15
Population pressure on social services	12
Population pressure on housing	12
Population pressure on agricultural system	5
Decrease in individual standard of living	4
Population density	3

SOURCE: Maxwell Stamper, "Population policy in development planning," *Reports on Population/Family Planning*, no. 13 (May 1973): 5.

It is clear that very few countries considered in their development planning the effect of demographic trends on even relatively short-term needs and demands in the different sectors. In addition, in his systematic analysis of these 70 development plans, Stamper found that:

> Most countries used very little demographic data in their plans. Estimates and projections of population sizes, rates of growth, and levels and trends of fertility and mortality were not mentioned by many countries. Most countries did not plan for the consequences of short-term population growth in their development plans. With regard to governmental services, most plans focused on current needs and shortages without looking at projected future needs, and they often did not view the demographic components of these shortages as partial causes. Of particular importance was the absence of short-range projections for the labor-force and school-age populations.[4]

Although no one is to be blamed for this situation, it is lamentable for it results in a fragmented attack on the basic problems of development. For

[1] A "population problem" is defined in this study as a current or future situation viewed by planners as a "problem" and whose cause is recognized as having some major demographic component. Although migration is a particularly important demographic factor in developing countries, it was excluded from this study because of the difficulty in searching the large volume of material.

example, if fertility levels are to be reduced, efforts must include socioeconomic techniques and approaches as well as clinical ones:

> Proposed strategies include improvement in literacy and the status of women; rural development; access to social and occupational mobility; redistribution of income to increase the possibility of achieving the consumption patterns of the next higher social class; imposition of the social costs of high fertility on those responsible; and adoption of population education and family planning programs.[5]

If development planning is to be successful, it must be based on both current demographic trends and future projections, and it must recognize the interactions between demographic processes and socioeconomic factors as they affect all sectors of the society and the economy.

The present volume is an effort to articulate these population-development planning interrelationships for specific planning sectors. Chapter One presents a brief review of approaches to development planning, the treatment of population in these approaches, and the interaction between economic and demographic factors at the aggregate macroeconomic level of analysis.

Chapter Two gives the reader a general overview of the dynamics of population change now at work in the developing world and a picture of likely future trends. One conclusion is unavoidable: by the year 2000 nearly all the countries of Asia, Africa, and Latin America will have populations double their present size. Even under the most optimistic assumption regarding fertility decline, zero growth or a stabilized population is further away yet. In their development planning, governments clearly will have to grapple for some time to come with the social, political, and economic consequences of this growth.

Labor force growth will follow a similar pattern, as Chapter Three points out. Because labor force size is a function of population size and age-sex structure, the growth rate will continue to be considerable for some time to come. But, because labor force size is also a function of age-sex-specific activity rates, and these may change as jobs become more or less readily available, there are shorter-run feedbacks from employment policy that can, in time, affect the underlying demographic trends. In addition, the nature of employment—factory, farm, cottage-industry, and so on—seems to have an impact on or at least an association with fertility. Here again, economic policy may have an impact on demographic trends.

In Chapter Four, we address ourselves to the relationship between educational needs and population trends. Clearly, the more children to be educated, the larger the budget required to finance additional materials, facilities, teachers, and teacher-training institutions. If the goal is also to increase the quality of education or the proportion of eligible children attending school, education's share of the gross national product and the government budget may prove to be an impossible burden. An understanding of future population trends is clearly essential for intelligent educational planning. Similarly, educational planning decisions and programs may have demographic implications. Population education—the inclusion of population content in the curriculum—is a deliberate effort in this direction, but there are more indirect, less well understood influences, too. These include the nature of the revenue-raising system to support schools, the location of the schools, and the concept of women's roles in society as they are either implicitly or explicitly reinforced by the educational system. All of these factors can be part of an educational policy aimed at affecting population size, growth, and distribution.

Housing needs, in terms of both numbers and sizes of dwellings, are also affected by demographic processes and trends. Changes in population size, age-sex structure, marriage patterns, fertility and mortality rates, family type and structure, and migration patterns all have impacts on housing needs and demands. In turn, housing conditions themselves—availability, location, rents, density, and type—also can affect demographic factors such as the decision to move, the timing of marriage, spacing and number of births, and family type. Chapter Five includes case studies of Singapore and Hong Kong to illustrate how two governments have met the demand for large numbers of low-cost, low-rent dwellings.

Increasingly, it is felt that a well-designed, comprehensive health program should include family planning services, both in an attempt to lower fertility and to reduce maternal and infant morbidity and mortality resulting from excessive childbearing and closely spaced births. Using case studies from Thailand and Sri Lanka, Chapter Six presents a model for projecting future health care needs and costs that demonstrates the savings to health care of declining fertility. The implication of these two case studies is that a large-scale family planning program would need to have only a relatively small independent effect on fertility rates to lead to savings in health costs that would exceed the cost of the program itself. The chapter also points out the importance of distinguishing between urban and rural areas in formulating goals for increasing ratios of health personnel and facilities to population. Because rural areas invariably have higher ratios to begin with, efforts should initially be concentrated on increasing the level of health care there, while holding service ratios constant in urban areas.

Population movement and distribution, the subject of Chapter Seven, are themselves demographic processes. Our present discussion makes two important points that are often not understood. First, short-run policies aimed at coping with the consequences of rural-to-urban migration may prove counter-productive in the long run. Making strenuous efforts to provide the minimum requirements in health care, education, and housing to recent migrants when such services are not available in rural areas and small towns will almost certainly encourage continued migration to cities. An economic policy that encourages or allows continued industrial development of urban areas will have the same effect, as will wage and price differentials between rural and urban areas. More fundamentally, such short-run policies will not strike at the source of the problem—continued

high rural fertility and the socioeconomic conditions that encourage such fertility. Second, in the short run, rural-urban migration may be a more serious problem than high fertility. Accordingly, methods of stemming the continued flow
of migrants to already overcrowded cities should be given priority, and all
planning decisions should be considered in relation to this goal.

Economic inequality in developing countries is considerable and shows no
signs of decreasing. The important effects of rapid population growth on economic inequality cannot be identified easily; they work their way through the
socioeconomic and legal structure of the society. Two relatively clear causes,
however, emerge from the discussion in Chapter Eight: the differential circumstances and rates of reproduction among social, regional, and economic groups.
High fertility under circumstances of poverty increases social and economic inequality over time and makes it persistent across generations. Lack of knowledge of effective ways to limit fertility, unavailability of family planning services, and high infant and child mortality combine to result in high fertility,
which in turn affects individual abilities and opportunities and their transmission
from parents to children through inadequate nutrition, health care, and education. In addition, a high population growth rate acts as a basic constraint on
a society's ability to meet the increasing demand for health care and education
without reducing quality or uniformity.

As Chapter Nine makes clear, foreign economic aspects of development
planning also have direct and indirect interrelationships with demographic factors. Population size and structure in relation to other factor endowments determine a country's fundamental economic strength relative to other countries in
respect to trade. Rapid population growth increases demand for imports while
decreasing marketable surplus for export. Indeed, a fairly wide range of short-
run balance of payments effects can be listed. Development planning decisions
have feedback effects on the external economic balance, also. Decisions on import or export taxes, on importation of foreign surplus food grains and other
products, and on the exchange rate policy may all affect domestic relative sectoral prices and incomes and, thereby, population movement and even fertility.
This area, however, like the demographic aspects of income distribution, is
relatively unexplored and needs considerably more research before definite links
can be established.

The general effect of rapid population growth and urbanization on resources and the environment seems clearcut: rapid population growth increases
resource requirements more quickly than they can be met; increased production
and consumption increases the pollution of the environment by the waste products thereof; and, as population density increases, so does pollution of the
environment. Resource and environmental factors in turn affect demographic
processes: the geographical distribution of economic activities influences population distribution; environmental quality can affect morbidity and mortality
rates and the rate and pattern of migration. An understanding of these and
other interactions explored in Chapter Ten is crucial to development planners,

particularly in making decisions involving economic growth. For example, the composition of the material goods produced and consumed plays an important role in determining both the character and the severity of resource and environmental problems. Because the composition of output and consumption tends to change with increasing per capita income—the goal of all developing countries —it is important that development planning include means of coping with or heading off problems resulting from these changes. The spatial distribution of economic activity and the choice of technology also determine the nature and extent of environmental problems and thus are areas of decision-making in which consequences should be considered and planned for.

The concluding chapter discusses general development objectives as they relate to and are affected by demographic processes. The appendixes at the end of the book deal briefly with two additional elements crucial to effective and meaningful development planning: demographic data collection and the methodology of population projections.

Some of the sector essays cover fairly familiar ground, while others are pioneering efforts to look into hitherto unexplored relationships. The essays are, in this sense, "uneven," but this is not, in our judgment, a serious liability. If these essays provoke further research on these areas; if they are a useful introduction to some of these problems for interested nontechnicians; and if they convince some policy-makers and planners that population variables are a crucial component of development planning, then they will serve a useful purpose.

8   INTRODUCTION

REFERENCES

1. For other discussions of what "population policy" means or ought to mean, see National Academy of Sciences, *Rapid Population Growth: Consequences and Policy Implications* (Baltimore, Md.: Johns Hopkins Press, 1971), pp. 70ff.; Bernard Berelson, "Population policy: Personal notes," *Population Studies* 25, no. 2 (1971); and George B. Baldwin, "Population policy in developed countries," *Finance and Development* 10, no. 4 (December 1973).
2. Dorothy Nortman, "Population and family planning programs: A factbook," *Reports on Population/Family Planning,* no. 2, 6th ed. (September 1974).
3. Maxwell Stamper, "Population policy in development planning: A study of seventy less developed countries," *Reports on Population/Family Planning,* no. 13 (May 1973): 4.
4. See ref. 3, p. 10.
5. See ref. 2, p. 3.

ONE

Planning, Population, and the Macro Framework

WARREN C. ROBINSON

PHILOSOPHIES OF PLANNING

There is no shortage of literature on the subject of development planning. A full-scale review of even the major works is beyond the scope of the present volume and peripheral to its objective. Nevertheless, a brief review of the main elements of planning is in order if we are to understand the relationship of the population variable to the development planning process.

There is some consensus on the reasons for planning, although no perfect agreement. Vernon[1] sees the purpose of planning as: (1) the optimal use of scarce resources or at least a more efficient use than would occur in the absence of planning; (2) the setting of clear-cut national economic objectives; (3) providing a political and social sense of purpose for the nation; (4) satisfying the ever-present foreign donor groups that the national government is making serious efforts to cope with its problems and is therefore worth assisting. Other reasons could be added, including perhaps the most important one of all—the exercise of planning educates planners and policy-makers to the reality of their situation and the degrees of choice they actually possess. Only the first of the four objectives is purely economic, and it is probably not dominant in the minds of most policy-makers. In fact, an economic plan is always a philosophical and political document, too, even if the politics and philosophy underlying it are buried deeply and covered over with plausible assumptions and subtle coefficients. The objectives of planning are inescapably political and social as well as economic. Some of the early literature on planning, by failing to see this or by imagining that economic development planning could be "neutral" with respect to the institutional setting, must be regarded as naive at best and reactionary at worst.

Vernon's second reason for planning—setting clear-cut economic objectives—has an economic meaning; however, it should be viewed in a broader sense. The plan is used to define a social welfare function—to establish the social welfare implications of the various potential combinations of private and social output. Targets are specified, and if these targets are met, it can be assumed that total social welfare has increased.

This planning objective can be pursued within the context of either of two sorts of economic orders. First, the economy may be one in which private ownership is predominant and, while in principle it might be capable of generating its own welfare-maximizing "solution" to resource and output allocation decisions, for various reasons it has proved incapable of doing so in practice. Many factors may explain such a "breakdown," including: (a) the inability of the market to take proper account of "externalities" of both production and consumption; (b) the limited time horizons of private decisions compared to the need for long-range vision to promote growth; (c) the relatively large scale of the capital investments required to launch development, together with an indivisibility or lumpiness in capital; (d) the inability of private financial and investment markets to actually accumulate and allocate to profitable uses the total social surplus of savings over consumption; and, most commonly, (e) the belief that prevailing prices are not market-clearing equilibrium ones and that, in the presence of such marked structural distortions, no maximizing solution will be forthcoming if the market is left to its own devices.[2]

All the above reasons are justifications for the belief that government intervention and planning are required even if one accepts that a laissez faire system can in principle promote maximum social welfare. Government intervenes to set the system right, as it were. This regulated or "mixed" capitalism has many advocates, and some see the contemporary United States as an example of such a system.[3]

The second type of economic order in which planning can occur is a system that emphasizes public ownership and control—in short, socialism. Socialism assumes that the capitalist system, even under perfect competition, cannot produce a real maximization of social welfare due to an inequitable distribution of income; that it will suffer periodic large-scale unemployment; and that it will inevitably tend toward monopoly to suppress technological progress. The democratic socialist version of this approach has much in common with the philosophy that holds that capitalism could work but does not. Indeed, at the hands of some of its theorists, the democratic socialist model became a revived, smoothly functioning market economy with decentralized profit-maximization by state enterprises, and consumer sovereignty the rule. Central direction was to be limited to control of investment and the setting of overall priorities in production.[4]

If this can be described as "right-wing" planning theory, then the "command" model must be the "left-wing" of this approach. The latter, which developed in practice in the USSR during the 1930s and 1940s without any previously articulated theory, stresses the need for: (a) total public control of all heavy industry through direct quantitative controls over material inputs; (b) setting detailed physical targets for industries; (c) restructuring consumer wants and tastes by emphasizing investment goods, so that allowing the consumer "free choice" becomes meaningless in practice; and (d) accepting "planners' preferences" as a good approximation of the social welfare function of the entire economy. This is the "Stalinist" model, which, in spite of the much-heralded "liberalization" of the 1960s, continues to hold sway in most Soviet bloc countries.[5]

The democratic socialist planning model was developed as an alternative to productive but troubled capitalism. Growth was not seen as the and stabilization. It was thus not really del, on the other hand, evolved out 's efforts to leap into industrialism nues to stress) development to the it is certainly a development model. f to the developing countries, regard-growth, at any cost, has often been

of most of the Third World there is a mixture ionist-capitalist thinking. Structural change and scalar growth resources are still mainly privately owned, and government intervention largely through implementation of the national economic plan.

Vernon suggests that a plan must be: (a) internally consistent; (b) comprehensive of most of the important processes and activities in the economy; and (c) optimal in the use it makes of the resources being allocated by the plan. Zelienski, writing from the socialist, command viewpoint, says that planning must begin with government control over the commanding heights of the economy (that is, heavy industry) and that the government must exercise effective control to insure compliance with the plan.[6] Planners working from a liberal capitalist philosophy stress the techniques of plan construction and the methodology of writing a good plan. They engage in endless discussions of interindustry models, linear programming, two-sector and three-gap models, and the like. The command economy planners tend to stress techniques of implementation and meeting targets, with less concern over whether short-run optimality is being insured. This difference in emphasis is fundamental to the command versus liberal plan philosophies.

The orthodox command models have largely ignored population. For many years the Stalinist-Marxist position was staunchly anti-Malthusian. Any suggestion that population growth might be as important (or even more important) than the social and economic organization of a society in determining future well-being and standard of living was opposed. There is no excess population under socialism, it was alleged. Thus, population growth affected planning targets only by the constraint imposed through labor force availability. The interaction of economic decisions and policies with population factors was not appreciated and certainly not employed as a part of planning. It is interesting to note, however, that in spite of this neglect of population, the socialist countries of Eastern Europe may be a classic example of indirect and accidental feedback effects from economic planning to population factors. In the 1950s and continuing up to the present, the push for investment and heavy industry has meant tight controls on consumption, chronic shortages of many goods, and great scarcity of housing space. These shortages almost certainly have had an effect on the marriage rate and fertility within marriage. The wider labor force opportunities open to women perhaps also have exerted a negative influence on fertility.[7]

Thus labor, housing, and other economic policies may have contributed to the decline in fertility in these countries even while the government was encouraging fertility with family allowances. The former policies seem to have had far more effect than the latter. Population has grown very slowly in these countries, and there is some concern about this on the part of these governments.

For those countries of Europe and elsewhere following a liberal planning philosophy, population was not a variable but rather a parameter. The objective of most planning was stabilization and employment, not growth. Hansen and others argued that population growth had been an important stimulus to Western European and American economic growth.[8] The cessation of this growth, or at least its slowing down, it was argued, was partly responsible for the apparently secular slowdown of these economies in the 1930s. However, Hansen and the other stagnation theorists offered no solution and did not suggest use of government plans or programs to increase fertility. Some governments did, in fact, attempt pronatalist subsidies, but they appear to have had very little effect.

In sum, the development of two major philosophies of planning occurred under particular historical circumstances such that the population factor was not important in the planning process. Population was viewed by one school as exerting a positive force on growth in that it stimulated demand; to the other school, population and labor force size were thought to constitute a resource limit on output and growth. To both, population was regarded as a parameter that was not likely to be much affected by any economic plans or policies.

Looked at this way, it is clear why both major philosophies of planning have, in fact, had so little of value to say to the policy planners in the developing world. For population factors—size, growth, density, movement, and composition—are at the heart of the development problem in the Third World. No doubt one could find other illustrations of incorrect emphasis and tone caused by borrowing from Western and Soviet planning philosophy. The emphasis on industry at the expense of agriculture and the concentration on urban problems rather than rural also occur to one. But the population factor is more fundamental yet.

This neglect of the population factor in economic philosophies of planning has led to a neglect of it at the operational level also. The leading economic planning models and frameworks have, until very recently, treated population as essentially a datum, something determined outside the system. More recently in the developing nations, family planning programs have gained wide acceptance. But true population planning is only now being developed at the conceptual and theoretical level, 25 years after the need for it arose.

THE MACROECONOMIC FRAMEWORK

Whatever the underlying philosophy or objectives, effective planning requires a knowledge of how the economy functions. Indeed, the development of social accounting techniques and the routine collection of data measuring gross output, income originating, investment, and other related magnitudes has proceeded hand in hand with the growing interest in interventionist, "corrective" economic planning in the nations of the West.

Planning without facts is not possible; or, rather, it is possible only when assumptions are substituted for a knowledge of past facts and when at least some qualitative, if not quantitative, indicators of performance under the plan can be devised.

The macro framework of a plan is its backbone, its core, and the link through which any sector or industry or even project is connected with the larger economy. The macro framework thus is a descriptive picture of the entire economy, planned and unplanned sectors, typically broken down to the major sectors, industries, and functional categories. A reasonably well-developed system of national accounts is, in practice, a prerequisite for macroeconomic planning. So, also, is some minimal data on population size, rate of growth, age-sex structure, and labor force participation.

Economic accounts are a series of definitional equations. Savings *ex post* is always equal to investment, but knowing the magnitude still tells us nothing about the dynamic process underlying these variables. Nevertheless, assuming that the recent past or the plan's base year are not highly atypical, disequilibrium observations of the macro framework, there are internal, structural relationships implied. The relationship of savings to total income—the propensity to save—is a key structural coefficient. Another is the relationship between total output and total employment. The ratio of total output to capital stock is yet another, and there are more. These relationships can be derived only from a reasonably well-developed set of aggregate economic accounts.

The accuracy and reliability of the national accounts data in developing areas is subject to wide variation. To begin with, there are serious conceptual problems in defining output, income, consumption, and savings in a largely subsistence, peasant agricultural economy. Where trade is in barter terms, it may be difficult to estimate monetary values. The most important commodities consumed may not be traded at all. Regions or provinces may be largely autonomous, and foreign trade may affect only a small "enclave" in the larger economy.

Even if these conceptual problems can be overcome, measuring the income and product flow accurately is never easy. If the available estimates are very far off, not only in magnitude but composition or structure, then a plan based on these estimates cannot achieve its objectives except by accident. Good planners, however, are lucky planners, and there seems general agreement that even bad data are better than no data. How bad they must be before one reaches the opposite conclusion is not clear.

Certain demographic data are also required if a reasonably consistent, meaningful plan is to be put together. Data on population size and growth rate, age-sex composition, and economic activity status are the minimal requirements for computing consumption needs, labor force size, and output. Since very often demographic data are available or can be collected even if economic data are missing, in practice the demographic data are an important input in estimating some of the economic magnitudes. For example, if labor force size is known and unemployment is not important, then with some estimate of productivity per worker the total product originating can be estimated, too. Such demographically based estimation techniques are, in fact, often used in estimating social accounts.

Beyond this, demographic data on population distribution, movement and migration streams, and regional variations in fertility and mortality are also very desirable if any disaggregated subnational planning is to be undertaken. (Appendix One of this book deals with the collection of demographic data.)

Planning as a macroeconomic exercise consists in large measure of projecting target values for some key aggregates—output, employment, exports—and then, on the basis of the established relationships, deducing what the other aggregate magnitudes must be in order to insure consistency. Policies and programs are then introduced to guarantee that the necessary values are, in fact, attained. Thus, macro planning involves iterative projections of the macroeconomic variables until a set of values is reached that is consistent with either some desired target in a key sector or a target of a desired magnitude. A target in income may be unattainable, given the available factors, the production relationships, and expected growth patterns over time. A plan calling for a technically unreachable target is a "bad" plan.

The most elementary form of planning is simply a straight-line projection of the past trend. Sooner or later, however, such planning will miss a crucial "turning point" and leave the economy (and the planners) in serious trouble. Thus, the first step toward dynamic planning is to convert the static, definitional macro framework into a model that attempts to show how the economy behaves over time, how the submagnitudes interact with one another, and how the structural coefficients themselves will change.

MACROECONOMIC MODELS AND POPULATION

The growth of national economic planning and the development of econometric macroeconomic models have proceeded hand in hand in the last several decades.

In discussing this evolution, the Dutch econometrician and Nobel Laureate, Jan Tinbergen, writes:

> The interdependence of the various economic and social phenomena had become so obvious that the need arose for a systematically arranged study of a number of simultaneous relationships. It also became clearly necessary, because of the great number of variables which characterized economic life and the comparatively modest knowledge of them, to simplify these systems, while at the same time preserving the most essential characteristics. . . . The term "economic model" came to be used more and more for these simplified systems. . . . The most recent development in models for planning is undoubtedly to be found in those spheres that are described in the West as social rather than economic in the narrow sense. . . . It is only recently that it has become clear that these social components of well-being have an influence . . . that cannot be neglected and that they consequently have to be integrated into economic planning.[9]

Thus, a macroeconomic growth model consists of a set of relationships among the key economic magnitudes of a national economy stated so that the effects of changes in any one variable on all the other interrelated variables can be traced out. The model is typically expressed as a set of equations with known or assumed coefficients of interrelationship and timing, and the whole is susceptible to empirical specification and testing.

The "first generation" of such models used for planning in the developing countries were very often of the Harrod-Domar[10] variety and assumed implicitly that capital accumulation and technical changes were the only factors that could cause increases in total output. Labor was, in effect, a free good and also had zero marginal product. Population growth affected the economic aggregate only when these aggregates were converted to per capita terms. Many early national plans were based on such theoretical frameworks.

A few pioneering efforts were made to show the long-run effect on per capita income of alternative population trends. That is, a growth model of the capital accumulation sort was used to project future levels of output, and then alternative (high, medium, low) population projections were constructed to illustrate their effect on per capita income. The justly famous Coale-Hoover study of India was of this variety.[11]

Such models can be said to have employed population illustratively, not substantively or analytically. They made no effort to show the effects of population growth on the year-by-year process of economic growth through its effect on relative factor prices, public investment decisions, consumption requirements, and the like. They showed, in effect, that if population has nothing to do with producing output, a smaller population is better than a larger population.

By the late 1950s a growing discontent with the restrictive nature of the Harrod-Domar framework led to a renewed interest in the so-called neoclassical model, in which output is made a function of labor as well as capital, plus various other inputs. This approach allows for a possible impact of population growth on factor proportions and on the technology employed (capital intensive or labor intensive), as well as an effect on per capita income. At a fairly high level of abstraction, Phelp's celebrated "Golden Rule" theorem falls into this category. In the population literature, neoclassical econometric growth models have been proposed by Enke, Lloyd, Ruprecht, and others. Many recent national economic growth models have employed this approach in constructing their macro framework and in making prospective plan projections.[12]

The role of population in macro models has changed even further in recent years. In general, the change has been from treating population as an exogenous parameter, determined by forces outside the economic system described by the model, to treating population as an endogenous variable, possibly determined by the system itself and also subject to policy manipulation by planners. This change in the treatment of population has occurred with the growth of planning experience in the developing nations. Models that could realistically be applied to these nations required more explicit treatment of population as a variable, and this has led to changes in the underlying structure of the models.

Most of the well-known models developed thus far focus on the effects of population growth on output and economic well-being. The "costs" to society of higher rather than lower birth rates are seen as the resources required to support the added population as well as the increase in output that such resources could have produced had they been employed for truly productive investment purposes. In other words, the "benefits" of fertility reduction are the social costs that would have been incurred had not birth rates been lowered. But these gross benefits must be netted against the stream of future outputs that the higher rather than the lower birth rate would have produced. (Of course, if the analysis is kept to the short run, say 20 years or less, births prevented today have only a minimal effect on output since it takes some 15 years for a birth cohort to reach the age of labor force participation.) The often asserted doctrine of "zero marginal productivity" of labor can be invoked to argue that additional members of the labor force add nothing to output and thus that no future "returns" are being foregone by preventing births.

So stringent an assumption is not required, however. As long as additional workers over their entire lifetime are producing little above their subsistence, then their net output (or net productivity) is zero and preventing their birth entails no loss of net output that could have been used for other purposes. At the same time, preventing such births will increase the ability of the economy to generate savings for capital formation. When the marginal product per worker is below the average product per worker, and both are falling, then it is inescapably the case that reducing the number of workers will increase the average product (and income) per worker. To put it another way, if the optimum population size (one in which, given the stock of other factors, output per worker is maximized) has already been exceeded, then any measures that prevent further increases in population must result in higher income per capita than otherwise would have been the case. The savings rate is sometimes assumed to be a rising function of per capita income; if true, this means that as per capita income rises, aggregate savings will rise also.

Likewise, as is well known, a falling birth rate brings about a shift in the age distribution of the population so that the proportion of nonproducers decreases. It seems a reasonable assumption that the expenditures required for many welfare (and social overhead) programs are a direct function of the proportion of nonearners in the population. Reducing this proportion will thus reduce the share of total available social investment funds that must go to relatively unproductive relief and social welfare programs and to maintaining a constant social overhead investment per capita. At the same time, a lower birth rate and a relative reduction in nonearners will allow a larger proportion of available investment funds to go to directly productive investments in agriculture or industry and to a rising level of social overhead investment (education, health, and so forth) per capita.

Thus, to summarize, a lower rather than a higher rate of population growth will be favorable to development except when: (1) marginal productivity exceeds average productivity per worker and both are rising; (2) the total supply of savings from any given total income is unrelated to the size of the population; and (3) the allocation of total savings is not affected by the age composition of the population. These conclusions flow from nearly all macroeconomic-demographic models constructed to date.

In spite of complexities and uncertainties, the general nature of the population-development relationship remains fairly clear. Whatever development problems a country has, rapid population growth complicates them. It tends to retard the accumulation of savings and investment, to lower per capita living standards, and to lead government to spend on nondevelopmental welfare programs. The possibly positive link between population growth and development in Western European history seems to have very little relevancy for the developing countries. For them, except in highly special and unlikely circumstances, population growth is a barrier to development. This much the macro models seem to make perfectly clear.

One further step logically is required for these models to become fully useful for economic-demographic planning. Just as population affects economic variables at each point along a growth path, so do economic variables affect population growth. Fertility, mortality, and other demographic processes are themselves "determined" by level of income, income distribution, the structure of production, and many other factors. To the list of economic determinants, one could also add the expenditures on family planning programs being undertaken by governments.

A truly satisfactory interactive economic-demographic macro model has yet to be developed. The revised TEMPO model is an effort in this direction, as are the International Labour Organisation's "BACHUE-1" and one or two others.[13] In practice, however, the notion of population planning as a separate sector, comparable to manpower planning or regional planning, is new and not widely accepted. Existing models are, in most regions, actually ahead of planning practice. (We return to this in Chapter Eleven.)

AN ILLUSTRATIVE MODEL

Rather than review all models that have been developed, we will present our own version of such a model, which draws on the others and can be explained easily.

The basic framework of this model is neoclassical to allow changes in population to influence the level of output directly. The model is a development model rather than a growth model. Dale W. Jorgenson described this distinction as follows:

> In the theory of development, emphasis is laid on the balance between capital accumulation and the growth of population, each adjusting to the other. In the theory of growth, the balance between investment and savings is all-important and the growth of population is treated as a constant or shunted aside as a qualification to the main argument. . . . In particular, limitation of the analysis to the situations in which there is effectively one producing sector rules out much of what is interesting about growth and development.[14]

The model must contain a demographic submodel indicating the determinants of population size, the proportion of the population in labor force ages, labor force participation rates, birth rates, death rates, and the impact of government expenditures on births and deaths. Since the point of view is long range, the neoclassical growth model is the most appropriate because it allows for changes in the capital/labor, capital/output, and labor/output ratios.

The heart of a neoclassical model is an aggregate production function. The typical function employed yields positive but diminishing returns to additional units of productive factors. The Cobb-Douglas function is usually preferred, although others can be employed. Furthermore, under competitive conditions, the parameters of this function determine the functional distribution of income.

Natural resources (including land) enter into the production function. The importance of this factor was pointed out by Demeny:

> It is obvious that the traditional sectors of underdeveloped countries exhibit a wide range of variations . . . that can be shown to be quite unrelated to differences in the rate of growth of the labor force but that are powerfully influenced by the fundamental endowments in traditional agriculture as inherited from the past. In other words, something uncomfortably akin to such old-fashioned and slippery notions as "population/resources ration," "population density," or even "overpopulation" or "population pressure" seems to reenter the scene and a more detailed analysis of the effects of alternative demographic processes on economic development is attempted.[15]

Figure 1.1 depicts the underlying structure of an economic-demographic macro model. The formal mathematical structural relationships and definitions are presented on pages 21–22.

Ideally, the model should distinguish between agricultural and nonagricultural output and between rural and urban population. Separating the population into rural and urban would also permit rural-to-urban migration and differential fertility and mortality to be dealt with explicitly. Unfortunately, such a model is too complicated to be illustrated in a single diagram. Splitting the production function into agriculture and nonagriculture would require two equations for each one now shown, plus equations to show the economic and demographic links between the sectors. Thus, for our purposes here, we will deal with a single aggregate production function.

This is a relatively complex model, requiring a considerable amount of data and a fairly elaborate computational facility to estimate. Nevertheless, it is a highly simple approximation of the subtle interactions that actually exist.

In this model, population enters into the model in the following ways:

1. Production is a function of labor force.

2. Labor force is a function of the size and age distribution of the population, output per capita, and the participation rate.

3. Population is a function of birth rates, which are a function of previous rates, output per capita, and government spending on family planning programs; and death rates, which are a function of per capita output, per capita government welfare spending, and previous death rates.

4. Savings is a function of population size as well as income.

5. Government spending on welfare programs is assumed as a figure per capita and then directly determined by population size. (Spending on family planning is not related to population size but is a "policy variable.")

These functional relationships are ones that most economic-demographic macro models would incorporate. Some are based on the growing body of empirical research on these topics, but some of the key relationships remain intuitive and theoretical rather than demonstrably true. For example, the relationship between population growth and savings remains very unclear, as does the effect of female labor force activity on fertility and the effect on fertility of government spending on family planning programs. Similarly, the precise nature of the assumed relationships between government spending on health and welfare programs and mortality is difficult to establish; the same may be said of the link between spending on what are often called "development-related" investments and total output or between development-related investments and the future flow of factors.

These five relationships describe a relatively complex macro planning model. Still, it does not take into account all the likely economic-demographic interactions. Other even less well-established but still likely relationships should perhaps also be built into a realistic macro model that aims at showing all economic-demographic interactions:

6. Output (yield per acre) is possibly a declining function of density through time.

Figure 1.1 An Interactive Economic-Demographic Macro Model

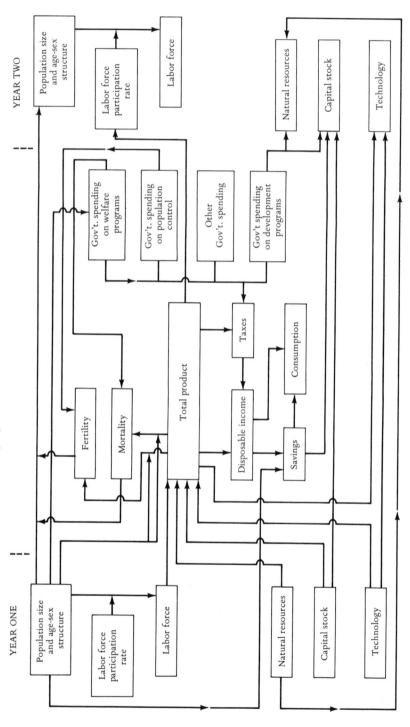

$$(1) \quad Q_t = \phi F_t \, L_t{}^\alpha \, K_t{}^\beta \, J_t{}^\Upsilon$$

$$(2) \quad F_t = f\left(\frac{\Delta Q_{t-1}}{Q_{t-1}}, t, F_{t-1}\right)$$

$$(3) \quad L_t = L\left(Z_t, \frac{Q_{t-1}}{P_{t-1}}, R_t\right)$$

$$(4) \quad b_{it} = b_i\left(b_{it}{}^1 G_{4_t}, \frac{Q_t}{Z_t}\right)$$
$$(i = 0 \ldots n)$$

$$(5) \quad B_t = \sum_i b_{it} \, H_{it}$$

$$(6) \quad H_{it} = B_{it} - \sum_{x=t-i}^{t} D_{ix}$$

$$(7) \quad D_{it} = d_{it} \, H_{it}$$

$$(8) \quad d_{it} = d_i\left(d_i{}^1, \frac{Q_t}{P_t}, \pi, t\right)$$

$$(9) \quad Z_i = \sum_{i=15}^{75} H_{it}$$

$$(10) \quad R_t = R\left(\sum_{i=0}^{5} \frac{H_{it}}{Z_{it}}\right)$$

$$(11) \quad P_t = \sum w_i \, H_{it}$$

$$(12) \quad K_i = K_{t-1} + I_i$$

$$(13) \quad I_i = S_t + \rho(G_2)$$

$$(14) \quad C_t = Q_t - S_t$$

$$(15) \quad S_i = J\{(Q_i - T_i), P_i\}$$

$$(16) \quad G_2 = \rho(G_2) + I - \rho(G_2)$$

$$(17) \quad G_{3_t} = \pi_t \, P_t$$

$$(18) \quad T_i = G_{1_t} + G_{2_t} + G_{3_t} + G_{4_t}$$

$$(19) \quad \Delta J = J\,(G_2 - \rho G_2)$$

$$(20) \quad J = J_i + \Delta J$$

EXOGENOUS VARIABLES

t time

G_1 nondevelopment, nonwelfare government spending

G_2 government development spending (capital investment and resource development)

G_4 government expenditures for family planning programs

PARAMETERS

ϕ constant used to convert to value units

α elasticity of productivity of labor

β elasticity of productivity of capital

Y elasticity of productivity of resources

b^1_i initial age-specific birth rates

d^1_i initial age-specific death rates

w_i age-specific consumption as a percent of adult consumption

σ average propensity to save out of per capita disposable income

π average government welfare expenditure per equivalent adult consumer

ρ percentage of total government development expenditures going to capital investment

CURRENT ENDOGENOUS VARIABLES

Q Production in value units

C Consumption

F Index of technical change

L Labor input in efficiency units

K Capital input in value units

J Resource input in physical units

Z Population over age 14

P Population in equivalent adult consumers

R Labor force participation rate

b_i Age-specific birth rate for the ith age group

B Births

H_i Persons in the ith age class

D_i Deaths in the ith age class

d_i Age-specific death rates for the ith age group

I Net investment and resource development

S Annual saving from current production

T Taxes

G_3 Government expenditures on welfare services

ΔJ Annual addition to the stock of resources

TG Total government expenditures

7. The composition of total output is partially a function of the age distribution and total size of the population.

8. The division of agricultural output between subsistence and marketable surplus is a function of the share of population in agriculture.

9. Industrial sector population and labor force are partially a function of migration, which in turn is a function of per capita income differences.

10. Government spending on housing and urban infrastructure is a function of the share of the population in urban areas.

11. Demand for imported consumer goods is partially a function of the proportion of consumers living in urban areas.

12. The female labor force participation rate is partially a function of past fertility.

The limitations of macro models as either valid theoretical constructs or useful guides to policy are well known. Gunnar Myrdal's critique is especially penetrating and severe.[16] Yet the macro model remains the only way in which population is related to most development plans. In advocating family planning programs, emphasis has usually been placed on showing the effects of high versus low fertility on income and consumption per capita. This tends to be a long-range relationship—20 years or so in the future, at the least, if the effect is to be marked enough to matter. As a result of such an emphasis, the impact of population growth is often regarded as exclusively long term. There has also been a tendency to focus on size and growth rate as the only important population variables and not to treat population composition, structure, and distribution in detail when analyzing the impact of population on development plans. This has obscured sector-specific impacts and relationships even more.

Macro models have served their purpose when they have sketched out the main relationships. To fully understand the practical impacts of population factors on development planning, one must move to the project or at least sector-specific level, where the most meaningful development planning occurs.

SECTOR-SPECIFIC PROBLEMS

Regardless of how logically compelling the macroeconomic picture is, in the end it is abstract. Even allowing for interactions and feedbacks, the overall negative effect of population growth on development is clear. This is true precisely because the macro framework and macro models are so highly aggregate and simplified.

At the working level, development decisions occur regarding particular projects and programs in particular sectors of the economy. To the civil servants, engineers, and budget people, the macro framework, the model, or the overall plan may seem very far removed. As a result, the population variable and its effects on development will also seem distant.

The very aggregative nature of such models tends to support this kind of thinking. Year-to-year changes in the demographically related or determined variables are not likely to be large. Even a 10 percent change in fertility or mortality from one year to the next will have relatively little effect on total population or labor force size or the other macro totals. It is this simple fact that leads some economists to argue that, while population factors matter "in the long run," they "don't matter next year." They may not matter next year in determining total output or total labor force, but they may matter in crucial ways to particular sectors, industries, regions, or ministries. What happens to migration between now and next year does matter to urban planning; what happens to birth rates does matter to health planners; what happens to rural population size does matter to marketable surplus and urban food prices; and so on. It can be shown that, even in the short run (less than five years), population does matter to specific sectors and problem areas.

This point is worth stressing: the emphasis thus far in relating population to economic development has been totally macro in level, relatively long-range in dimension, and also linked strongly to the model-building approach to planning. Yet it is at the working level—in terms of specific sectors, projects, industries, and regions—that the actual day-to-day work of development is occurring. The effort to integrate an awareness of the population factor into the economic development planning process has been partially successful at the macro level, but it has not resulted in much day-to-day awareness or recognition of the problem at the working level. In fact, for nearly all areas of even very short-run development planning, population questions loom large. In the series of specific sector studies that make up the core of this book, we will attempt to show this to be true.

REFERENCES

1. Raymond Vernon, "Comprehensive model-building in the planning process," *Economic Journal* 76 (March 1966): 57–69.
   The literature on planning is too vast and complex for us to attempt any summary here. Among the better collections of essays on planning are Everett Hagen, ed., *Planning Economic Development* (Homewood, Ill.: Irwin, 1964); Bertram Gross, ed., *Action under Planning* (New York: McGraw-Hill, 1967); Albert Waterston, *Development Planning: The Lessons of Experience* (Baltimore: Johns Hopkins Press, 1969); and Jan Tinbergen, *Development Planning* (New York: McGraw-Hill, 1967).
2. Frances Bator, "The anatomy of market failure," *Quarterly Journal of Economics* 72 (August 1958): 351–379.
3. See Paul Samuelson, *Economics,* 5th ed. (New York: McGraw-Hill, 1961), chap. 3.
4. Abba Lerner's book is still perhaps the classic statement of this point of view: *The Economics of Control* (New York: Macmillan Co., 1962). See also Oskar Lange, *Essays on Economic Planning* (Bombay: Asia Publishing House, 1967).
5. Alec Nove, *The Soviet Economy* (London: George Allen & Unwin, 1962); George R. Feiwel, *The Soviet Quest for Economic Efficiency* (New York: Praeger, 1967).
6. Zelienski, "Are there laws of planning?" *Economics of Planning* 5, nos. 1–2 (1965): 43–52.
7. See Alfred Sauvy, "Population theories," in *International Encyclopedia of the Social Sciences,* vol. 12 (New York: Macmillan, 1968), pp. 349–358; and James Brackett, "The evolution of Marxist theories of population," *Demography* 5 (1968): 158–173.
8. A. H. Hansen, "Economic progress and declining population growth," *American Economic Review* 29 (March 1939): 1–15.
9. Jan Tinbergen, *Development Planning* (New York: McGraw-Hill, 1967).
10. For a description, see H. Y. Wan, Jr., *Economic Growth* (New York: Harcourt, Brace, Jovanovich, 1971), chap. 1.
11. Ansley J. Coale and Edgar M. Hoover, *Population Growth and Economic Development in Low-Income Countries: A Case Study of India's Prospects* (Princeton, N.J.: Princeton University Press, 1958).
12. This literature is summarized in several recent papers; see W. C. Robinson and David E. Horlacher, "Population growth and economic welfare," *Reports on Population/Family Planning,* no. 6 (February 1971); Geoffrey McNicoll, "An aggregative economic model and population policy," Working Paper no. 18 (Honolulu: East-West Population Institute, East-West Center, October 1971).
13. TEMPO Technical Information Center, *Description of the Economic-Demographic Model,* 68 TMP-120 (Santa Barbara: General Electric Company, Center for Advanced Studies, 1971); R. Blandy and R. Wery, "BACHUE-1—The dynamic economic-demographic model of the Population and Employment Project of the World Employment Programme," in *International Population Conference, Liege, 1973* (Liege: International Union for the Scientific Study of Population, 1973). See also US Bureau of the Census, International Statistical

Program, Socioeconomic Analysis Staff, "LRPM2—A system of perspective planning sub-models," Staff Paper no. 72-3 (Washington, D.C.: Government Printing Office, 1972); and Jose Encarnacion, Jr., "An economic-demographic model of the Philippines," in Augustin Kintanar, ed., *Economic and Demographic Studies of the Philippines* (Quezon City: University of the Philippines, 1974).

14. Dale Jorgensen, "The structure of multi-sectoral dynamic models," *International Economic Review* 2 (September 1961) : 277.

15. Paul Demeny, "Notes on economic considerations influencing population policies in underdeveloped countries" (unpublished, 1968).

16. Gunnar Myrdal, *Asian Drama* (New York: Random House, 1968), vol. 3, app. 3, pp. 1941-2004.

T W O

The Demographic Background to Development Planning

TOMAS FREJKA

This chapter will discuss, as background for subsequent chapters, emerging demographic trends and possible paths of the demographic transition in the nations of the developing world. Important conclusions reached in this chapter include the following:

1. Population growth of a considerable volume can be expected in the developing countries throughout the remainder of this century.

2. This population growth is the outcome of a historically unparalleled constellation of fertility and mortality levels and trends.

3. There is a reasonable likelihood that, even at the turn of the century, population growth rates of many developing countries will still be of a higher order than they were for developed countries during most of their history.

4. Given that populations of the developing countries are going to grow, their growth will be relatively small or large, depending on the type of fertility trends that are (inadvertently or purposefully) generated.

5. By definition, countries experiencing rapid population growth are in a period of transition; the question is: under what circumstances will a substantial decline in their population growth rates occur?

THE DEMOGRAPHIC TRANSITION IN THE DEVELOPED COUNTRIES

Demographers use the term "demographic transition" (occasionally, "demographic revolution" or "vital revolution") to designate a process of fundamental change in the demographic behavior of populations. Traditional high levels of mortality and fertility, resulting in low growth rates, are gradually transformed into relatively low levels of mortality and fertility. Often there is a time lag in the fertility decline compared to the mortality decline, however, resulting in high population growth rates. This process has been observed in practically all the so-called developed countries.[1]

Originally, the demographic transition was a European phenomenon, but it has spread to Asia, Latin America, Africa, and Oceania as well (see Table 2.1). However, the decline in population growth that began to occur about 1900 in Europe and America as a result of lowered fertility has been distinctly limited to those regions. Most of the rest of the world is still undergoing declines in mortality levels, while fertility remains correspondingly high.

Although the specific features of the demographic transition differed from country to country, and although there is still much uncertainty about the interplay of causes that brought about the transition, several important circumstances underlying the changes in mortality and fertility can be observed.

The decline in mortality that began in Europe and North America during the nineteenth century was the result of gradual but marked changes in life styles, living standards, and environment that have occurred between medieval and modern times: decreasing direct dependence on the vagaries of nature; advances in science, medicine, and technology; the spread of education; the industrialization of production; the improvement of agricultural technology; the growth of urban centers; the implementation and enforcement of public health measures; the development of modern means of transportation and communication; and the increased interdependence in many aspects of life of areas within a country as well as of countries. These and many other changes were an integral part of the process called modernization. And it was during this process that, as a result of improving health conditions (diet, hygiene, working conditions, medicine, and so on), people began to survive to increasingly higher ages. It is believed that in medieval times as many as 25 percent of all babies died before they were one year old and 50 percent of the children failed to reach the age of 20.[2] This would correspond to an average life expectancy at birth of about 25–30 years. At present, in the developed countries only about 2–3 percent of babies die before they reach their first birthday, and about 95 percent of children survive to age 20.

Childbearing behavior has radically changed also. Existing evidence, though sparse, points to an average completed fertility of around five births per woman in premodern times in Western European countries.[3] Although the fertility decline in the currently developed countries varied considerably from country to country[4], in Western Europe after the 1920s the average number of children born to women during their childbearing period was between two and three. Trends of the 1960s and levels around 1970 seem to indicate that childbearing patterns in the vicinity of two children per family are becoming widespread.

Table 2.1   Estimates of World Population by Regions, 1650–1970

Year	World total	Africa	North America	Latin America	Asia	Europe and USSR	Oceania
			Estimated Population (in millions)				
1650	553	60	1	10	380	100	2
1750	726	68	1	15	500	140	2
1850	1,325	88	26	35	900	274	2
1900	1,663	110	81	63	980	423	6
1920	1,810	140	117	91	966	487	9
1940	2,249	176	146	131	1,212	573	11
1950	2,486	217	166	162	1,355	572	13
1960	2,982	270	199	213	1,645	639	16
1970	3,632	344	228	283	2,056	705	19
			Population Growth Rates (percent per year)				
1650–1750	0.3	0.1	0.0	0.4	0.3	0.3	0.0
1750–1850	0.6	0.3	3.3	0.9	0.6	0.7	0.0
1850–1900	0.5	0.4	2.3	1.2	0.2	0.9	2.2
1900–1920	0.4	1.2	1.9	1.9	-0.1	0.7	2.0
1920–1940	1.1	1.2	1.1	1.8	1.1	0.8	1.0
1940–1950	1.0	2.1	1.3	2.1	1.1	-0.0	1.7
1950–1960	1.8	2.2	1.8	2.8	2.0	1.1	2.1
1960–1970	2.0	2.5	1.4	2.9	2.3	1.0	1.7

SOURCES: Goran Ohlin, "Historical outline of world population growth (Paper presented to the United Nations World Population Conference, Belgrade, Yugoslavia, 30 August–10 September 1965), p. 30. United Nations, Statistical Office, Demographic Yearbook, 1970 (New York: United Nations, 1971), p. 105.

POPULATION GROWTH IN THE DEVELOPING COUNTRIES

For most of the developing countries, available statistics on fertility and mortality levels and trends are less than completely adequate. In addition, there is a wide range in the values of mortality and fertility characteristics in these countries. Still, one can make some generalizations.

Mortality levels in the late 1960s were highest in most of tropical Africa—an average female life expectancy at birth of 40–45 years. In North Africa and in most of Asia, the female life expectancy was probably around 50–55 years, and in some places more. Mortality was lowest in most countries in Latin America, the female life expectancy in many countries being around or above 60 years.

At present there is considerable variation in fertility levels in the developing countries; about two-thirds, however, had a gross reproduction rate of around 3.0 or more in the 1960s (Table 2.2).[1] The available evidence seems to indicate that fertility was highest in Africa, and somewhat lower in Latin America and Asia.

Table 2.2   Number of Countries in Africa, Asia, and Latin America by Estimated Gross Reproduction Rate, 1960s

Gross reproduction rate	Africa	Asia	Latin America	Total
2.4 and under	2	6	6	14
2.5–2.8	6	7	4	17
2.9–3.2	19	6	13	38
3.3–3.6	13	9	2	24
3.7 and over	0	1	0	1
Total	40	29	25	94

SOURCES: United Nations, Statistical Office, *Demographic Yearbook, 1970* (New York: United Nations, 1971); and United Nations, Statistical Office, *Population and Vital Statistics Report,* Series A, vol. XXIV, no. 1 (New York: United Nations, 1972).

Even less information exists on long-term mortality and fertility trends. We will present two examples, not necessarily typical. As Figure 2.1 illustrates, the crude death rate in Sri Lanka (formerly Ceylon) fluctuated between 25 and 35 deaths per 1,000 population per year from 1900 through the early 1920s; a slight decline in mortality followed, which lasted through the 1930s. There was a sharp drop in mortality after World War II, and, by the late 1950s, the crude death rate was below 10 per 1,000. In Costa Rica, the crude death rate

[1] The formulations are intentionally vague to indicate the low degree of reliability of the data underlying our statements. Nevertheless, it is believed that the overall picture does resemble reality.

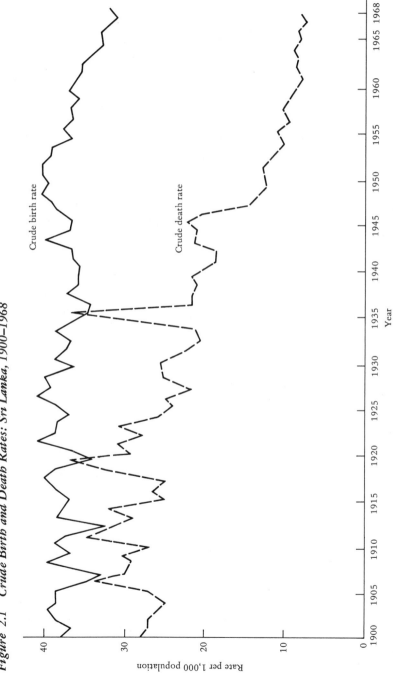

Figure 2.1 *Crude Birth and Death Rates: Sri Lanka, 1900–1968*

SOURCES: O.E.R. Abhayaratne and C.H.S. Jayewardene, *Fertility Trends in Ceylon* (Colombo, 1967), pp. 22, 24. Department of Census and Statistics, *Statistical Abstract of Ceylon, 1969* (Colombo, 1970), pp. 56, 61.

was around 29 per 1,000 until 1920; within 40 years it also dropped below 10 (Figure 2.2). For many other countries we lack data, but the fact has been established that in a large number of the developing countries mortality commenced a steady decline after World War II if it had not started earlier. This is true for almost every country in Latin America and Asia and for many African countries.

A vailable evidence on current fertility trends in the developing countries does allow the formulation of some observations. There is firm evidence from 15 countries that fertility has started to decline: such a trend can be documented for Hong Kong, Singapore, Taiwan, Republic of Korea, Sri Lanka, and West Malaysia in Asia; Barbados, Chile, Costa Rica, Trinidad and Tobago, Jamaica, and Puerto Rico in Latin America; and Mauritius, Egypt, and Tunisia in Africa. For eight other countries, including the People's Republic of China, there has possibly been a decline, but to date no hard evidence is available. Thus far it is very difficult to judge how widespread the fertility decline is among the developing countries.

Figure 2.2   Crude Birth and Death Rates: Costa Rica, 1895–1969

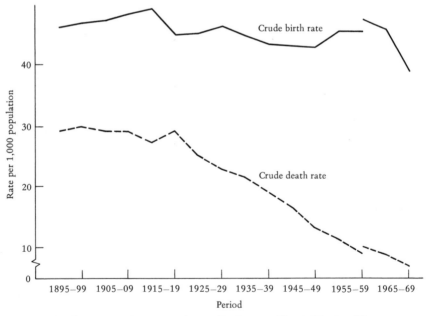

SOURCES: Andrew O. Collver, *Birth Rates in Latin America: New Estimates of Historical Trends and Fluctuations* (Berkeley: University of California, Institute of International Studies, 1965), p. 101. Direccion General de Estadistica y Censos, *Anuario Estadistico de Costa Rica, 1968* (Ministerio de Industria y Comercio, 1970), p. 19. United Nations, Population and Vital Statistics Report, Series A, vol. 34, no. 1 (New York: United Nations, 1972), p. 11.

Dudley Kirk has attempted to establish important features of the demographic transition in the developing countries. Noting that his conclusions are "based primarily on the experience of relatively few countries with good data," Kirk argues that a "new or renewed demographic transition" is evident in the developing countries:

> 1. A growing number of countries have been entering the demographic transition on the natality side since World War II and after a lapse of 25 years in which no major country entered this transition.
> 2. Once a sustained reduction of the birth rate has begun, it proceeds at a much more rapid pace than it did historically in Europe and among Europeans overseas.
> 3. The "new" countries may reduce birth rates quite rapidly despite higher levels than existed historically in Western Europe.[5]

To what extent Kirk's observations can be applied to the majority of the developing countries remains to be seen in the years to come.

In addition to fertility and mortality levels, another important demographic feature that must be considered in development planning is the age structure of the population. Populations with high fertility typically have a "young" age structure, that is, a large proportion of the population is in the child age groups. For example, it is estimated that in Thailand in 1947, 42 percent of the population were under age 15. As a result of high infant and child mortality, however, a significant proportion of these children did not survive into adulthood. With the conspicuous decline in mortality since the late 1940s, increasingly larger proportions of children survive to adult ages.[2] Thus, as Figure 2.3 illustrates, in Thailand large generations are going to enter into the childbearing years during the 1970s and the 1980s because well over 50 percent of the population was under age 20 in the mid-1960s. As health and living conditions improve, a significant portion of these young people will survive to form families and have children.

In sum, by 1970 several developing countries had actually started on the path of the demographic transition. But, while the transition of mortality from high to low levels is well under way, clear signs of a decline in fertility are evident only in a relatively small number of countries on each continent. Consequently, most developing countries have large generations of children and teenagers that are going to enter the childbearing ages and the labor force in the years to come. Given the current situation in the developing countries, let us discuss some of the alternative paths the demographic transition could take.

---

[2] In a population that has a constant expectation of life at birth of 40 years, the probability of surviving to age 20 is around 0.65. But in a population that has a permanent expectation of life at birth of 60 years, the probability of surviving to age 20 is around 0.85.

Figure 2.3   Age Composition of the Population of Thailand, 1947, 1960, and 1966

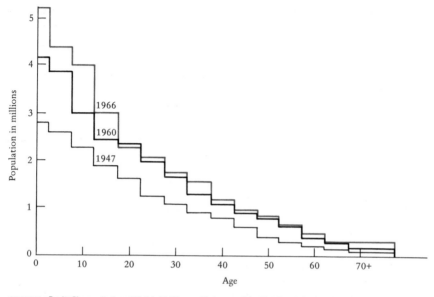

SOURCES: Pradit Charsombuti and Melvin M. Wagner, *Estimates of the Thai Population, 1947-1976, and Some Agricultural Implications* (Bangkok: Kasetsart University, 1969), p. 17. National Statistical Office, *The Survey of Population Change, 1964-1967,* Publication Series E-SuR, no. 1 (Bangkok: Office of the Prime Minister, 1970).

POSSIBLE PATHS OF THE DEMOGRAPHIC TRANSITION

In order to be able to illustrate possible paths of the demographic transition in the developing countries, one has to establish a framework of assumptions for the computation of projections. The fundamental assumptions are: (1) mortality will continue to decline; (2) eventually an average family size of two children will be the norm; and (3) once the two-child family norm is attained, the corresponding level of fertility will be maintained.

To accept the two-child family as a benchmark value is justified both historically and theoretically. The historical evidence is that, since the 1930s, fertility in several developed countries has been fluctuating around this level, and especially during the 1960s fertility trends for many more developed countries have been converging on this value. The theoretical justification is that if a population with low mortality adopts a fertility behavior norm of roughly two children per woman, this population will eventually cease to grow—the number of deaths will equal the number of births, and a balance of low death rates and low birth rates will be achieved.[3]

---

[3] The concept of the two-child family as a benchmark value must be qualified. When mortality is low, as in Sweden, an average of 2.1 children per woman will provide a

Technical details on the methods applied and on the assumptions will not be elaborated here but can be found in the literature.[6] The projections start with the estimated 1970 size and age structure of the population. The average mortality level of the late 1960s is assumed to decline further, at first at a rate similar to the recent past and later slowing down until it reaches approximately the level of contemporary Sweden (1969 female expectation of life at birth, 76.5; 1973 infant mortality rate, 11.1).

Variations among five different projections are the result of applying five different trends of fertility decline, which in each case settle roughly at the level of two children born per woman during childbearing age. Let us take the example of Sri Lanka (see Figure 2.4). During the late 1960s the average total fertility rate was around 4.5. Under the five projections, total fertility rate is assumed to decline to a value slightly above 2 as follows:

In Projection 1, in 1970–1975
In Projection 2, in 1980–1985
In Projection 3, in 2000–2005
In Projection 4, in 2020–2025
In Projection 5, in 2040–2045

One can see how rapidly fertility would have to decline if Projections 1 and 2 were to take place; clearly, even Projections 4 and 5 represent a meaningful decline. It is important to note that Sri Lanka is one of the rare populations where a fertility decline started during the 1960s. In addition, the level of fertility was lower in Sri Lanka before the start of the decline than in most other countries. Therefore, whatever one's impression about the steepness of the fertility decline of the individual projections for Sri Lanka, the assumed fertility decline in most other countries would be relatively steeper.

It is also important to mention that the constructed framework of assumptions is based on only the most basic interrelations of demographic processes. Several aspects of the demographic behavior of populations are not analyzed separately, but outlined fertility trends are considered to implicitly contain effects of these processes, for instance, the effects of changes in marriage patterns.

Trends in Population Size

Figure 2.5 illustrates growth trends for the population of Sri Lanka under three different assumptions.[7] The hypothetical trend of population growth of Projection 1 is especially interesting. Although an average fertility level of two

---

sufficient flow of births to replace all deaths. However, in a country where mortality is still high, more than two children would have to be born per woman to compensate for higher, especially infant, mortality. Therefore, in those cases where a rapid fertility decline is assumed, but mortality is still declining, we are assuming a fertility level somewhat higher than two children per woman; for instance, with a female life expectancy at birth of 55 years, 2.6 children per woman are assumed.

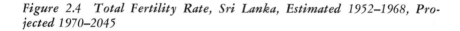

Figure 2.4 Total Fertility Rate, Sri Lanka, Estimated 1952–1968, Projected 1970–2045

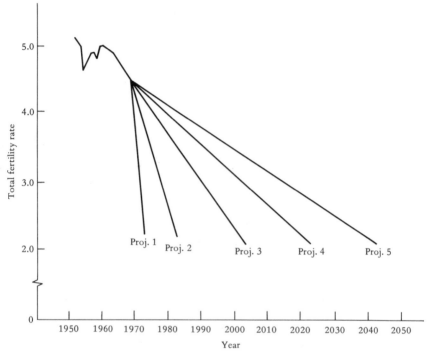

SOURCES: O. E. R. Abhayaratne and C. H. S. Jayewardene, *Fertility Trends in Ceylon* (Colombo, 1967), p. 119; and Nicholas H. Wright, "Ceylon: The relationship of demographic factors and marital fertility to the recent fertility decline," *Studies in Family Planning* 1, no. 59 (November 1970): 17-20.

children per woman is assumed to be adopted immediately—a most extreme assumption—the population of Sri Lanka would increase by 40 percent by the end of this century. Even thereafter, growth would continue, and it would not level off until around the middle of the next century, at which time the population would be about 70 percent larger than in 1970.

Assuming a more gradual fertility decline, with the two-child family generally adopted by the year 2000 (Projection 3) and maintained thereafter, the total population of Sri Lanka would be about 80 percent larger by the end of this century, and around the year 2050 it would be about two-and-one-half times its 1970 size.

If the fertility decline were stretched out over a period of 70 years (Projection 5), in the year 2000 the population of Sri Lanka would be two times larger than in 1970, and by the year 2050 it could be four times larger than in 1970.

Table 2.3 contains computations based on identical assumptions for Costa

Figure 2.5   *Alternative Projections of Population Growth: Sri Lanka,*
1970–2100

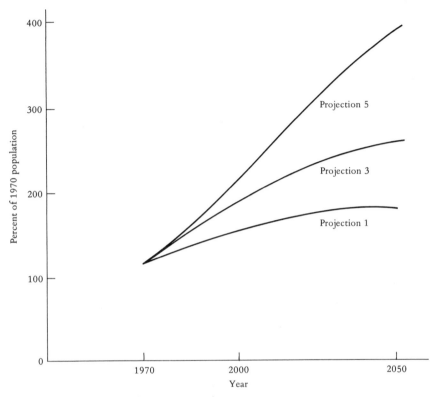

Projection 1: Two children per woman[a] by 1970.
Projection 3: Two children per woman[a] by 2000.
Projection 5: Two children per woman[a] by 2040.

[a]See footnote 3.

Rica, Iran, and Ghana. These data give an idea of the range of possibilities that lie ahead for different types of developing countries. In each of these countries, the population would grow faster than that of Sri Lanka. Assuming a rapid fertility decline (Projection 3), by the year 2000 the population of Ghana would have grown by about 90 percent, that of Iran by 100 percent, and that of Costa Rica by over 110 percent. By the year 2050, the range of possible growth for these countries is between 2.8 and 3.3 times their 1970 size. The results of applying the assumptions of Projection 5 show that all these populations would more than double by the year 2000. In fact, the population of Costa Rica could grow by a factor of 2.5. By the year 2050, one could expect the population of Ghana

Table 2.3   Alternative Population Projections with Differing Assumptions of Fertility Decline for Four Countries, 1970–2050

	An assumed fertility decline from current level to 2 children per woman[a] in					
	1970–1975 (Projection 1)		2000–2005 (Projection 3)		2040–2045 (Projection 5)	
Country and year	Absolute size[b]	Index[c]	Absolute size[b]	Index[c]	Absolute size[b]	Index[c]
Sri Lanka						
1970	12.1	100	12.1	100	12.1	100
2000	17.4	143	21.8	180	24.5	202
2050	20.4	169	30.2	249	47.3	390
Costa Rica						
1970	1.7	100	1.7	100	1.7	100
2000	2.6	151	3.7	213	4.4	254
2050	3.3	188	5.7	329	10.8	624
Ghana						
1970	9.0	100	9.0	100	9.0	100
2000	12.3	136	16.8	187	20.2	225
2050	15.1	168	24.8	276	49.8	555
Iran						
1970	27.9	100	27.9	100	27.9	100
2000	39.2	140	56.2	201	68.4	245
2050	48.2	173	85.9	307	179.8	644

[a] See footnote 3.
[b] In millions.
[c] 1970 = 100.

to be 5.5 times larger than in 1970 and that of Iran to be 6.5 times larger than in 1970.

Having presented some results, let us point out in a more concrete way how these data can be interpreted. Projection 1 is an illustration of most unlikely if not impossible developments. Projection 3 is an illustration of developments that might take place if the demographic transition, mainly the fertility decline, is relatively fast and the transition of fertility behavior from "traditional" to "modern" is attained in roughly one generation. Projection 5 is an illustration of developments that might occur if the demographic transition takes as much time as it did in countries of Western Europe in the nineteenth and beginning of the twentieth centuries.

As an adjunct to this section, let us indicate for one country what these rates of population growth would mean in terms of population density. In 1970 the average population density of Sri Lanka was about 180 persons per square kilometer. Under the assumptions of Projections 3 and 5, by the year 2000 the average density would grow to 330 or 370 persons per square kilometer, respectively. By the middle of the next century, according to Projection 3, the crude population density would be around 460, whereas Projection 5 would bring the population density to over 720 persons per square kilometer.

Trends in Vital Rates and Growth Rates

We will continue with the example of Sri Lanka. The crude death rate is at present very low and it will have a tendency to remain around 6 per 1,000 for a number of decades. Even if the crude birth rate declines rather rapidly (Projection 3), it will still be significantly higher than the crude death rate during at least the whole period of the fertility decline. As a result, the rate of natural increase is likely to diminish but will not be trivial for several decades. With the assumptions of Projection 3, the rate of natural increase would still be around 1 percent per year by the year 2000.

Should fertility decline at a moderate rate (Projection 5), the crude birth rate around the turn of the century would still be over 25 per 1,000 population, and thus the annual rate of natural increase would be around 2 percent.

In Iran, the crude death rate is around 15 and in Ghana probably around 20 per 1,000 population. It is reasonable to assume that it will decline in both countries. It is much more difficult to judge the direction of future fertility trends for these two countries. In any event, what seems to be fairly probable is that, even with a rapid fertility decline (Projection 3), there would still be an annual growth rate of around 1.5 percent per year in both Iran and Ghana at the end of this century (see Table 2.4). Naturally, a less rapid fertility decline would mean a higher rate of population growth.

Changes in Age Structure

At present the developing countries have large proportions of their populations in the young age groups and small proportions in the old age groups. For instance, in Iran in 1970, 46 percent of the population were in the 0–14 age group, 4 percent were in the 65 and over age group, and 50 percent were in the 15–64 age group (see Table 2.5). How the age structure of a population changes depends very much on its fertility trend. In Iran, with a rapid fertility decline (Projection 3), the 0–14 age group in 1985 could be reduced from 46 to 41 percent of the population; with a moderate fertility decline (Projection 5), it could decline to 44 percent; and by the year 2000 the proportion in this age group could be 34 or 42 percent, respectively. Clearly, the rate of fertility decline, insofar as it affects the age structure of a population, has important ramifications for the making of development plans—for example, in estimating the future need for educational facilities.

A more detailed view of the consequences of rapid versus slow fertility de-

Table 2.4   Alternative Projections of Vital Rates with Differing Assumptions of Fertility Decline for Four Countries, 1970–2050

| Country and period | An assumed fertility decline from the current level to 2 children per woman[a] in | | | | | |
| | 2000–2005 (Projection 3) | | | 2040–2045 (Projection 5) | | |
	CBR [b]	CDR [c]	CRNI [d]	CBR[b]	CDR [c]	CRNI [d]
Sri Lanka						
1965–1970	31.9	7.0	2.5	31.9	7.0	2.5
1975–1980	29.1	6.0	2.3	31.5	6.0	2.6
1985–1990	25.2	5.8	1.9	29.5	5.6	2.4
1995–2000	19.8	6.2	1.4	26.3	5.8	2.1
2005–2010	17.2	6.8	1.0	24.2	5.9	1.8
2025–2030	14.7	9.1	0.6	19.4	6.9	1.3
2045–2050	13.8	11.6	0.2	15.5	8.4	0.7
Costa Rica						
1965–1970	38.3	6.2	3.2	38.3	6.2	3.2
1975–1980	34.9	4.9	3.0	38.4	4.9	3.3
1985–1990	29.7	4.5	2.5	36.3	4.4	3.2
1995–2000	21.9	4.5	1.7	32.4	4.2	2.8
2005–2010	18.1	4.8	1.3	29.2	4.1	2.5
2025–2030	14.8	6.9	0.8	22.1	4.8	1.7
2045–2050	13.5	10.4	0.3	16.2	6.5	1.0
Ghana						
1965–1970	48.0	22.3	2.6	48.0	22.3	2.6
1975–1980	40.2	16.4	2.4	44.1	16.9	2.7
1985–1990	33.9	12.4	2.1	41.2	12.8	2.8
1995–2000	25.0	9.8	1.5	36.8	10.0	2.7
2005–2010	20.3	8.8	1.2	32.9	8.2	2.5
2025–2030	16.4	9.1	0.7	24.4	6.6	1.8
2045–2050	14.6	11.6	0.3	17.2	7.4	1.0
Iran						
1965–1970	43.9	14.7	2.9	43.9	14.7	2.9
1975–1980	37.6	10.8	2.7	41.5	11.0	3.1
1985–1990	32.3	8.3	2.4	39.8	8.4	3.1
1995–2000	23.7	7.0	1.7	35.6	6.7	2.9
2005–2010	19.2	6.5	1.3	32.1	5.5	2.7
2025–2030	15.6	7.9	0.8	23.9	5.1	1.9
2045–2050	14.1	10.8	0.3	16.9	6.4	1.1

[a] See footnote 3.
[b] CBR = crude birth rate (per 1,000).
[c] CDR = crude death rate (per 1,000).
[d] CRNI = crude rate of natural increase (per 100).

Table 2.5   Percentage Distribution of the Population by Age under Two Different Assumptions of Fertility Decline: Iran, 1970–2000

	An assumed fertility decline from the current level to 2 children per woman[a] in					
	2000–2005 (Projection 3)			2040–2045 (Projection 5)		
Year	0–14	15–64	65+	0–14	15–64	65+
1970	46.2	49.8	4.0	46.2	49.8	4.0
1985	41.0	56.0	3.0	44.2	53.0	2.8
2000	33.5	62.3	4.2	42.1	54.5	3.4

[a] See footnote 3.

cline on the age structure of a population can be attained by following the changes in a single age group through time under different conditions of fertility. Let us first follow the 5–9 age group in Iran (Table 2.6). This age group provides a good, although rough, approximation of the number of children who will be in need of primary education. With a rapid fertility decline (Projection 3), the size of this age group in Iran would grow moderately during the 1970s and the 1980s and stabilize during the 1990s. If fertility were to decline slowly (Projection 5), this age group would grow faster, and by the year 2000 it would be over 50 percent larger than under the conditions of Projection 3.

Another age group that warrants observation is the population aged 15–19. This age group is a good approximation of the number of labor force entrants and the number of women who will enter into the childbearing period of their lives. It is important to note that persons who are going to enter the labor force or the childbearing stage of their lives during the next 15–20 years are already alive at the time of initial observation. Therefore, a decline in fertility does not influence the growth of this age group until after 15 years. For example, only after 1985 will fertility trends of the 1970s be detectable in the labor force entrants group (Table 2.6). By the end of the century, the size of this age group will be significantly influenced by current fertility trends. A relatively rapid decline of fertility (Projection 3) would generate an average annual growth rate of 2 percent in the 1990s, whereas a moderate fertility decline (Projection 5) would mean that the 15–19 age group would still be growing at more than 3 percent per year.

SUMMARY

The demographic transition in most developing countries has already begun. There are not many populations whose mortality rate is currently as high as it was in "pre-modern" times in the populations of the now developed countries

Table 2.6 Growth of Selected Age Groups with Differing Assumptions of Fertility Decline: Iran, 1970–2000

Year	Assumed fertility decline from the current level to 2 children per woman[a] in				
	2000–2005 (Projection 3)	2040–2045 (Projection 5)	Period	2000–2005 (Projection 3)	2040–2045 (Projection 5)
	Absolute numbers (1,000s)			Annual rate of growth (%)	
Age group 5–9					
1970	2,027	2,027	1970–1980	+2.3	+2.8
1980	2,553	2,693	1980–1990	+1.9	+3.3
1990	3,587	3,731	1990–2000	+0.4	+2.5
2000	3,097	4,799			
Age group 15–19					
1970	1,398	1,398	1970–1980	+3.4	+3.4
1980	1,971	1,971	1980–1990	+2.4	+2.9
1990	2,503	2,640	1990–2000	+2.0	+3.3
2000	3,045	3,681			

[a] See footnote 3.

(an expectation of life at birth of 25–30 years and an infant mortality rate around 250 per 1,000 births). As of the early 1970s, however, there is evidence of a certain fertility decline in only a few developing countries.

Historical trends of mortality seem to indicate that once mortality starts to decline it continues to do so until it reaches levels common in the contemporary developed countries—a life expectancy of around 70 years. There is, of course, no guarantee that this generalization will be applicable indefinitely into the future; recent trends in the developing countries, however, seem to confirm this historical experience. The decline of mortality might be rapid in one country and slow in another, but the direction of the trend is relatively clear.

The future trends of fertility are considerably more complex and uncertain. Based on our discussion, however, we can draw the following general conclusions:

1. Even with a very rapid rate of fertility decline, populations of the developing countries will continue to grow.

2. If, for instance, the average fertility patterns that are currently becoming commonplace in the developed countries are achieved in the developing countries by the end of this century, their populations will still double in size by the end of this century, and they might reach three times their 1970 size by the middle of the next century.

3. If the transition period to "modern" fertility patterns in the developing countries is stretched out over a period of about 70 years, the populations of these countries will grow by a factor of 2.0–2.5 by the end of this century, and by the year 2050 they will be more than five or six times larger than in 1970.

4. The rate of fertility decline will determine long-term changes in the age structure. If fertility declines slowly, populations will continue to have high proportions of children (that is, over 40 percent of the population will be under age 15 throughout the remainder of this century). With a rapid fertility decline, the proportion of the population under age 15 could be around 30 percent by the year 2000.

Thus, the typical developing country in Asia, Africa, and Latin America will have a population by the year 2000 double its present size, even if a moderate fertility decline occurs. Ultimate population stabilization—the much-discussed goal of zero population growth—seems far away for such a country and will occur when the population is several times its present size. Population growth is inevitable, and government policy in many areas will have to grapple with the implications of this growth for many years to come.

REFERENCES

1. See Ansley J. Coale and Edgar M. Hoover, *Population Growth and Economic Development in Low-Income Countries: A Case Study of India's Prospects* (Princeton, N.J.: Princeton University Press, 1958), chaps. 2, 3.
2. Cf. Pierre Goubert, "Recent theories and research in French population between 1500 and 1700," in David Glass and D.E.C. Eversley, eds., *Population in History* (Chicago: Aldine, 1965), p. 468.
3. See David Glass and D.E.C. Eversley, eds., *Population in History,* chaps. 13, 18, 20, and 26; Solvi Sogner, "Aspects of the demographic situation in 17 parishes in Shropshire 1711–60: An exercise based on parish registers," *Population Studies* 17, no. 2 (November 1963): 137.
4. Cf. Dudley Kirk, "A new demographic transition?" in National Academy of Sciences, *Rapid Population Growth* (Baltimore, Md.: Johns Hopkins Press, 1971), pp. 123–147.
5. See ref. 4, p. 145.
6. Tomas Frejka, "Reflections on the demographic conditions needed to establish a U.S. stationary population growth," *Population Studies* 22, no. 3 (November 1968): 379–397; Tomas Frejka, *The Future of Population Growth: Alternative Paths to Equilibrium* (New York: John Wiley & Sons, Inc., 1973).
7. Similar illustrative projections have been prepared for nearly every country possessing any usable demographic data. See Tomas Frejka, *Reference Tables to "The Future of Population Growth: Alternative Paths to Equilibrium"* (New York: The Population Council, 1973).

THREE

Population Growth, Manpower, and Employment

GHAZI M. FAROOQ

Manpower is a primary factor in the production of all goods and services and, as such, is a basic component of development planning. The problems of availability, development, and utilization of human resources have recently assumed even greater importance in socioeconomic planning because of the chronic imbalance that now exists and is growing between the supply of and demand for labor in most developing countries.[1] In almost every case, rapid population growth, which adds to the supply of labor at a much faster rate than can effectively be absorbed in employment, is singled out as the main reason for this imbalance.

In this chapter we will first discuss the mechanisms that determine labor force size and growth, both short- and long-term. In the second part, the focus will

ACKNOWLEDGMENTS: The author is grateful to Gavin Jones, Ann R. Miller, Lloyd Reynolds, and Vincent H. Whitney for their comments, criticisms, and suggested improvements of an earlier draft.

[1] For the sake of simplicity, "manpower supply," "labor supply," "economically active population," and "labor force" are treated here as equivalent terms and refer to the total number of persons available for the production of GNP, including persons working and persons looking for work. A more refined measure of labor supply would be a flow variable formed by translating the labor force size into the total number of man-hours available during a specified period.

Our use of the terms "demand" and "supply" does not imply the existence of an organized market in which labor is traded. "Supply" means simply availability—persons who are working, desire to work, or would work; "demand" means only the potential for useful application of labor in the productive processes. The economy may be made up completely of self-employed persons and unpaid family labor, and yet labor available—or supply—may exceed the amount that can be used, given the supply of other factors and the technology being used—the demand.

be on the imbalance between labor supply and demand or, to use a more comprehensive term, on manpower utilization. There will also be a brief discussion of some of the more important demand factors and their implications for employment strategy. The main emphasis throughout will be on the role of population size and growth in determining potential labor supply and demand; in order to present a more complete picture, however, some essential nondemographic variables and their interplay will be included.

FACTORS DETERMINING MANPOWER SUPPLY

The size or supply of the labor force is determined by three factors: the size and age-sex structure of the population, which are the result of the interplay of the demographic forces of fertility, mortality, and migration; and the age-sex-specific activity rates (the percentage of male or female population in a given age group actually or potentially engaged in economic activity), which are influenced by a complex of economic, social, and cultural factors, and possibly by demographic factors also. The relationships between these factors are portrayed in Figure 3.1 by a simplified flow diagram.[1] Demand for labor is taken

Figure 3.1   Flow Diagram of Basic Determinants of Labor Force Size

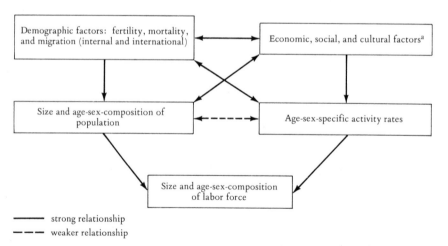

————— strong relationship

— — — weaker relationship

[a]Economic factors: Per capita GNP, average earning level for workers, employment opportunities and their geographical distribution, industrial structure, occupational structure, organization of production, and so forth. Social factors: Educational opportunities, educational attainment, urbanization, marital laws and characteristics, and so forth.
Cultural and other factors: Traditional attitudes toward participation of different groups, particularly women, in economic activity, religious influences on attitudes to work, and so forth.

SOURCE: Ghazi M. Farooq, "An aggregative model of labor force participation in Pakistan, "*The Developing Economies* 10, no. 3 (September 1972): 267-269.

as an implicit determinant of labor supply and is contained under "economic factors." This model emphasizes the disaggregation of the population into different age-sex groups in order to study each group as a separate entity.[2] The rationale for this approach is that the labor force participation of each group is determined differently and that different groups contribute to GNP to a different degree. Also, the nature and complexity of the interrelations vary with the particular group under study.[3]

There are significant interactions among the factors determining labor activity, as illustrated by the flow diagram. For example, migration may be largely motivated by economic factors. Also, economic factors may profoundly influence social and cultural factors and vice versa, particularly in the initial stages of modernization. There also may be a direct relationship between demographic factors and age-sex-specific activity rates, particularly for women; fertility and female work participation in the middle-adult age groups may be interrelated. Ideally, the inclusion of a framework similar to that in Figure 3.1 in the statistical apparatus of development planning would greatly improve the formulation of long-term manpower strategy.[4]

Changes in fertility have an impact on labor force size only in the long run. Age distributions do, of course, reflect past fertility and mortality conditions, but in the short run they may be taken as "given." Two countries with the same total population size and age-specific activity rates but different age distributions could differ significantly in size of labor force. The same is true of two countries with the same population size and age distributions but different age-specific activity rates.

Age Structure

The effect of age structure and age-sex-specific activity rates on labor force size can be seen by comparing the population pyramids of the three developing countries with that of Sweden, shown in Figure 3.2. The proportion of the total

---

[2] The different age-sex groups suggested are: males 10–19, 20–59, 60 and over; females 10–19; married women, 20 and over; single women, 20 and over; and other women, 20 and over.

[3] For example, the quantitative determination of child labor can be expected to be relatively simple. A United Nations study using data for 30 countries found an almost one-to-one functional relationship between the activity rates for young persons and the combined factors of school attendance and the degree of industrialization (the latter measured as the percentage of active males in agriculture and related activities). Coefficients of determination were, respectively, 0.89 and 0.94 for males aged 10–14 and 15–19.[2] On the other hand, the determinants of female economic activity may be very complex.

[4] With the necessary data available, the relationships advanced in this framework can be expressed as estimated regressions. And, applying simultaneous equation solutions (accounting for interactions) to the resulting matrix of coefficients, the complexity of which would depend on the data, projections of labor force dimensions and various subcategories can be made.[3]

Figure 3.2 Population and Labor Force by Age and Sex: Selected Countries (Figures in brackets are percentages in labor force for respective age groups)

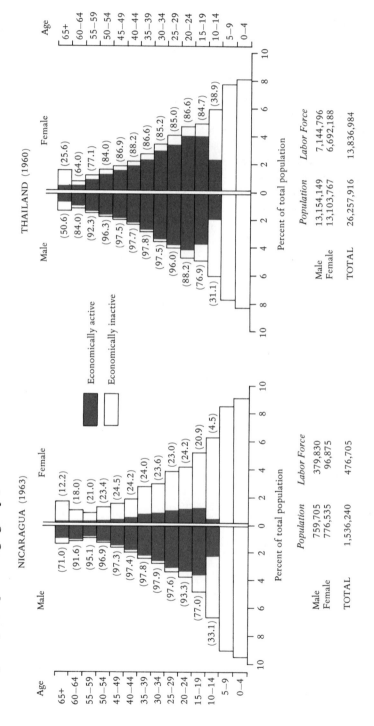

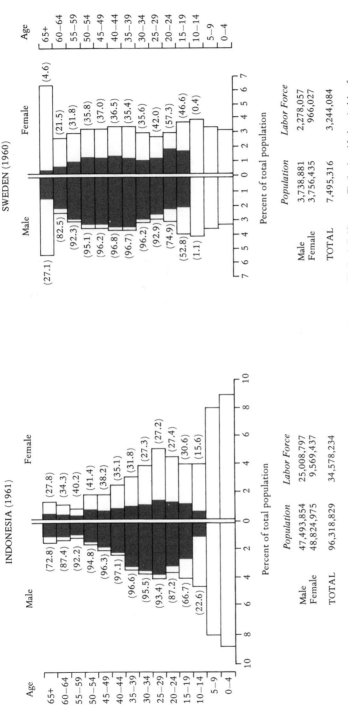

INDONESIA (1961)

SWEDEN (1960)

Age: 65+, 60–64, 55–59, 50–54, 45–49, 40–44, 35–39, 30–34, 25–29, 20–24, 15–19, 10–14, 5–9, 0–4

Male — Female

Percent of total population

Indonesia

	Population	Labor Force
Male	47,493,854	25,008,797
Female	48,824,975	9,569,437
TOTAL	96,318,829	34,578,234

Sweden

	Population	Labor Force
Male	3,738,881	2,278,057
Female	3,756,435	966,027
TOTAL	7,495,316	3,244,084

NOTE: Minimum age limit for economic enumeration is 10 years in Nicaragua, Indonesia, and Sweden, and 11 years in Thailand. In Nicaragua, Thailand, and Indonesia, labor force data for the middle-adult age groups are reported by 10-year age groups instead of 5-year. The quinquennial activity rates were interpolated from free-hand, smooth activity curves, which were drawn on the basis of reported rates. These quinquennial rates were checked and adjusted by applying them to the population in the respective age groups.

SOURCE: United Nations, *Demographic Yearbook*, 1963, 1964, and 1965 (New York: United Nations, 1964, 1965, and 1966).

population in the inactive age group of under 15 years in Nicaragua, Thailand, and Indonesia is about twice as large as in Sweden.[5] This is the primary reason why the overall crude male activity rate (defined as the percentage of the total male population in the labor force) in these countries is much lower than that of Sweden (see Table 3.1), despite their larger activity rates for almost every age group. If, however, each of these countries, with its present schedule of activity rates, were to assume the same age composition as Sweden, its crude male activity rate would greatly increase. This is shown in Table 3.1, where an age-standardized activity rate has been computed for each country, using the age structure of the Swedish population as a standard. The influence of age composition on labor force size can be further elaborated in proportionate terms by the "age structure index"[6] (Table 3.1, last column), computed here for the total population. The total age structure index means that, in Indonesia, for example, with its present age-sex activity schedule, the labor force is 26 percent smaller (100 minus 74) than it would be if the age structure of its population were the same as that of Sweden. In addition, standardization procedures can be used to show numerically the influences of different age structures on labor supply as separate from differences in activity rates.[5]

Table 3.1   Crude and Standardized Activity Rates by Sex, Selected Countries (in percents)

Country	Male Crude	Male Standardized	Female Crude	Female Standardized	Both sexes Crude	Both sexes Standardized	Total age-structure index
Nicaragua (1963)	50.0	72.9	12.5	16.9	31.0	44.8	69
Thailand (1960)	54.3	69.5	51.1	61.1	52.7	65.3	81
Indonesia (1961)	52.7	69.9	19.6	26.8	35.9	48.3	74
Sweden (1960)	60.9	60.9	25.7	25.7	43.3	43.3	100

SOURCES: United Nations, *Demographic Yearbook, 1963* and *Demographic Yearbook, 1965* (New York: United Nations, 1964 and 1965).

---

[5] The proportion of the population in the other inactive age group (65 and over) is comparatively smaller in developing countries; in many developing countries, such as Nicaragua and Indonesia, substantial activity rates in ages 65 and over are reported, particularly for males. However, given the agrarian nature of those economies, it has been suggested that economic participation in these ages may be only nominal.[4]

[6] Age-structure index is simply a ratio of the crude to the standardized rate multiplied by 100.

Since most new entrants to the labor force for the next 15–20 years have already been born, the present age composition of a country's population contains crucial information about potential labor supply for the planner.[7] An age structure with more than 40 percent of the total population under age 15, as is typical of developing countries,[8] means a large number of labor force entrants during a relatively short period of time.

Determinants of Labor Force Participation

As the flow diagram in Figure 3.1 shows, age-sex-specific activity rates are determined by economic, social, and cultural factors, as well as demographic factors. The shaded portions of the population pyramids in Figure 3.2 illustrate the results of variations in such factors from country to country. In Sweden, as in all industrialized countries, the average age of entry into the labor force is higher and the average age of retirement is lower than in those developing countries that are largely agricultural.[8] Thus, the proportion of the male population under age 24 and over age 59 who are economically active is smaller in Sweden than in these three developing countries. Between the ages of 25 and 59, however, there is little or no difference between these four countries in the proportion of the male population who are economically active. For males, age is the single most important determinant of labor activity. This, of course, is the result of the universal social custom of assigning to men the role of breadwinner.

The relationship between age and labor force participation is more or less absent in the case of women. Although Nicaragua, Indonesia, and Thailand have similar economic structures and comparable degrees of economic development, each shows a distinct pattern of female labor force participation. In Nicaragua, women appear to be all but inhibited from participating in economic activity. Women in Thailand, on the other hand, are reported to be contributing to the labor force almost as much as men, and female age-specific activity rates follow almost the same pattern as do those of males. Female labor activity in Indonesia is somewhere between that of Nicaragua and Thailand and resembles more the Swedish pattern.

We must be careful in interpreting the reported level of female labor activity. It is now well established that the reporting of female economic activity is more influenced by traits of culture and tradition, by differences in concepts, definitions, and enumeration procedures, and by reporting biases than by economic

---

[7] If age-specific mortality rates are available along with age-specific activity rates and the age distribution of a population, measurement of new entries and separations—and hence new additions to labor force over a period of, for example, 15 years—is feasible.[6]

[8] In 1965, about 42 percent of the population in the developing regions were under age 15, as compared to 28 percent in the more developed areas (25 percent in Europe and 31 percent in North America).[7]

factors. One study has shown that in many Catholic and Muslim countries, underreporting was partly responsible for the low reported female participation rates.[9] But this does not rule out substantial real differences, which, for example, do exist between Thailand and other Muslim countries in their urban female labor force participation rates[10] and the considerable differences that sometimes exist between ethnic and other subgroups within countries such as Malaya.[11] This emphasizes the importance of social, cultural, and institutional factors in conditioning the attitudes of a society toward female work participation.[12] In fact, factors influencing female labor force participation are a lot more complex than suggested in most economic models.

The young age structures found in most developing countries have important implications for those involved in development planning. A country with sustained high fertility and declining mortality develops a high child dependency ratio (defined as the ratio of the population under age 15 to the population aged 15 and over). Despite the higher labor force activity rates found in many developing countries in the younger and older age groups, the labor force is growing at a slower rate than the total population. The disproportion between the economically active and the economically inactive is further enlarged when the demand for labor does not keep pace with the rate at which the labor force is growing.[9]

Impact of Fertility and Mortality on Manpower Supply

Given data on the initial population size and age structure and an assumed trend in age-sex-specific activity rates, the separate and combined effects of changes in fertility and mortality levels on future manpower supply can be quantified over an extended period of time. In cases where external migration is important, its impact on labor force size can also be estimated.

As an illustrative example, Tables 3.2A and 3.2B give projections of changes, both absolute and relative, in the Brazilian male population and labor force over the period 1950–1980 under different sets of mortality, fertility, and activity schedule assumptions.[10] If the 1950 conditions were maintained, both male population and labor force would almost double by 1980. Considering the recent trend in mortality levels, however, an assumption of declining mortality is more realistic. If this assumed decline were accompanied by constant fertility and the present activity schedule, it would produce a significantly larger male population (by 6.4 million) and labor force (by 2.7 million) than would exist under the "no change" assumption. It is interesting to observe that since decreasing mortality leads to rejuvenation at the base of the population (see part A, column 4), the relative

---

[9] This has been particularly true in Latin American countries.[13]

[10] A similar exercise has been carried out for Algeria, Tunisia, Brazil, Mexico, Sri Lanka, India, and the Philippines.[14]

increase in labor force would be slightly smaller than that in the total population, as also shown by the reduction of 1.5 percentage points in the crude activity rate. The effects of this assumption on population and labor force size reflect the conditions generated in the "transitional period," which many developing countries are currently undergoing. In fact, as a result of this phenomenon, the tremendous population increases of the 1950s and 1960s will be transformed into a labor force explosion in the 1970s and 1980s.

Table 3.2A   Analytical Projections of Male Population under Three Different Assumptions: Brazil, 1950–1980

	Increase in population, 1950–1980[b]		Percent change in age structure from 1950[c]		
Assumptions[a]	Number ('000)	As % of 1950 population	0–14	15–59	60+
Constant mortality and fertility	24,687	95.3	—	−0.4	+0.4
Declining mortality and constant fertility	31,066	119.9	+1.4	−2.3	+0.9
Declining mortality and fertility	23,411	90.4	−4.2	+2.6	+1.6

[a] The decline in mortality is such as to increase expectation of life at birth from an estimated level of 44.1 years in 1950–1955 to 56.6 years in 1975–1980. The decline in fertility is such as to lower the age-sex adjusted birth rate from an estimated level of 43.0 per thousand in 1950–1955 to 31.6 in 1975–1980. The decline in age-specific male activity rates is such as to approximate by 1980 the corresponding values of the 1950 activity schedule of Sweden.

[b] Total male population in 1950 was 25.9 million.

[c] Percent distribution of male population in 1950 by the three broad age groups was 41.9, 53.9, and 4.2, respectively.

SOURCES: United Nations, Department of Economic and Social Affairs, *Methods of Analyzing Census Data on Economic Activities of the Population*, ST/SOA/Series A/43 (New York: United Nations, 1968), Table 12; United Nations, Department of Economic and Social Affairs, *Future Population Estimates by Sex and Age, Report II: The Population of South America, 1950–1980* (New York: United Nations, 1955), p. 35, 74.

The effects of declining mortality can be modified significantly if there is also a decline in the fertility level. In the case of Brazil, the assumed decline in fertility overcompensates for the decline in mortality and considerably moderates the population and labor force growth rates. It also causes a shift in the age structure, increasing the proportion of the population in the adult age groups,

Table 3.2B   Analytical Projections of Male Labor Force under Six Different Assumptions: Brazil, 1950–1980

Assumptions[a]	Increase in labor force, 1950–1980[b]		Crude activity rate[c]	
	Number ('000)	As % of 1950 labor force	1980	Relative change from 1950
Constant mortality, fertility, and activity rates	13,972	95.6	56.5	+0.1
Constant mortality and fertility with declining activity rates	11,392	78.0	51.4	−5.0
Declining mortality with constant fertility and activity rates	16,686	114.2	54.9	−1.5
Declining mortality and activity rates with constant fertility	13,721	93.9	49.7	−6.7
Declining mortality and fertility with constant activity rates	14,941	102.3	59.9	+3.5
Declining mortality, fertility, and activity rates	12,431	85.1	54.8	−1.6

[a] The decline in mortality is such as to increase expectation of life at birth from an estimated level of 44.1 years in 1950–1955 to 56.6 years in 1975–1980. The decline in fertility is such as to lower the age-sex adjusted birth rate from an estimated level of 43.0 per thousand in 1950–1955 to 31.6 in 1975–1980. The decline in age-specific male activity rates is such as to approximate by 1980 the corresponding values of the 1950 activity schedule of Sweden.

[b] Total male labor force in 1950 was 14.6 million.

[c] Male crude activity rate in 1950 was 56.4 percent.

SOURCES: United Nations, Department of Economic and Social Affairs, *Methods of Analyzing Census Data on Economic Activities of the Population*, ST/SOA/Series A/43 (New York: United Nations, 1968), Table 12; United Nations, Department of Economic and Social Affairs, *Future Population Estimates by Sex and Age, Report II: The Population of South America, 1950–1980* (New York: United Nations, 1955), p. 35, 74.

which further results in an increase of 3.5 percentage points in the crude activity rate.

It is quite probable that if industrialization, urbanization, and general economic and social development occur during the 1950–1980 period, the activity schedule will be modified in the direction of later entrance into economic activity and earlier retirement. The effects of declining activity rates are shown in Table 3.2 by assuming that by 1980 the activity schedule of Brazil would be the same as that of Sweden in 1950. The actual changes are more likely to fall somewhere in the range between the constant and declining activity rate assumptions.

There may be a separate influence of population size and growth on manpower supply through the altering of specific labor force participation rates. A relatively high population growth rate that is the result of high fertility will have a depressing effect on work participation among married women. High population growth in combination with already high levels of unemployment and underemployment may also have diverse long-term effects on the participation rates of different population groups. One such result may be the intensification of the "discouraged worker" effect, that is, lack of job opportunities deterring a potential worker from entering the job market, thus lowering the activity rate. This effect seems to be strongest among the young age groups, especially in urban areas.[15] At the same time, however, there may be positive influences on participation rates of certain other groups. For example, many women may seek paid jobs in order to increase family income, which is declining because of high unemployment and/or lower work participation among males. Known as the "additional worker" effect, this may raise the female participation rate.[11] Unfortunately, few data exist to establish and quantify these diverse influences of population growth on specific participation rates.

MANPOWER DEMAND AND UTILIZATION

After obtaining knowledge about the existing level of manpower or labor supply and ascertaining its plausible trend over a future period of time, the planner's next task is to plan for its utilization through increased employment opportunities. A common development strategy has been to concentrate on increasing GNP, with the implied assumption that this would automatically provide enough jobs for new entrants into the labor force. In a number of countries, the naivety of this strategy became apparent when the gulf between labor supply and employment (usually referred to as the employment gap) continued to increase despite modest to large increases in output growth.[12]

In most developing countries, manpower resources are available in an amount adequate to meet any conceivable increase in labor demand in the short run as well as in the long run. The real policy problem, and the one that is assuming

---

[11] High unemployment in Bogota was found to be associated with a decrease in the labor force participation rate of working-age men, an increase in the participation rate of working-age women, and a decrease in net participation in labor activity.[16]

[12] Depending on the mode of production and the technologies adopted, the same growth rate in GNP in two countries may be associated with two very different employment growth rates. And sometimes it is possible that transferring from labor-intensive to capital-intensive production techniques may reduce the employment level despite the gains in output growth. The strategy of concentrating on GNP aspects alone has also had unfavorable implications for income distribution.

primary importance in development planning, is the generation of maximum employment, often including productivity improvements. This in no way implies that the planner should ignore or give less attention to the determinants of labor supply discussed earlier. A knowledge of these, particularly when labor supply is increasing rapidly and the degree of potential underutilization is large, is absolutely essential for the proper formulation of goals and targets and for economic and social welfare considerations applying to the population as a whole.

Labor demand is, theoretically, the total number of jobs an economy has available at a specified point in time, and it can be measured in either of the following ways (assuming that a large number of jobs do not remain unfilled): (1) by taking a count of persons gainfully employed, or (2) by estimating unemployment and underemployment and excluding these from the total labor supply. The second method gives a direct measure of the extent of manpower underutilization and may provide a more appropriate estimate of the employment level in developing countries. In those economies with miniscule modern sectors and predominantly traditional, family-owned and family-operated enterprise systems in both agricultural and nonagricultural sectors, almost every labor force participant may seem to be working and hence be reported as employed. Reported unemployment rates may be low, but underemployment may be rampant.[13] In such countries, the first method would obviously give a biased estimate of the employment level.

Problems in Measuring Unemployment

An internationally used criterion of unemployment is "not working but seeking work." The concept of unemployment gained prominence during the Great Depression and has mainly been relevant in the context of advanced economies, which are essentially full-employment economies dominated by organized labor markets (that is, by the "employee"—wage or salaried worker—category).

The employment problems of developing countries are quite different from those of the more developed countries, and often the concepts and methods derived from the latter do not apply to the problems of the former. The nature of the economy in a developing country is such that its labor force usually has a heterogeneous character. With a predominance of "self-employed" or "own-account worker" and substantial "unpaid family worker" categories, the concept of unemployment as defined above is theoretically not relevant to most of the labor force. Also, it is generally difficult to make a clear-cut distinction be-

---

[13] For example, the 1961 Pakistan census reported an overall unemployment rate of only 3.3 percent. It was admitted by the Planning Commission, however, that, "Underemployment is fairly widespread in rural areas at present. The labour force is estimated at about 37 million workers in 1965, of whom over 20 percent would be idle if the rest were to be fully employed."[17]

tween "seeking work" and "not seeking work." When available employment opportunities are limited compared to labor supply, many persons who are without jobs but desire to be economically active may report themselves as not seeking work because they believe that work is not available. This kind of "misreporting" can lead to a considerable distortion in the size of the labor force and in the estimate of unemployment. Therefore, a better criterion may be "available for work," whether seeking work or not. For example, in rounds 11 through 15 of the National Sample Survey in India, the inclusion of the category "not seeking but available for work" significantly increased the estimates of unemployment, particularly in the rural areas.[14] This modification also increased the unemployment rate significantly in the Philippines (October 1965 round of the Statistical Survey of Households) and in Sri Lanka.[19]

The modified concept of unemployment as "available for work but not working" can, of course, be applied to the modern, nonagricultural urban sector with an organized labor market and to contractual workers in the agricultural and traditional nonagricultural sectors in both rural and urban areas. But more importantly, it can be applied to the self-employed category by including among unemployed, "self-employed but currently without work." And it may provide a better measure of seasonal unemployment, that is, unemployment due to seasonally recurring factors, particularly in the agricultural sector.

The Special Problem of Underemployment

The problem of underutilization of manpower in developing countries is largely one of underemployment rather than open unemployment. The notion of underemployment, however, has been beset with controversy. Much has been written on this subject; a tremendous amount of research is going on; and new concepts and measurement procedures are being evolved—often leading to new controversies. A thorough investigation of all the concepts of underemployment, although perhaps essential, is beyond the scope of the present study. Only a few of the basic and less controversial approaches will be discussed.[20]

The International Labour Organisation (ILO) defines two major categories of underemployment:

(a) *Visible underemployment*, which involves persons involuntarily working part time for shorter than normal periods of work;

(b) *Invisible underemployment*, which exists when a person's working time is not abnormally reduced but whose employment is inadequate in other respects such as: (1) when his job does not permit full use of his highest existing skill or capacity; (2) when his earnings from employment are abnormally low; (3) when he is employed in an establishment or economic unit whose productivity is abnormally low. Underemployment in the situation (b)(1) and (2) is some-

---

[14] This category was about 37 percent of the total rural unemployed and 13 percent of the total urban unemployed in the 15th NSS Round (1959–1960).[18]

times referred to as *disguised underemployment*, while that in the situation (b)(3) is described as *potential underemployment*.[21]

A review by Robinson provides a set of categories of invisible or disguised underemployment that are especially relevant for the agricultural sector in a typical developing country:

TYPE ONE: Unrealized potential output per worker due to low nutritional and health levels of the labor force.

TYPE TWO: Low levels of output per labour input due to inadequate motivations for the cultivators to pursue maximization.

TYPE THREE: Low aspirations for material income as compared to leisure may result in the supply of labour being well below the full employment potential of the work force.

TYPE FOUR: Given relatively fixed factor proportions and a very large supply of one factor relative to the others, unemployment of some of the abundant factor will result.

TYPE FIVE: A highly seasonal pattern of agriculture may result in labour being unused for several months a year.[22]

The above concepts of underemployment, as well as others, have been applied in varying forms in developing countries.[23] For example, in Latin America it was found that underemployment is a more serious problem than open unemployment in both rural and urban areas.[24] In the early 1960s, underemployment exceeded 20 percent in cities in Chile, El Salvador, Panama, and Peru. There was "an abundance of 'fringe' occupations, in which those who cannot find more productive employment can eke out a living—petty hawking, shoe shining, personal service, and so forth."[25] Underemployment in the agricultural sector is partly associated with land shortages. According to Elizaga, a farm of less than two hectares is not economical because it cannot fully absorb the total work capacity of an average farm family. Yet as early as 1951, one-third of the farms in Colombia were less than two hectares. Agricultural censuses taken around 1960 show that 47 percent of the farms in El Salvador were less than 1.42 hectares; 28 percent in Brazil and 20 percent in Panama were less than two hectares.[26] A 1959 study of agricultural underemployment in Mexico showed that over one-half of workers were employed for only 145 days or less a year.[27] Underemployment is as serious, if not worse, in many Asian and African countries. Cho's study of South Korea, for example, concluded that approximately 30 percent of the total annual labor time available in the agricultural sector was unused.[28]

Recently, Hauser and others have suggested measuring manpower potential and its utilization with a multifaceted concept of "underemployed" involving: (a) total unemployment; (b) excessive low average hours worked per week; (c) excessive low average productivity; (d) obvious mismatch of employment with skill and/or training; and (e) discouraged workers who have stopped looking for work.[29]

To this could be added the waste of educational resources and manpower that result from youth delaying their entrance into the labor force and remaining in school because of poor expectations regarding employment. Too often, after completing advanced degrees, they remain either unemployed or over-educated for existing jobs.

Estimation of Employment Generation

A convenient and still quite popular method among planners of estimating the number of additional jobs that would be created over a specified plan period is to apply to the projected GNP growth an output-employment or income-employment growth coefficient (or sometimes, an additional-worker-per-unit-of-investment growth coefficient) as observed over some past period. The assumption is that such coefficients remain more or less stable over an extended period of time.

An income-employment growth coefficient, however, cannot be applied uniformly to the whole economy. Each major sector, as well as subsectors and even minor industry categories, may vary a great deal in the degree of underemployment. For example, within the major industry group of "commerce" are included the relatively modern subcategory of "finance, insurance, etc.," in which underemployment is likely to be low, and the more traditional subcategory of "retail trade," in which underemployment is likely to be high. Productivity levels also vary significantly among industrial groups. Hence, it is essential to obtain relevant income-employment coefficients by detailed industry groups at the two-digit if not at the three-digit level.

In fact, these coefficients vary not only from industry to industry but also from time to time within a specific industry group; that is, when the incremental productivity level is different from the existing industry average.[15] Possibilities of changes in organization and technology add to the instability of income-employment coefficients. A significant reallocation of workers among major sec-

---

[15] This point is further elaborated in the following:

Income-employment growth coefficient $= R_y/R_e$,

where: $R_y =$ income or output (Y) growth rate
$R_e =$ employment (E) growth rate

By definition, then, $R_y/R_e = \dfrac{\Delta Y}{Y} \Big/ \dfrac{\Delta E}{E} = \dfrac{E}{Y} \cdot \dfrac{\Delta Y}{\Delta E}$

In the above equation, the average productivity level is given by the reciprocal of E/Y, and marginal or incremental productivity by $\Delta Y/\Delta E$. Changes in the income-employment growth coefficient are a direct function of changes in marginal productivity relative to the existing average level.[30]

tors may also make application of such coefficients unrealistic.[16] Thus, there are serious problems with this approach.

Income-employment growth coefficients or investment-labor ratios, however, can be used to estimate manpower requirements for relatively modern subsectors (as characterized by relatively more-organized labor markets and well-defined modes of production), primarily in the industrial sector, with the condition that these coefficients or ratios be adjusted for price and productivity changes whenever necessary.[17]

We want to stress the relevance of estimation of employment generation by the analytical approach—analyzing directly the factors governing employment opportunities (by occupation) in different industry and subindustry groups. Each group should be divided into relatively traditional and modern subcategories. The former type contains mainly unskilled or semi-skilled labor and is basically a case of labor supply affecting the level of employment. The latter type contains significantly larger numbers of highly skilled manpower. The demand for high-level manpower categories (professional and technical, administrative and managerial, and clerical) depends largely on industry-specific targets in the development plan, particularly in the more modern subsectors, and on the modernization drive in, for example, the agricultural sector (that is, introducing modern production methods, agricultural extension and development services, irrigation work, and, where necessary, land settlement and land reforms). It should be emphasized that estimation of job creation is essential not only by sector but also by occupation. Actually, translation of both manpower supply and manpower requirements in terms of occupational (or skill) categories is necessary for obtaining consistency between employment policies and educational and vocational training policies. In retrospect, the singular phenomenon of the educated unemployed in developing countries could only have developed because of a lack of consideration of skills and occupational patterns in previous manpower planning.

The analytical method can be augmented, particularly in the industrial sector and its subgroups, by taking into account the experience of other countries at different stages of economic development. This is more commonly known as the international comparison approach and may be essential if data are deficient in the country under consideration.[32] However, since a recent United Nations study provides an adequate discussion of these approaches to estimating job cre-

---

[16] For example, in Japan and Taiwan, employment in agriculture has been declining absolutely with a massive transfer of workers to the modern urban sector. And the income-employment growth coefficient for the agricultural sector has even become negative.[31]

[17] It is also important to note that if there are significant distortions in factor markets, that is, if factor prices misrepresent relative scarcities (discussed in detail later), then the use of investment or capital labor ratios is misleading and may even result in the adoption of inefficient investment strategies.

ation or manpower requirements and recommends specific methods for different sectors and subsectors, details will not be given here.[33]

Demand Considerations and Potential Manpower Utilization

As mentioned before, one primary objective in developing countries has been the maximization of GNP growth. But sometimes this goal can be shown to be in direct conflict with the goal of increasing employment. Income distribution is also a dimension and an objective in these matters. Decisions on priorities have to be made, usually at the sector or subsector level, and involve two basic decisions: first, a decision on the economic ranking among sectors and sub-sectors; and second, a decision on the optimal technique of production for each industrial activity.

The second decision, that is, the choice of production method to be used in an industry to increase output, is between two broad categories: (1) capital-intensive (labor-saving)—raising the capital/labor ratio and thereby increasing the output/worker ratio; or (2) labor-intensive—increasing the amount of labor, that is, lowering the capital/labor ratio. Or the technique of production chosen may fall somewhere between these two poles.

The relative uses of capital and labor in an industry are a direct function of the production techniques available and relative factor prices. For some in-dustries, such as chemical and pharmaceutical, petroleum, and electrical engi-neering, there may be little possibility of variation in the techniques used, whereas in many others the range of choice is wide. Within that range there is often a trade-off between increasing employment opportunities and raising the output growth rate through relatively capital-intensive methods. Japan's experi-ence during its early development period is an example of a conscious decision to increase employment in the manufacturing industries in order to absorb ex-cess industrial labor and to relieve the population pressure on the agricultural sector. The government "actively intervened to transfer second-hand capital assets, which were considered to be inefficient for the higher level of modern technologies, from the larger firms which owned them to smaller firms, thus enabling the latter to lower their capital costs."[34] Such encouragement of "dualism" in the industrial sector may be the most satisfactory way in the short run of reconciling the goals of increasing both output and employment levels.

With regard to the first decision, that is, setting priorities among sectors, it is important to note that relatively more-modern industries tend to be capital-intensive (labor-saving) to a higher degree than are traditional ones over the range of technologies available to them, and that larger output increases in the former are required to generate one additional job. Therefore, in deciding which sectors or industries should receive priority in their development, the planner must realize the implications for employment. For example, Taiwan first de-veloped its labor-intensive agricultural sector and absorbed new entrants to the labor force there. More recently, it has been able to shift workers from the rapidly developing agricultural sector (which has the lowest productivity level) to more-modern nonagricultural industries (which have higher productivity levels). Conversely, India and the Philippines first attempted to promote modern manufacturing industries and have been facing severe employment problems.[35] The implication here is not that one development strategy is necessarily superior to the other, but that they have different consequences in terms of potential manpower utilization as well as productivity and output growth. These choices also represent choices regarding the structure of employment and, implicitly, income distribution. This, in turn, feeds back into the pattern of consumer demand and offsets output.

Factor Pricing and Factor Proportions

Factor pricing, except perhaps in a fully planned economy, plays a crucial role in the choice of technology and organization of production, and hence in determining factor proportions. It is now well known that relative factor prices are distorted in many developing countries. Low interest rates along with easy credit policies make the market price of capital (especially industrial capital) much lower than its scarcity value or opportunity cost. Further, the usual liberal capital import policies in combination with unrealistic exchange rates (that is, overvalued domestic currencies) artificially lower the market price of imported capital. At the micro-firm level, this tends to encourage a higher capital intensity in production than would have been warranted from an efficiency point of view. At the macro level there is a cumulative negative effect on employment. The cheapening of capital also has led to its underutilization, particularly in the industrial sector as illustrated by the absence of multiple shifts. In other words, entrepreneurs find it cheaper to duplicate plants rather than employ more than one shift in existing plants. Capital underutilization and, consequently, lost industrial employment are quite substantial in developing countries.[36]

Wage control policies (for example, minimum industrial wage laws), collective bargaining, and, in some cases, generous wage scales in government services, which create higher standards for other job categories, have led to distortions in the labor market also. Overall, wages in the modern urban sector have tended to be much above the opportunity cost of labor, creating a bias for labor-saving techniques. Also, the existence of a rural-urban wage differential (even after correcting for cost of living differences) has led to large rural-urban migrations. This has resulted in the expansion of the traditional urban sector, which often is merely a counterpart of the agricultural sector, and in higher levels of unemployment.

Hence, as a result of distortions in both the capital and labor markets and the use of suboptimal factor proportions,[18] increasing population size, with its

---

[18] In the traditional agricultural sector population growth exerts the most direct influence on factor proportions by increasing labor/land ratios (and perhaps labor/capital ratios).

resulting growth in the labor force, is in many cases being translated into increasing unemployment and underemployment.

Besides the above considerations, there are also important relationships between potential manpower utilization or employment level on the one hand, and policies regarding education, population distribution, income distribution, and fiscal and international trade policies on the other. An understanding of all of these is vital for formulating a consistent set of policies to meet the challenge posed by the continuing rapid expansion of the potential labor supply.

SUMMARY AND CONCLUSION

In the developing world, an unprecedented rate of population growth during the 1950s and 1960s has led to an explosion of growth in the labor force in the 1970s that will continue through the 1980s. In most countries, there are no signs of a significant slackening in the population growth rate. Even if fertility levels are reduced to replacement level in the feasible near future, however, adequate employment generation will remain a serious problem for the remainder of this century.

In the short run, given a particular age-sex-specific activity schedule, labor force size is basically a function of the size and age composition of a population. In fact, age composition data contain crucial information on the present level of manpower supply and, perhaps more importantly, on the probable magnitude of manpower supply in the future, since most new entrants into the labor force for the next 15–20 years have already been born.

Impacts of changes in fertility and mortality levels on manpower supply via their altering of population size and age structure are essentially long term. The crucial role of demographic variables in determining potential manpower supply can be highlighted by examining the situation in a typical developing country. A country with a high population growth rate due to sustained high fertility and significantly declining mortality faces two basic problems: (1) age structure becomes more inefficient (that is, there is an increasing proportion of the population in the young, inactive age groups) and causes the labor force to grow at a slower rate than the population; and (2) although labor force growth is slower than population growth, it is too rapid in relation to the capacity of the economy to generate employment. High population growth by itself, and in combination with economic factors such as unemployment, may also affect manpower supply through altering specific labor force participation rates, although the direction and magnitude of these changes are not easy to predict.

Given the deficient ability of a developing economy to generate employment, there is a direct relationship between population growth and the level of manpower underutilization. This relationship is most clearly evident in the agricultural sector. At least in countries with already high farm population densities, rapid population growth results in a lowering of the land/labor ratio and, even if the capital/labor ratio is maintained, in a reduction of the use of the relatively more abundant factor, labor. High population growth is also among the major factors responsible, at least indirectly, for the abundance of fringe occupations in urban areas. Proportionately, the larger part of underutilized manpower takes the form of underemployment, rather than open unemployment.

Among the policy conclusions emerging from the discussion in this chapter is the need to check rapid population growth in order to reduce future employment problems. However, population control by itself will not be sufficient. In order to improve employment prospects, it is essential that the distortions in the factor markets be removed; that the present low levels of capital utilization be raised to their maximum; and that the fundamental policy pursued be one of adopting technologies fitted to factor endowments rather than tailoring endowments to fit technology.[37] Special emphasis should be placed on developing the agricultural sector, which is still the single most important source of employment in most developing countries. In a number of countries, new agricultural technology has been quite effective in rapidly increasing agricultural output, but its increased potential for employment has not been sufficiently tapped. But again, for countries having a majority of subsistence farms, if population growth is not reduced, this technological change will relieve the employment problem only temporarily.

REFERENCES

1. For a detailed discussion of this model, see Ghazi M. Farooq, "An aggregative model of labor force participation in Pakistan," *The Developing Economics* 10, no. 3 (September 1972): 267–289.
2. United Nations, Department of Economic and Social Affairs, *Population Growth and Manpower in the Philippines,* ST/SOA/Series A/32 (New York: United Nations, 1960), p. 50.
3. For a discussion, with examples, of some methods of projecting labor supply, see United Nations, Department of Economic and Social Affairs, *Methods of Projecting the Economically Active Population,* Manual V, ST/SOA/Series A/46 (New York: United Nations, 1971), pt. 1.
4. For example, see Lee L. Bean, "Demographic aspects of potential labor force growth in Pakistan," in International Union for the Scientific Study of Population, *Sydney Conference, 1967, Contributed Papers* (Sydney: IUSSP, 1967), p. 91.
5. For methods of standardization, see United Nations, Department of Economic and Social Affairs, *Methods of Analysing Census Data on Economic Activities of the Population,* ST/SOA/Series A/43 (New York: United Nations, 1968), sect. 2.
6. For methods and an example, see ref. 3, pp. 35–38, and ref. 5, pp. 29–34.
7. United Nations, Department of Economic and Social Affairs, *The World Population Situation in 1970,* ST/SOA/Series A/49 (New York: United Nations, 1971), chap. 5, sect. D, table 19.
8. For details, see United Nations, Department of Economic and Social Affairs, *Demographic Aspects of Manpower, Sex and Age Patterns of Participation in Economic Activities,* ST/SOA/Series A/32 (New York: United Nations, 1962), chap. 3.
9. Ghazi M. Farooq, "Dimensions and structure of labor force and their changes in the process of economic development: A case study of Pakistan" (Ph.D. diss., University of Pennsylvania, 1970), sect. 2.4.
10. See, for example, John D. Durand, "Regional patterns in international variations of women's participation in the labor force," mimeographed (Philadelphia: University of Pennsylvania, Population Studies Center, 1971); and "Manpower demography of countries in Asia and the Far East," in United Nations, Economic Commission for Asia and the Far East, *Interrelation Between Population and Manpower Problems: A Joint ECAFE/ILO Regional Seminar,* Asian Population Studies Series no. 7, E/CN.11/1015 (Bangkok: ECAFE, 1972).
11. G. W. Jones, "Female participation in the labor force in a plural economy: The Malayan example," *Malayan Economic Review* 10, no. 2 (October 1965): 61–82.
12. A very important reference on this subject is Easter Boserup, *Women's Role in Economic Development* (London: George Allen & Unwin, 1970).
13. See Gavin W. Jones, "Underutilization of manpower and demographic trends in Latin America," *International Labour Review* 98, no. 5 (November 1968): 451–469.
14. Mahmoud Seklani, "Variations de la structure par age et changes de la popula-

tion active dans les pays sous-developpes," in International Union for the Scientific Study of Population, *International Population Conference, New York, 1961* (London: IUSSP, 1963), pp. 527–531.

15. For details and some case situations, see David Turnham, "The employment problem in less developed countries: A review of evidence," Employment Series, no. 1 (Paris: Development Centre of the Organisation for Economic Co-operation and Development, 1971), pp. 41–43.

16. Miguel Urrutia, "Metodoes para medir los differentes tipos de sub-empleo y de desempleo en Colombia," in Centro de Estudios sobre Desarrollo Economico, *Empleo y Desempleo en Colombia* (Bogota: Ediciones Universidad de los Andes, 1968), pp. 47–52.

17. Planning Commission, Government of Pakistan, *The Third Year Plan (1965–70)* (Karachi: The Manager of Publications, 1967), p. 25. The true level may be even higher than this estimate. See F. G. Seib, "Manpower planning in Pakistan" (Paper presented to the Seminar on Population Problems in the Economic Development of Pakistan, Karachi, Pakistan Institute of Development Economics, 1967), pp. 28–29. Also note that the Planning Commission estimate apparently did not include underemployment in urban areas. For a detailed discussion on the quality of nonagricultural employment in Pakistan, see ref. 9, sect. 5.2.1.

18. Planning Commission of India, *Report of the Committee of Experts on Unemployment Estimates* (Chandigarh: Government Press, 1970), app. 1.

19. ILO Reports and Inquiries, "A survey of employment, unemployment and underemployment in Ceylon," *International Labour Review* 87, no. 3 (March 1963): 247–257. In Santiago, Chile, unemployment without this correction was reported to be 5.6 percent, and with it, 11.5 percent. Organization of American States, Department of Social Affairs, *Employment and Unemployment Trends in Chile*, UP/Series H/7.65 (Washington, D.C.: General Secretaries of the OAS, September 1968).

20. For a very useful and detailed analysis of the concepts of measurement of unemployment and underemployment and some statistical data, see ref. 15, chap. 3.

21. ILO, *Report of the Meeting of Experts on the Measurement of Underemployment*, Document M.E.M.U./D.4 (Geneva, 1963), para. 22; also ILO, *Measurement of Underemployment: Concepts and Methods*, Eleventh International Conference of Labour Statisticians, Report no. 4 (Geneva, 1966).

22. Warren C. Robinson, "Types of disguised rural unemployment and some policy implications," *Oxford Economic Papers* 21, no. 3 (November 1969): 375–379. Two approaches more popularly used by economists for studying underemployment are "marginal productivity" and "labor force reserve." For a concise discussion of these and their drawbacks, see Kailas C. Doctor, "Recent progress in underemployment statistics and analysis," *Proceedings of the World Population Conference, 1965* (New York: United Nations, 1967), vol. 4, pp. 348–354.

23. See ref. 15, chap. 3.

24. For discussion and estimates of unemployment and underemployment for individual countries in Latin America, see ref. 13, pp. 456–469.

25. See ref. 13, pp. 458–459.

26. Juan C. Elizaga, "The demographic aspects of unemployment and underemploy-

ment in Latin America," *Proceedings of the World Population Conference, 1965* (New York: United Nations, 1967), vol. 4, p. 264. See also ILO, *Manpower Planning and Employment Policy in Economic Development,* Report no. 2, Eighth Conference on American States Members of the International Labour Organisation, Ottawa, 1966 (Geneva, 1966).

It is interesting to mention briefly the controversy over using farm size as a norm for determining underemployment. A study by Paglin purported to show that in India, which has frequently been cited as a classic example of underemployment in agriculture, labor on small farms was efficiently employed. The farms (even those of less than five acres) used a significant amount of hired work, although a smaller percentage than did larger farms. And this hired labor added considerably to output. Morton Paglin, "Surplus agricultural labor and development: Facts and theories," *American Economic Review* 4, no. 4 (September 1965): 815–834. This, however, is not to detract from the problem of underutilization of manpower in agriculture, which is certainly a serious problem in most developing countries.

27. Arthur F. Neef, *Labor in Mexico,* B.L.S. Report no. 25 (Washington, D.C.: US Department of Labor, 1963), pp. 39–40.

28. Yong Sam Cho, *Disguised Unemployment in Underdeveloped Areas* (Berkeley: University of California Press, 1963), p. 78.

29. Philip M. Hauser, "A new approach to the measurement of the work force in developing areas" (Paper prepared for Conference on Manpower Problems in East and Southeast Asia, Singapore, May 1971).

30. For a more detailed discussion of income-employment growth coefficients, limitations, and some estimates, see Harry T. Oshima, "Labor absorption in East and Southeast Asia: A summary with interpretation of postwar experience," *The Mayalan Economic Review* 16, no. 2 (October 1971): 63–74.

31. Harry T. Oshima, "Growth and unemployment in Singapore," *The Malayan Economic Review* 12, no. 2 (October 1967): 39.

32. M. A. Horowitz, M. Zymelman, and I. L. Herrnstadt, *Manpower Requirements for Planning: An International Comparison Approach* (Boston: Northeastern University, 1966), vols. 1, 2. For limitations of the international comparison approach, see A. S. Bhalla, "Manpower planning in the context of perspective economic planning in Pakistan," *International Labour Review* 96, no. 5 (November 1967): 479–480. For a critique of this approach and a discussion of alternative approaches as related to educational planning, see R. M. Sundown, "Manpower and educational development in East and Southeast Asia: A summary of conference proceedings," *Malayan Economic Review* 16, no. 2 (October 1971): 78–90.

33. See ref. 3, pp. 47–85.

34. T. Watanabe, "Economic aspects of dualism in the industrial development of Japan," *Economic Development and Cultural Change* 13 (April 1965): 300. Also see G. Ranis, "Allocation criteria and population growth," *American Economic Review* 53, no. 2 (May 1963): 619–633.

35. See ref. 31, p. 39.

36. For details, see Ghazi M. Farooq and Gordon C. Winston, "Shift working, employment, and economic development: A study of industrial workers in Pakistan," Research Memorandum no. 60, Center for Development Economics, Wil-

liams College, July 1974; Gordon C. Winston, "Capital utilization in economic development," *Economic Journal* 81, no. 321 (March 1971) : 36–60; and "Over-invoicing, underutilization, and distorted industrial growth," *Pakistan Development Review* 10, no. 4 (Winter 1970) : 405–421. For some estimates of underutilization of capital, see United Nations, "The process of industrialization in Latin America," ST/ECLA/Conf. 23/L2/Add. 2, mimeographed (New York, January 1966), Statistical Annex; and "Industrial excess capacity and its utilization for exports," UNIDO/IPPD/1, mimeographed (October 1967).

37. See ref. 15, pp. 11–15 and references therein.

FOUR

Educational Planning and Population Growth

GAVIN W. JONES

Education occupies a highly important place in most plans for economic and social development. However you look at it, the education sector is important: as a percentage of the total budget; as a supplier of the trained manpower that is a prerequisite for the accomplishment of other development goals; as an employer of that same trained manpower; as the main sector through whose activities national identity and national goals and aspirations are given meaning and reality among the people. Educational needs are obviously also very closely related to population growth.

There has been a persistent tendency in the past two decades for education's share of gross national product and of government budgets to increase. This has been true of both developed and developing countries, but the rise has been particularly sharp in the developing countries, most of which appear to have doubled or even trebled their public expenditure on education in a period of five to ten years. Most countries in Asia were spending between 1 and 3 percent of total output on education in 1955, and no country was spending more than 3 percent; by 1969, only half these countries were still devoting less than 3 percent of total output to education, and in some the proportion exceeded 5 percent.

These rapidly increasing expenditures on education have been associated with enormous increases in student enrollments and sharp increases in the proportion of eligible children attending school. Expenditures per pupil, however, have remained very low and, in fact, probably fell in Asia during the 1960s.[1] It seems

---

[1] That is, if we look separately at the primary and secondary levels of education. A higher proportion of pupils is now in secondary schools, where costs per head are much higher.

fair to say that in most developing countries the main effort during the past decade has been directed toward realization of quantitative goals for education, and in many countries the quality of education, however it is measured, remains very deficient. In other words, although rapidly rising educational expenditures have more than kept pace with increases in the population to be educated, the average quality of human resources produced by the school system may not have risen.

Cost-benefit studies on education in developing countries tend to indicate that returns to investment in education have been high and the increasing public investment in education not misplaced.[1] However, some studies show poorer returns, particularly for higher education.[2] In any event, education's share in government budgets cannot go on increasing indefinitely, and criteria for deciding the best allocation of funds between education and other areas of the budget are urgently needed.

Unfortunately, neither cost-benefit analysis in its present state of development nor the more commonly used "manpower requirements" approach give completely reliable guidelines. More subjective criteria therefore come into play, cluding felt pressures from the electorate, desire to reach levels reached in other countries, and so forth. International pressures are felt through means such as UNESCO-sponsored meetings of ministers of education, which have adopted resolutions whose influence on national education policies appears to have been considerable. Quantitative targets for expansion of enrollments have been set at these meetings, and the goal of universal primary education was adopted at a meeting of Asian ministers of education in Tokyo, April 1962. Target dates were not specified, but it was envisaged that most Asian countries could meet the goal before 1980.

The key problems facing a national planning agency with regard to educational development are how much of the government's budget should be allocated to education, and how funds expended on education can be utilized most effectively to realize national development goals. These two questions should not be considered separately. The total sum to be allocated to education cannot be gauged correctly in isolation from considerations of educational development strategy. For example, if a promising and balanced educational development strategy requires more funds than are planned, consideration should be given to raising the allocation for education. If we are realistic, however, we will admit that typically budgets are allocated less on the basis of grand, long-term development strategy than on the following simple formula, applied to all government ministries: allocation to the ministry or department in the previous year plus a decent (but restrained) markup to allow for inflation and necessary expansion. Sudden shifts in the composition of government expenditures are very unusual in most countries. Therefore, while stressing the need for regular and systematic reevaluation of budget priorities, we recognize that most of the time planners must work within rather inflexible limits on expenditures. In these circumstances, they must be concerned chiefly with the internal ordering of each economic and social sector, with a view to achieving higher returns from a given expenditure.

These educational planning decisions should also relate some overall manpower utilization scheme. Manpower and educational planning should, in fact, be two sides of the same coin. More often, they are totally different procedures.[3]

Finally, population growth and change have a variety of effects on educational needs and educational planning decisions. Educational planning itself also has feedback effects on population. We return to these below.

DEMOGRAPHY AND EDUCATIONAL PLANNING

Demographic calculus must be an integral component of all educational planning. For one thing, the stated aims of educational development usually include a demographic component. This is true, for example, of the aim of reaching universal primary education within a given length of time, or of lowering dropout rates at certain grades, or of supplying enough trained people to meet the manpower needs of sectoral development plans. In analyzing the implications of these goals, demographic analysis is obviously necessary. But even if the aims of education are not stated in specifically demographic terms, demographic analysis is no less necessary in educational planning Education is a highly people-oriented investment. Its main inputs are people—students and teachers. Its outputs are also people (or, if we like, knowledge embodied in people). Study of the flow of students through a school system is parallel to the study of the dynamics of a population. Entrants to the lowest grade proceed through and out of the system, facing at any given time measurable risks of repeating a grade, promotion to a higher grade, dropout before reaching a recognized terminal point, or graduation at a recognized terminal point. Dropouts and graduates represent the output of the system, people who in their turn become inputs into other subsectors of the population, particularly the labor force.

Because of the close relationship between population dynamics and the dynamics of the educational system, educational planning becomes in large part an exercise in applied demography, and sophisticated techniques have been developed for tracing through the effects of certain policy changes on the subsequent structure of the student population, the requirements for teachers with various qualifications, and so forth.[4] What is often ignored, however, is the possible effects of alternative paths of demographic development and, in particular, alternative trends in birth rates. At the present time, birth rates are beginning to decline in some developing countries, but the onset and rapidity of such declines are difficult to forecast. It is particularly important to specifically incorporate this uncertainty into the educational planning process by allowing for a variety of alternative population trends.

When the aims of educational development are expressed in a way that implies bringing a certain proportion of an age group into the school system (as in the aim of reaching universal primary education, or raising the intake rate of six-year-olds into the first grade, or lowering the dropout rate after a given grade), changes in birth rates or in child mortality rates will directly, although not immediately, change the numbers implied by these aims.

Imagine two developing countries of 10 million people, each with 1.8 million children in the primary school ages, of whom 60 percent (1.1 million) are in school. Both aim to reach complete enrollment of primary school-age children in 15 years. In Country A, the birth rate remains steady at 45 per thousand, whereas in Country B, the birth rate falls to 32 during the 15-year period. The result is that Country A must find school places for 1.8 million additional children, compared with 1.5 million in Country B. The increase in both cases is well above the total base-year enrollment and the difference between them not very marked. But it would be more marked if we compared only six-year-old entrants to primary school or if we considered a longer time period.

Educational planning must consider not only the needs of the nation as a whole, but also the needs of different provinces and regions within the nation. Preparation of subnational population projections requires an analysis of migration patterns and an informed judgment as to whether, and in what ways, differential population growth rates in the past will change in the future. In countries where school enrollment rates are much higher in cities than in rural areas, any change in the rate of rural-urban migration will have a marked effect on the need for educational investment.

An educational planning agency would not feel that it had done its job unless it had presented the policy-makers with estimates of costs and logistic requirements of a variety of alternative paths of educational development. By the same token, the planning agency should not be satisfied unless it has incorporated into its calculations a range of possible future demographic trends. This is not particularly difficult to do, as the remainder of this chapter will demonstrate. Therefore, there is really no reason for neglecting to examine alternative population trends in medium- and long-range educational planning. As well as highlighting the uncertainties of future trends (about which all planners need to be constantly reminded), use of projections with alternative demographic trends also makes it possible to isolate the savings to educational budgets or, alternatively, the additional accomplishments possible with a given budget, when the birth rate declines.

The main propositions established in this chapter so far, then, are that (1) educational planning must include a large dose of applied demography; and (2) alternative population trends should be considered in medium- and long-term educational planning. One other important interrelationship between population and education must also be considered: (3) educational planning can be an important tool in the hands of government to affect population growth rates through curriculum content, the financing scheme employed, and the location of the facilities.

The remainder of this chapter will be concerned with summarizing methods for integrating demographic analysis with educational planning, presenting results from some studies that have examined the implications for educational planning of alternative population trends, and exploring possible effects of educational planning on fertility. There are obviously many other important areas of educational planning that we do not treat at all.

THE DEMOGRAPHIC OBSTACLE TO EDUCATIONAL PROGRESS

Age Structure and Its Effects

If the countries of the world are grouped into the educationally advanced and the educationally underdeveloped, it is found that birth rates and rates of population growth are substantially higher in the educationally underdeveloped countries. One consequence of high fertility is that the proportion of the population in the schoolgoing age groups is much higher. The share of total population aged 5–14 varied in 1965 from a median of 16 percent in the educationally more advanced countries to a median of 27 percent in the educationally less advanced countries. Similar differences can be observed if we relate the numbers in the schoolgoing ages to numbers in the working ages (roughly ages 15–64), the fruits of whose labor must finance educational development efforts.

On the average, the developing countries devote a smaller proportion of their national product to education than do the wealthier countries. But even if a developing country manages to spend as large a share of the national product on education as a wealthier country, as a result of the age structure of its population, a developing country still devotes a substantially lower share per head to the school-age population. And, of course, because of its much lower per capita product level, the actual dollar amount spent on education per head of the school-age population will be very much lower still. We can summarize, then, by saying that countries that are underdeveloped educationally are precisely those whose age structure creates the greatest barrier to further educational progress.

It is clear that the inhibiting effects of age structure on educational development will be greatly reduced if a rapid decline in fertility can be brought about. Using three hypothetical population projections, the first with constant, high fertility, the second with gradually declining fertility, and the third with rapidly declining fertility, Figure 4.1 gives a rough indication of the reduced burden of education as fertility rates decline, by showing the change over time in the number of potential workers (persons aged 15–64) for every potential student (persons aged 5–14). Many potential students are older than 14 and many persons aged 15–64 will not be working, but, nevertheless, the two broad messages of the figure are incontestible: populations with low birth rates have more workers per potential student than do populations with high birth rates; and a

Figure 4.1 *Number of Potential Workers (persons aged 15–64) per Potential Student (persons aged 5–14), Alternative Population Projections, Hypothetical Developing Country*

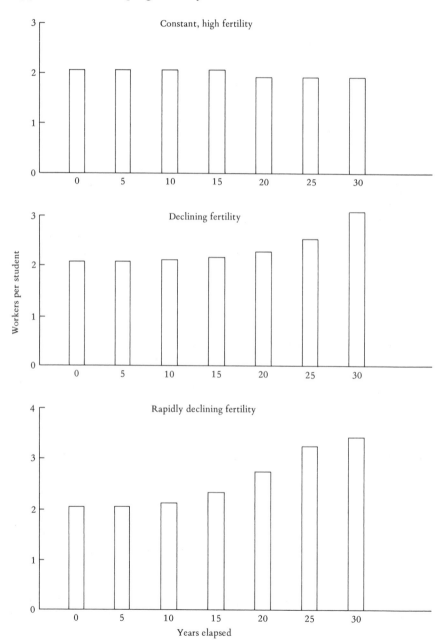

rapid decline in the birth rate makes for a substantial rise in the worker/potential student ratio within 20 years, a rise that continues until the age structure of the population finally "settles down" to the level appropriate to the new, lower birth rate. In the constant fertility projection, the worker/potential student ratio after 30 years is 1.9; with a rapid decline in fertility, it has risen to 3.4.

Effects of Alternative Fertility Trends on Educational Requirements

It is very important for each country to conduct its own educational planning studies, related to its own special conditions, including studies of the different effects of alternative longer-term population trends on educational requirements. A number of such studies have now been done in various countries, and it may be useful to summarize some of the major findings that seem to have general application.[5] The discussion will focus on the effects of a significant decline in fertility, as compared with a situation in which fertility declines more slowly or remains constant.

The effect of a decline in fertility on enrollments is delayed, because children typically do not enter school until they are aged six. At upper levels of education, the lag is even greater: children born this year will not begin secondary school until the end of the 1980s. Over time, however, the effect of a decline in fertility on school enrollments is quite marked. Take, for example, the case of Ghana. If we assume a rise in the primary school enrollment rate from 73 percent in 1975 to 83 percent in 1990, then the percentage increases in enrollments in five-year periods will differ as follows, according to whether fertility rates remain constant or decline (the total fertility rate is assumed to decline linearly from 6.9 in 1975 to 3.0 by the year 2015):

Fertility level	Percentage increase in enrollments		
	1975–1980	1980–1985	1985–1990
High	23.9	28.2	28.3
Declining	23.9	23.7	14.2

Within ten to fifteen years of the onset of fertility decline, the growth of primary school enrollments has dropped substantially, to a rate almost half that in the high fertility projection. The implications of this sharp difference for educational planning are clear.

A similar example for Pakistan, assuming an even more rapid increase in school enrollment rates, shows the delayed effect of fertility decline on secondary school enrollments compared with primary school enrollments. During the 15-year period following 1965, the increase in enrollments is as follows:

Primary School
    High fertility   208%
    Declining fertility   135%
Secondary School
    High fertility   260%
    Declining fertility   234%

By 1980, the effect of fertility decline has just begun to show at the secondary level, whereas at the primary school level the absolute annual increase in enrollments is less than half that in the high fertility projection.

The absolute savings in enrollments resulting from a decline in fertility are, of course, greater if enrollment rates are being raised. However, the relative savings in enrollments are precisely the same whether or not enrollment rates are raised. Viewed in this light, a rapid rise in enrollment rates does not even slightly dilute the enrollment advantage of reduced fertility. The relative savings in enrollments caused in any given time period by a decline in fertility can be altered only by altering the speed of that decline.

The savings in enrollments resulting from a decline in fertility are translated directly into savings in requirements for teachers if teacher/pupil ratios are left unchanged. It is here that the major savings in educational costs are realized, because teacher salary costs typically constitute 60–80 percent of the total recurrent costs of an educational system.

However, beyond the question of teacher requirements *per se*, there are a number of quality aspects that are also of crucial concern to educational planners. For example, will it be possible to increase the ratio of fully trained to untrained teachers? If the rate at which trained teachers are produced by the teacher training colleges is constant, then a slower increase in pupil numbers resulting from a decline in fertility will clearly lead to a more rapid increase in the proportion of trained teachers in the school system. But the educational goal may be different from this. For example, the goal may be to ensure that all new teachers entering the teaching force are fully trained. What will be the required number of enrollments in teacher training colleges from year to year to ensure that this goal is realized?

In answering this kind of question, the weakness of the "enrollment rate" approach becomes evident (see appendix, p. 85). By estimating annual enrollments and teaching force required, using the "grade cohort" approach, it is possible to project backward the enrollments in teacher training institutes necessary to yield the required number of teachers each year. Appropriate assumptions of course must be made as to attrition rates, rates of reentry of former teachers, and the like. The results of such an exercise for Sri Lanka are shown in Figure 4.2. The goal in this example is that all new primary school teachers after 1971 should have two years' training.[2] (At the beginning of 1970, 25 percent of all primary school teachers were uncertified.) The influence of alternative paths of fertility decline is strikingly apparent. For example, in 1980, in the example assuming rapidly rising enrollment rates, there would need to be 15,358 students enrolled in teacher training institutes in Projection 3 (delayed fertility decline), compared with 10,680 in Projection 2 (steady fertility decline), and 4,360 in Projection 1 (early and rapid fertility decline). In the ten-year period 1975–1985, well over four times as many teachers would need to be graduated from teacher training institutes in Projection 3 as in Projection 1. The reason for these very large differences is that teacher training requirements are heavily influenced by changes in the number of pupils, and alternative paths of fertility have a much sharper effect on the increment to the student population than on the absolute size of that population.

The second part of Figure 4.2 shows that when there is no attempt to improve enrollment rates, Projection 1 would require little increase in recent enrollments in teacher education institutes to ensure that all new teachers are fully trained; in fact, from about 1975 to 1988 even fewer enrollments would be required than previously. By contrast, Projection 3 would require more than a doubling of such enrollments by 1980. In the example with improving enrollment rates, the absolute gap between Projections 1 and 3 is even wider. This illustrates the great importance of the particular time path of fertility decline that is followed.

Other qualitative aspects of future educational needs and plans are even more difficult to project using these more-or-less mechanical models. For example, many countries are experimenting with greater use of nonformal educational techniques, adult literacy schemes, and more imaginative and extensive use of audiovisual equipment, even teaching by radio and television. Indeed, the motivation to such innovative approaches is often the realization that traditional approaches are inadequate to cope with needs, given budgetary constraints and continued rapid population growth. The input-to-output coefficients for such educational plans are radically different from traditional approaches and are difficult to project. However, regardless of the nature of the educational program, its emphasis, or its strategic objectives, what has been said about the demographic obstacle to educational development remains valid.

---

[2] The following assumptions were used in these calculations:

 a. That dropout from the teaching force is 4 percent per annum.

 b. That entry into the teaching force of trained teachers other than those just graduating from teacher training institutes is 1 percent per annum. (These would be mostly former teachers reentering the service.)

 c. That dropout from each year of the teacher training course is 3 percent per annum.

Figure 4.2   Required Enrollments in Teacher Education Institutes, 1970–1991, To Ensure That All New Primary School Teachers after 1971 Are Fully Trained: Sri Lanka

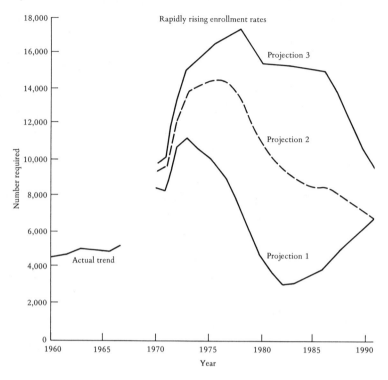

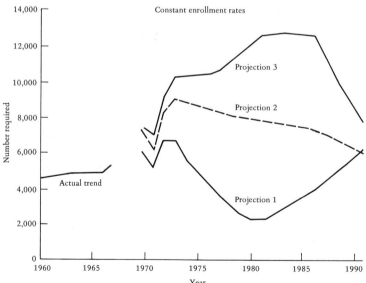

Projection 1: Early and rapid fertility decline.
Projection 2: Steady fertility decline.
Projection 3: Delayed fertility decline.

SAVINGS IN EDUCATIONAL COSTS RESULTING FROM LOWERED FERTILITY

By making reasonable assumptions about trends in certain key components of educational costs (for example, teacher salaries by category of teacher, other recurrent costs, capital costs per pupil-place), it is possible to project the costs of meeting given educational goals, according to different trends in population growth, and hence to derive estimates of the savings resulting from lowered fertility. Of course, increases in the dollar costs of education, or in the dollar savings in educational costs resulting from lowered fertility, have little meaning in isolation: the national product and government budgets can also be expected to increase substantially over time. The key variables that should interest the planner are the projected trends in educational costs as a *proportion of government budgets and of national product,* and the projected savings resulting from lowered fertility as a proportion of budgets and GNP.

The results of such a study done for Thailand are given in Figure 4.3. In this study it was assumed that the growth of total GNP would not be affected by the trend in fertility. This implies that per capita income will grow faster in the projection that assumes a more rapid fertility decline. This is consistent with the results of macroeconomic models discussed in Chapter One; however, other assumptions could also be used without greatly affecting the results.

Figure 4.3   Total Costs of Education as a Percent of GNP under Three Projections, Assuming Improving Enrollment Rates: Thailand, 1970–2000

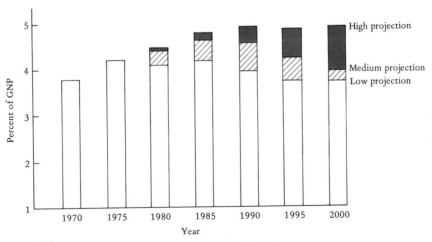

SOURCE: Gavin W. Jones and Vallobh Tantivejakul, "The effect of alternative population trends on the attainment of educational goals in Thailand" (Bangkok: Manpower Planning Division, National Economic Development Board, 1971).

The three population projections for Thailand in Figure 4.3 all assume a decline in fertility, although the decline is assumed to be rather slow in the high population projection. Therefore, the savings shown result from either a moderate or rapid fertility decline as opposed to a slow decline, not from a comparison of declining fertility with a state of constant, high fertility.

Two facts emerge from this example: first, there is a considerable lag (about a decade) before fertility decline has a substantial effect on educational costs; second, the savings build up, over time, to very significant proportions. In Thailand, the projected increases in enrollment rates would require an increase of 25 percent in education's share of GNP by the mid 1980s if the high population projection obtains, but of only 10 percent if the low projection obtains. By the end of the projection period (the year 2000) education's share of GNP in the high projection exceeds that in the low projection by 32 percent, a difference amounting to more than 1 percent of the total GNP. Yet, in both these projections, the proportion of school-age population enrolled at the different levels of education is identical.

The Thailand case study yields results consistent with those of other case studies. Given the aim of gradually improving school enrollment rates, annual educational costs were higher by the following percentages in the higher as compared with the lower fertility projection in studies done for these countries:

Country	After 15 years (percent)	After 25 years (percent)
Republic of Korea		
Compared with rapid fertility decline	20	72
Compared with slower fertility decline	18	29
Ghana	7	25
Pakistan	10	30
Thailand	16	33
Sri Lanka	17	54

The wide differences in these figures are caused primarily by differences in the assumed speed of the fertility decline in the respective "low" projections. In Ghana, only a relatively modest decline in fertility was assumed.

The higher costs of education that result from high fertility constitute a real drain on national resources: a significantly higher share of national resources is needed to achieve the same improvements in the average educational level of the young adult population than when fertility levels are lower.

In the context of a strong commitment by governments of most developing countries to broaden the coverage and improve the quality of their educational systems, a very important result of a decline in fertility is to widen the options available to planners. They can achieve a given improvement in the coverage and quality of the school system with a smaller commitment of the nation's resources than if the fertility level were higher. The resources saved could be used to further improve the coverage and quality of the educational system, on other developmental activities, or on some combination of the two.

The experience of Singapore, which has undergone a sharp decline in fertility along with rapid expansion of the educational system, especially at the higher levels, and steady increases in costs, indicates that fertility decline should not be expected to halt the upward trend in educational costs. But the important point is that the rising educational expenditures in such a country are achieving notable improvements in the quality of the educational system, whereas in a country with 3 percent population growth per annum, rising expenditures may be doing little more than keeping pace with burgeoning numbers of children.

Relative Importance of Population Growth
in Increasing Educational Costs

The examples given above demonstrate clearly that population growth greatly increases the magnitude of the task of expanding and upgrading educational systems and that a decline in fertility leads to important savings in the costs of meeting educational goals. Nevertheless, a number of other factors also contribute to the rise in educational costs; therefore, we should make some attempt to compare the effect of rapid population growth on educational costs with the effects of other factors. One study in which this has been attempted finds that population growth is likely to contribute between 30 and 50 percent of the total increase in educational costs in most developing countries during the next decades.[6] A number of country case studies indicate an even higher contribution of population growth to the increase in recurrent costs of primary education over a 20-year projection period, the share varying between 50 and 70 percent.[7]

It will perhaps be useful to present here the results of calculations showing the relative contribution of population growth to the rise in educational costs in Thailand, information which complements that given in Figure 4.3. At each level of education, the relative shares of the different contributory factors differ. We will only show the relative shares for two of the major levels of education, primary and secondary, in an example assuming improving enrollment rates. The analysis will be limited to recurrent costs, although it must be emphasized that the difference in the relative contribution of population growth to rising capital costs between the high and the low population projections will be even greater.

Very substantial increases in the recurrent costs of primary education will occur between 1970 and 1990 (see Table 4.1). The 1970 costs will be multiplied by a coefficient ranging from 3.4 to 4.3, depending on the population projection. Even greater increases will occur by the year 2000, the 1970 costs being multiplied by a coefficient ranging from 5.9 to 7.9.

Five different factors account for the variation in total recurrent costs in this

Table 4.1 Total Increase and Coefficients of Increase Attributable to the Various Factors that Influence the Increase of Total Recurrent Educational Costs (Assuming Improving Enrollment Rates): Thailand

Factor	1970–1990 (20 years)			1970–2000 (30 years)		
	Low projection	Medium projection	High projection	Low projection	Medium projection	High projection
Primary Education						
Population growth	1.386	1.647	1.777	1.521	1.766	2.253
Increase in enrollment rate	1.274	1.274	1.274	1.264	1.265	1.263
Increase in pupil/teacher ratio	.963	.963	.963	.963	.963	.963
Increase in teacher salaries	1.912	1.885	1.886	3.011	2.837	2.760
Change in the total costs/teacher costs ratio	1.042	1.042	1.042	1.061	1.042	1.042
Total increase	3.385	3.968	4.283	5.916	6.355	7.917
Secondary Education						
Population growth	1.602	1.772	1.772	1.722	2.016	2.294
Increase in enrollment rate	2.086	2.086	2.086	2.327	2.327	2.327
Increase in pupil/teacher ratio	1.067	1.067	1.067	1.067	1.067	1.067
Increase in teacher salaries	1.361	1.343	1.343	2.144	2.020	1.971
Change in the total costs/teacher costs ratio	1.091	1.091	1.092	1.092	1.091	1.091
Total increase	5.297	5.779	5.763	10.006	11.033	12.251
Total increase in GNP	3.864	3.864	3.864	7.602	7.602	7.602

NOTE: The total increase in costs is equal to the product of the coefficients of increase attributable to each of the factors.

example. The coefficients attributable to each of these factors may be interpreted as the change in total costs that would result if this factor operated in isolation. When all the factors operate simultaneously, the coefficients are multiplied by each other and the total variation is equal to the product of the coefficients. A coefficient greater than unity means that the corresponding factor is causing an increase in costs; a coefficient less than unity means a decrease.

Over any given time period, the rise in costs attributable to enrollment rate changes is the same for all three projections, whereas the rise attributable to population growth is of course greater in the projection with the highest birth rate. At the primary level, population growth causes a greater increase in costs than does an increase in enrollment rates; the rapid rise in enrollment rates at the upper primary level is partly offset by a decline in enrollment rates at the lower primary level. Apart from population growth, the other factor responsible for major cost increases is increase in teacher salaries. Ideally, this category should be divided into the cost increase caused by an increased level of teacher qualifications and the cost increase caused by rising salaries for any given level of teacher qualification. This is not possible, however, because the distribution of teachers by qualification levels was not projected beyond 1980.

At the secondary level, enrollment rate changes are a far more important factor in raising costs than at the primary level. Even over the first 20 years, these changes alone would be responsible for a doubling of costs. Except in the high population projection, the population growth coefficient is also higher than at the primary level because a decline in fertility takes longer to slow the increase in numbers at secondary school ages. The teacher salaries coefficient is lower than at the primary level: teacher salaries are held down by the influx of young teachers at the lower end of the salary scale.

Population growth is clearly one of the major factors in raising educational costs in Thailand. Over a 20-year period, primary education costs would increase by about 3.4 times under the low population projection, whereas the increase in the high projection would be 4.3 times. The former figure is lower than the projected increase in GNP over the period, whereas the latter figure is higher. This means that with slower population growth, the share of GNP required for primary education would fall; with rapid population growth, it would rise.

Similarly, over a 20-year period, secondary education costs would increase by about 5.3 times under the low population projection, whereas the increase in the high projection would be 5.8 times. Again, population growth would cause the rise in educational costs to exceed the growth in GNP.

Comparing the total increases in educational costs at the primary level with the projected increase in GNP, we see that only in the high population projection do educational costs grow more rapidly than GNP. On the other hand, total costs of secondary education rise more rapidly than GNP in all three population projections. The main reasons for the difference are that a more rapid rise is postulated in secondary than in primary educational enrollment rates, and that falling birth rates take longer to slow the numbers entering the secondary than the primary school ages.

EFFECTS OF EDUCATIONAL DECISIONS
ON POPULATION GROWTH

Thus far, we have concentrated on the measurable effects of fertility trends on educational needs and costs. It is necessary now to draw attention briefly to some of the other complex interactions between population growth, educational progress, and economic development.[8] Not only does declining fertility facilitate more rapid educational development, but educational planning can, in turn, facilitate a decline in fertility. This can occur in several ways.

First, population education can be made part of the curriculum in primary and secondary schools as well as in adult education and training courses. Population education as a sub-area in education is only beginning to take shape, but it holds great promise, even if its impact will be felt mainly over the long run.[9] Technical and financial assistance for designing and implementing a population education program within an educational plan is available from several donor agencies, including UNESCO. There is no reason for a well-balanced educational plan to ignore this component since it need not compete with any other goals.

Some parents' educational aspirations for their children have been shown to affect desired family size and, in consequence, willingness to adopt family planning. For fertility reduction, the optimum educational plan might be one that aimed at exposing all couples entering or in the early stages of their family formation to a full understanding of the educational possibilities open to their children. This implies a system that reaches all classes, regions, and groups and offers equally to all at least access to a system through which upward advancement by merit to even the level of higher education is possible. This is, of course, a frequently stated objective for other reasons as well. The goal, to repeat, should be the kindling of a desire by parents for considerable education for their children, together with the realization that the more children they have, the more difficult this may become.

Third, the burden of educational costs must be related somehow in the minds of the parents to their family size. The more indirect and hidden are the taxes and charges that parents (and others) pay to finance the educational system, the less incentive they will feel to limit family size. The use of a direct school charge or a tax related to children to be educated should serve as a powerful stimulus to reduce future fertility. Evidence from some countries suggests that such direct school charges falling on the parents have already functioned this way. Resorting to educational financing that falls on the parents rather than the larger society may run counter to some widely accepted notions of social equity and distributive justice and may not be acceptable for some countries, but the possible depressing effect on fertility makes it worth serious consideration.

The extent to which these reinforcing feedbacks will operate undoubtedly will depend on the total development context within which they occur. Likewise, the total development context will influence the extent to which declining fertility and educational development will facilitate more rapid economic development. These feedbacks are most important and need to be taken into account in establishing the appropriate program of educational development. But it is difficult to derive quantitative estimates of their importance.

CONCLUSION

The clear implication of the studies summarized in this chapter is that upgrading a country's human resources through education can be achieved more quickly and at less cost if the birth rate is lowered. The additional costs of high birth rates, in terms of improving the education received by successive cohorts of young people, are substantial.

It is not unfair to say that the techniques available to educational planners are well in advance of those commonly used in educational planning in developing countries. Sometimes this is because of insufficient recognition at high government levels of the importance of planning, sometimes because of shortage of personnel trained in educational planning techniques, sometimes because an inadequate data base prevents the use of more complex planning models. Narrowing the gap between potential and reality in planning will help to avoid costly mistakes in educational strategy based on inadequate evidence or faulty interpretation. Integration of alternative population projections into educational planning models will serve both to underline the uncertainty of demographic trends and to demonstrate the significant long-term benefits resulting from lowered fertility.

The possible feedback effects on fertility of the design and content of an educational system also need to be taken into account. Fertility reduction can be accelerated by educational planning decisions, and no such opportunity should be lost.

APPENDIX: Use of Models in Educational Planning

Any comprehensive educational plan involves the use of models, whether simple or more complex. Without the use of some kind of model, it is impossible to compress the great complexity of an educational system into a set of data that can be purposively analyzed.

The kind of educational planning model that will be most useful to planners in a given developing country clearly depends on a number of factors, including the kind and quality of data available, the uses to which the results will be put, the nature of the educational system itself, and the capacity of the planning agency to work with complex models.[3] However, a few general points are worth making.

LINKS BETWEEN GOALS AND ENROLLMENT TARGETS

Educational goals may be expressed in a variety of different ways. Sometimes they are expressed in terms of required output (that is, number of successful school-leavers) by level and type of education; sometimes they focus on a particular level of education (for example, "to introduce compulsory education of six-years' duration within the next 15 years"); and sometimes they are expressed in the form of a general policy statement (for example, "to enlarge considerably vocational and technical education at the secondary level"; or "to eliminate the disparity between enrollment of boys and girls"; or "to ensure that secondary school places are available to at least 60 percent of those completing primary school").

As stated succinctly in a UNESCO document, these educational goals, in whatever form they are expressed, must be converted into enrollment targets for each relevant level and type of education.[10] Obviously, the planner must respect the internal consistency and the structural balance of the educational system, as well as the time-lags caused by the duration of each level and type of education, and spread the required increase in enrollments over the plan period in a realistic way. The conversion of desirable goals into enrollment targets is a complicated and time-consuming operation because of the many links and interrelationships within the educational system. For example, a decision to double the output of college graduates requires not only a doubling in enrollments in the years preceding the target year, but might call for an increase in teacher-training institutes in order to supply the required number of teachers. Similarly, a decision to enlarge technical education at the secondary level might influence the number of students available, after several years, for entry to institutions of higher education.

Future enrollments at each level and for each type of education are affected by changes in several factors: progression rates within each level; transition rates from one level to another; the distribution of enrollments within a given level by type of education; and the number of new entrants into the educational system. The last variable is, in turn, affected by such educational measures as increasing school facilities and improving the quality of teachers, teaching methods, and teacher supervision. Enrollment targets should therefore be elaborated in several alternatives, using different assumptions as to changes in each of the

---

[3] The capacity to work with complex models will depend, in turn, on the qualifications of the staff, the number of personnel who can be spared for educational planning work, access to computers, and funds available.

above factors, and testing their implications for the whole educational system, including implications for recurring and capital costs.

What kind of model will best enable the planner to meet these requirements? The two major families of models will be described below, but first it may be worth stressing the problems that may be faced in the use of complex models.[11]

LIMITATIONS OF COMPLEX MODELS

In the mid-1960s, UNESCO planners and statisticians prepared a model of educational development, one version of which has come to be known as the Asian model.[12] This complex model, using the grade-cohort approach (to be described below), was used to prepare general guidelines for the development of education in the Asian region during the subsequent 15 years. Those guidelines were examined and approved by the Conference of Ministers of Education and Ministers Responsible for Economic Planning of Member States in Asia, held in Bangkok, November 1965. Financial implications of different educational development strategies were considered, and the strategy finally adopted, although ambitious, was considered to be feasible in terms of its financial and personnel requirements.

The report prepared by UNESCO was a good start. It helped to identify the implications of alternative paths of educational development and to set broad limits to what was feasible. However, one aim stated in preparing the model— that it should be used in educational planning within different Asian member countries of UNESCO—was not realized. A simplified version of the model has been applied to one Asian country, but not by that country's educational planners [13], and work is currently in progress on applying a much-altered version of the more complex model in Thailand.

Why has the Asian model not been used by Asian countries? The answer to this question is important, because the fate of the Asian model is likely to be the fate of other complex models as well. The reasons would seem to be:

1. The data requirements of the model are too great. Most Asian countries do not have data such as repetition rates by grade and sex, age and qualification of teacher force by level of education, and many other variables necessary to apply the detailed model.

2. Application of the detailed model requires a large-capacity computer, planners who understand the dynamics of the model, and computer programmers who can make the necessary adaptations to get it running under local conditions.

3. In many countries, the team working on educational planning within the ministry of education or within the national planning agency is very small and lacking in staff with the technical skills and experience necessary to apply such a model.

4. The pressures of day-to-day planning push long-range planning into the background.

In the future, as educational data and planning skills are improved, the usefulness of such complex models will be greater. In the meantime, it is necessary to recognize that for some time, in many countries, decisions affecting long-term development of the educational system will be made without studying in detail the implications of alternative development paths through the use of complex models. This raises the question whether simpler models are available that will do just as well. In seeking an answer to this question, we will examine briefly the characteristics of the two main types of educational planning models —the grade-cohort method and the enrollment rate method.

THE GRADE-COHORT APPROACH

The Asian model is an example of a model using the grade-cohort approach. This type of model traces the progress of an entry cohort of pupils (that is, the group entering grade one in a given year) through the school system from year to year, taking note of the proportions of pupils dropping out, graduating at certain key cut-off points, repeating a grade, or being promoted to the next higher grade. A schematic presentation is given in Figure 4.4 for the first four grades. This model closely simulates what actually happens within the school system, and the planner can experiment with changes in a number of key variables, singly or in combination, to discover what the effects would be over time on enrollments, numbers graduating, and so forth. Sub-models can project teacher-training requirements, building requirements, and educational costs.

The key advantage of this type of model is that it allows the planner to focus on specific changes he might want to make (for example, lowering repetition rates at certain grades) and isolate the effect of these changes on costs, teacher-training requirements, and so forth.

The point at which fertility trends affect the numbers in this model is at the entry of pupils into grade one. For example, if the aim is to allow 70 percent of six-year-olds to enter grade one, the numbers entering will depend on the size of the six-year-old age group. (Where late entry is common, as it is in many developing countries, the numbers entering grade one are derived from more than one age group.) Thereafter, the numbers remaining in the system are determined by the pattern of dropout, repeater, and promotion rates assumed.

In cases where educational statistics are not adequate to the task of calculating dropout, repeater, and promotion rates at each grade, it is possible to preserve the dynamic features of this model by using a simplified progression rate calculated from year to year from a time series of data on total enrollments in each grade. These data are usually available even when data on repeater and dropout rates are not.[14]

The problem with interpretation of progression rates is that a given pro-

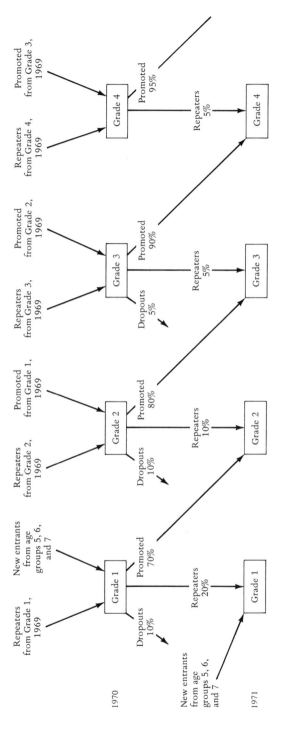

Figure 4.4 Schematic Presentation of Flow of Pupils Through Lower Primary Grades

gression rate can result from an indefinite variety of combinations of promotion, repeater, and dropout rates; and a rise in the progression rate is similarly subject to a variety of possible interpretations. However, in a developing school system characterized initially by high repeater rates, it is reasonable to assume that as the system is improved, the repeater rates at all grades will (at worst) be held constant or (more likely) decline. In either case, a rise in progression rates can then be safely interpreted to indicate a rise in promotion rates or a fall in dropout rates, or both.

The drawbacks to the grade-cohort approach have already been mentioned in the previous section. One is that, because of the enormous number of calculations required, its application over a time period of any length requires use of a computer.[4] A computer is especially necessary if the effects of a variety of alternative population trends are to be tested, because such testing requires that most or all of the educational projections be run through for each set of population projections. In most planning situations in developing countries, development of a computer model and generation of results require a much longer lead-time than does the generation of results from simpler models that lend themselves to use of calculating machines. However, once a suitable computer model has been developed and tested, the lead-time is much shorter for subsequent runs with altered assumptions. Therefore, in many developing countries, work on a computer model for use in educational planning would be well justified. However, even in such countries, work with a simpler model would probably also be useful.

THE ENROLLMENT RATE APPROACH

The enrollment rate approach to educational planning, rather than simulating the internal dynamics of the progression of pupils through the educational system, takes a series of snapshots of the educational system at different times (normally five-year intervals). It may examine the proportions of children in different age groups who are enrolled in school at different times. Or, in the many countries for which data on the ages of students enrolled in different grades are not available, the calculation may have to relate enrollments at a given educational level (for example, primary school) to the national age group from which students at this level are supposed to be drawn. Using the primary school level as an example, enrollment rate under such circumstances would be calculated as follows:

$$\frac{\text{number enrolled in primary school}}{\text{number in official primary school age range}} \times 100$$

---

[4] The calculations can be done on desk calculators, but only with a very large investment of labor. Moreover, the man-hours are difficult to forecast because a mistake in an early section of the computations requires that most subsequent calculations be revised.

If we assume that in this example the primary school age range is 6–12 years, the "proxy" enrollment rate will overstate the proportion of children aged 6–12 who are in school to the extent that children under 6 and over 12 are enrolled in primary school.

However, trends in enrollment rates over time have more meaning, because the rates calculated at different times will all be affected by the inclusion of over-age pupils and therefore will be roughly comparable. The only situation in which this would not be true is one in which there is a marked change over time in the proportion of over-age pupils. If, for example, the proportion of primary pupils who are over-age falls sharply over time, then the rise measured in the "proxy" enrollment rate will understate the real rise in the proportion of children in school in the main primary school age groups.

Provided this problem is recognized, models based on enrollment rates remain a useful tool for educational planning purposes, and especially for quickly discovering some of the implications of alternative population trends for educational requirements. Governments sometimes express their educational goals in ways that make the enrollment rate approach very relevant—for example, "raising the proportion of primary school age children in school from 40 to 65 percent within 10 years."

The key disadvantage of the enrollment rate approach is that it is too aggregative and does not touch some of the variables that may particularly concern the planner. For example, it does not provide a suitable framework for the planner who wants to identify the effects of various combinations of changes in repetition rates at different grades. For "fine tuning" of the educational system, there is no alternative to the grade-cohort approach; but for identifying some of the broad, long-range problems of educational development, especially those stemming from population growth, and presenting them in a way that is meaningful to political leaders, the enrollment rate approach has its uses.

POPULATION PROJECTIONS REQUIRED IN EDUCATIONAL PLANNING

Educational planning, even if for only two or three years ahead, requires some kind of population projections. For short-term planning, population projections can be expected to forecast accurately the numbers in the schoolgoing ages if one has accurate data on the base population, divided into age groups, and a fairly accurate picture of mortality. These data are not available, of course, for many developing countries, but at least errors in forecasting trends in vital rates will contribute far less to inaccuracies in projections than will errors in the estimate of the base population and vital rates.

For longer-term planning, the basis for projection becomes less precise, because the longer the period considered, the less likely that assumptions about fertility, mortality, and migration will forecast accurately what actually happens.

Hence the need to select a range of alternatives within which reality can be expected to fall.

The type of population projection required will depend on the form of educational planning model to be used. If a simple enrollment rate approach requiring only five-year time intervals is used, then a standard cohort population projection by five-year age groups and five-year time intervals will suffice. Data on age groups that differ from the standard 5–9, 10–14, 15–19, and so forth, can be interpolated using Sprague multipliers or another technique of interpolation. On the other hand, if the grade-cohort approach is used, projections of population by single-year time intervals and single years of age are required. Such detailed data are at present available in very few developing countries. It is possible, however, to make do with a projection by five-year age groups and five-year intervals. Single-year intervals can be interpolated, as can single-year age groups.

Construction of population projections are discussed in numerous books that are readily available and that describe interpolation techniques and the calculation of population projections with particular reference to their use in educational planning.[15]

REFERENCES

1. Marcelo Selowsky, "Education and economic growth: Some international comparisons," *Economic Development,* Project for Quantitative Research in Economic Development, Report no. 83, mimeographed (Harvard University, December 1967); Martin Carnoy, "Rates of return to schooling in Latin America," *Journal of Human Resources* (Fall 1967): 517–537; R. N. Stroup and B. M. Hargrove, "Earnings and education in rural South Vietnam," *Journal of Human Resources* (Spring 1969).

2. M. Blaug, P. R. G. Layard, and M. Woodhall, *The Causes of Graduate Unemployment in India* (London: Allen Lane, Penguin Press, 1969); O. D. Hoerr, "Education, income and equity in Malaysia," *Economic Development and Cultural Change* 21, no. 2 (January 1973): 247–273.

3. For a summary of these relationships, see R. M. Sundrum, "Manpower and educational development in East and Southeast Asia," *Malayan Economic Review* 16, no. 2 (October 1971).

4. See, for example, B. A. Liu, *Estimating Future School Enrollment in Developing Countries: A Manual of Methodology* (UNESCO, 1966). For a briefer discussion see Inter-Agency Working Group on Demographic Projections, "Projections in the field of education: Plans, methods and assumptions" (UNESCO/WGDP/1, 1968).

5. For example, Meredith Burke and Gavin Jones, "The demographic obstacle to the attainment of educational goals in the Republic of Korea," in Ministry of Health and Social Affairs, *Population and Family Planning in the Republic of Korea,* vol. 1 (Republic of Korea, 1970); Gavin W. Jones, "Educational goals in tropical Africa," in S. H. Ominde and C. W. Ejiogu, eds., *Population Growth and Economic Development in Africa* (London: Heinemann, 1972); Thomas W. Merrick, "Population growth and the costs of expanding and maintaining the Brazilian education system, 1965–2000" (Paper presented to the annual meeting of the Population Association of America, Atlanta, Georgia, April 1970); Gavin W. Jones and Vallobh Tantivejakul, "The effect of alternative population trends on the attainment of educational goals in Thailand," mimeographed (Bangkok: Manpower Planning Division, National Economic Development Board, 1971); Gavin W. Jones and Ashraf K. Kayani, *Population Growth and Educational Progress in Ceylon* (Colombo: Caxton Printers, 1971); Ta Ngoc Châu, *Population Growth and Costs of Education in Developing Countries* (Paris: UNESCO, International Institute for Educational Planning, 1972); Eduardo E. Arriaga, "Impact of population changes on education costs," *Demography* 9, no. 2 (May 1972).

6. Gavin W. Jones, *Population Growth and Educational Development in Developing Nations* (New York: Halsted Press/Wiley, 1975), chap. 9.

7. See ref. 6.

8. For a full treatment, including a diagrammatic presentation of some of the interactions, see ref. 6, chaps. 10, 11.

9. For a good summary of the emerging field, see *Population and Family Education: Report of an Asian Workshop* (Bangkok: UNESCO Regional Office, 1971).

10. See ref. 4, Inter-Agency Working Group, p. 5.

11. For a detailed discussion of educational planning models, see J. D. Chesswas, *Methodologies of Educational Planning for Developing Countries,* 2 vols. (Paris: UNESCO, International Institute for Educational Planning, 1969).

12. UNESCO, *An Asian Model of Educational Development: Perspectives for 1965–1980* (Paris, 1966). For a recent revision of the model, see UNESCO, "The UNESCO educational simulation model," COM/WS/149, mimeographed (Paris, 1970).

13. See ref. 5, Jones and Kayani. The model has been applied to a number of non-Asian developing countries—Rwanda, Kenya, and Chile.

14. For an application of this approach, see ref. 5, Jones and Kayani.

15. United Nations, "Methods for population projections by sex and age," Manual 3, ST/SOA/Series A (New York, 1965); Ta Ngoc Châu, *Demographic Aspects of Educational Planning* (Paris: UNESCO, International Institute for Educational Planning, 1969); Frederic C. Shorter, *Computational Methods for Population Projections: With Particular Reference to Development Planning* (New York: The Population Council, 1974).

F I V E

Population Change
and Housing Needs

BENJAMIN N. MOK

The demand for housing can be immediately affected by any change in population—number, location, or composition. Changes in fertility, marriage patterns, migration, and mortality also immediately affect housing needs. In the developing countries of the world, fertility, mortality, and migration trends during the last several decades have created a housing demand of enormous proportions. Changes in marriage and divorce patterns, age structure of the population, and average household size have added to the demand. Finally, the problem is exacerbated by a large backlog of unmet housing needs and the continual depletion of housing stock.

This chapter will discuss the effect of specific population variables on housing needs and assess current and future demand in the developing countries. Case studies of Singapore and Hong Kong illustrate how two governments have met the difficult challenge of providing large numbers of people with low-rent, public housing.

FERTILITY, MORTALITY, AND AGE STRUCTURE

Many countries in the world experienced an increase in fertility after World War II. Some experienced it during the late 1940s, but for others it was delayed until the early 1950s. The babies born in the immediate postwar era are now reaching marriageable age. According to data compiled by the Economic Commission for Asia and the Far East (ECAFE), the number of persons aged 15–24 in this region[1] amounted to 379 million in 1970 and will increase to 469 million in

---

[1] The term "ECAFE region" includes the following countries: Afghanistan, Australia, Brunei, Burma, British Solomon Islands, Sri Lanka, Republic of China (Taiwan), Fiji,

1980, an increase of 24 percent.[*1*] It is also estimated that this age group will continue to increase at a faster rate than the total population for the next three decades. Clearly, the immediate and direct effect of such an increase in this age group will be an unusually heavy demand for housing. Some of these persons will marry and want to establish their own households; others will find employment, leave their parents' households, and need small living quarters for themselves.

Almost all of the developing countries have experienced a substantial decline in mortality since World War II. In many of these countries, crude death rates have been reduced by nearly one-half during the last 20 years and are rapidly approaching the levels recorded in the economically most advanced countries. As a result, the proportion of older persons in the population can be expected to increase for the next several decades. It is estimated that the proportion of the population aged 60 and over in the ECAFE region will increase from 5.8 to 6.3 percent between 1970 and 1980 alone. This age group also has special housing needs that must be considered by planners.

MIGRATION AND URBANIZATION

Internal migration normally results in the splitting up of extended-family units and the creation of small family groups. This of course increases the need for housing. The effect from international migration, on the other hand, is less significant, mainly because most countries have adopted a controlled immigration policy.

Internal migration, almost entirely from agricultural communities to cities and towns, is the main contributor to the anticipated increase in the urban proportion of the population. According to an estimate made by the ECAFE Secretariat, the proportion of the population in urban areas in the ECAFE region will probably increase from about 25 percent of the total population in 1970 to about 44 percent in the year 2000. However, the increase of urban population in terms of absolute numbers is even more alarming—from 507 million in 1970 to 1,561 million in 2000.[*2*]

These large increases have serious implications for economic and social development and pose a serious challenge to urban and rural planners in solving housing problems. A number of people will move with their families to the urban areas, but even more single men and women will go there seeking better jobs and a higher living standard. As a result, there will be an increasing need for one-person households in the urban areas. People's housing needs change, however, and as these young people marry and have children, they will need

Hong Kong, India, Indonesia, Iran, Japan, Khmer Republic, Republic of Korea, Laos, Malaysia, Mongolia, Nauru, Nepal, New Zealand, Pakistan, Papua and New Guinea, Philippines, Singapore, Thailand, Tonga and Western Samoa, Republic of Vietnam. When the developing countries are referred to, Australia, Japan, and New Zealand are excluded.

larger dwellings. Still, the formation of many small households in urban areas and the breaking up of larger family units in rural areas will clearly contribute to a lower average household size.

NUMBER AND SIZE OF HOUSEHOLDS

Although the number of households and total population do not necessarily grow at the same rate, it is possible to project the future number and size of households on the basis of the rate of population growth, the age structure of the population, household headship rate, and the rate of rural-urban migration, as well as other social and economic factors (for example, the average size of households tends to decline with social and economic development).

In the ECAFE region, the growth in the number of households over the next decade, which could be taken as an indicator of the growth of housing needs, is expected to be faster than the growth of population. According to the projected figures given in Table 5.1, the number of households in the ECAFE region will increase by 31.9 percent or 126 million between 1970 and 1980. The most important reason for this high growth rate is that the population aged 25–64, for which household headship rates are high, is growing faster than the total population. Furthermore, as a result of the increased nuclearization of families, age-sex-specific headship rates have also increased.

Table 5.1 Projected Number and Size of Households by Region, 1970–1980

Households	High fertility countries	Japan	Australia New Zealand	Total ECAFE	Western Europe
Number (thousands)					
1970	361,856	28,297	4,375	394,528	50,040
1980	476,988	37,704	5,628	520,320	55,450
Percent increase	31.8	33.2	28.6	31.9	10.8
Size					
1970	5.18	3.66	3.51	5.05	2.97
1980	4.95	3.09	3.34	4.80	2.85
Percent decrease	4.4	15.6	4.8	5.0	4.0

SOURCE: Calculated from United Nations, Population Division, "Analysis and projections of households and families," Working Paper no. 28, Revision 1, POP/Sem PASD/ BP/1 (1971), table 6.

Economic conditions and the availability of housing affect household size and number. A shortage of housing or low income may cause people to delay marriage or the formation of a new household or to share living quarters with others. An increase in income may occasionally lead to an increase in fertility and thus in average household size; more often, however, increased income will motivate people to buy privacy and promote the break-up of extended families, thus increasing the number of households and reducing average household size. The increasing divorce and separation rates experienced in some countries in this region will have at least a marginal effect in increasing the demand for housing. The housing demand of old people is growing because more people tend to live separately from their parents and because both the proportion and number of old people is increasing.

PRESENT REPLACEMENT NEEDS

Besides population changes, housing needs are determined by the accumulated backlog of demand caused by insufficient or inadequate housing and the depletion of housing stock through obsolescence or demolition.

A great part of the world population is housed in unfit and unhealthy dwellings. Housing output has consistently lagged behind needs during the First Development Decade (1960–1970).[3] According to the 1965 United Nations estimates given in Table 5.2, the developing areas of Africa, Asia, and Latin America together require construction of 391.9 million housing units during the period 1960–1975 or an average of 26.1 million per annum. Asia requires nearly three-quarters of this total; an average of 19.4 million housing units will have to be constructed annually to cope with population increase, replacement of obsolescent stock, and elimination of existing shortages in Asia.

Available statistics for Asia and the Far East show that, in most countries, less than two housing units per thousand population were built each year during the 1960s, while the estimated requirement for this region is eleven units per thousand population.[4] In some metropolitan areas, as much as one-third of the population are squatters.[5] In Latin America, the housing deficit is about 20 million units; in Asia and the Far East, it is about 22 million in urban areas and 125 million in rural areas (as of 1960).[6]

The housing situation in most countries of Asia presents a discouraging picture. The housing deficit has accumulated mainly in the low-income groups, and this will make it more difficult to clear the backlog. In India, the urban housing shortage, which was 9.3 million units in 1961, was expected to increase to 13.3 million by 1971. In cities of India with a population of 500,000 and over, 30 percent of the population live in slums. In rural areas, it was estimated that approximately 50 million houses needed to be reconditioned or entirely rebuilt.[7] In Pakistan, it was estimated that a total of 1.1 million units would have to be built in urban areas during the second five-year plan (1960–1965), but only 150,000 had been built by the end of 1965. During the third plan period (1965–1970), the accumulated backlog of 950,000 plus the new projected need of 600,000 units due to population increase gave a new estimated five-year total need of 1.55 million. The Planning Commission, handicapped by

Table 5.2 *Estimated Housing Needs of Africa, Asia, and Latin America, 1960–1975 (in millions of dwelling units)*

Housing required to provide for:	Average annual requirements						Total requirements 1960–1975	
	1960–1965		1965–1970		1970–1975			
	Urban	Rural	Urban	Rural	Urban	Rural	Urban	Rural
Population increase								
Africa	0.4	0.9	0.5	1.0	0.7	1.1	7.8	14.7
Asia	2.2	4.0	2.7	4.2	3.2	4.5	41.0	62.1
Latin America	0.9	0.4	1.3	0.3	1.5	0.3	18.7	4.8
Sub-total	3.5	5.3	4.5	5.5	5.4	5.7	67.5	81.6
Replacement of obsolescent stock								
Africa	0.1	1.1	0.1	1.1	0.1	1.1	1.8	16.1
Asia	1.1	6.3	1.1	6.3	1.1	6.3	16.5	94.0
Latin America	0.3	0.7	0.3	0.7	0.3	0.7	4.1	10.3
Sub-total	1.5	8.1	1.5	8.1	1.5	8.1	22.4	120.4
Elimination of existing shortages								
Africa	0.1	0.7	0.1	0.7	0.1	0.7	1.8	10.7
Asia	0.7	4.2	0.7	4.2	0.7	4.2	14.6	62.6
Latin America	0.2	0.5	0.2	0.5	0.2	0.5	3.4	6.9
Sub-total	1.0	5.4	1.0	5.4	1.0	5.4	19.8	80.2
Total	6.0	18.8	7.0	18.0	7.9	19.2	109.7	282.2

SOURCE: United Nations, *World Housing Conditions and Estimates of Housing Requirements*, No. 65.IV.8 (New York: United Nations, 1965), table 1.

lack of funds, was only able to recommend the construction of 292,500 units in response to this need, 80,000 by the government and the rest by the private sector.[8]

MEETING HOUSING NEEDS

Due to the effects of population changes, changes in household size and number, the accumulated backlog of housing need, and the depletion of housing stock, the developing countries are now facing serious housing problems. Especially critical are the problems of the large cities, which are overcrowded as a result not only of the increasing number of permanent residents brought about by rapid population growth, but also of migration of large numbers from rural areas. Prospects for providing their expanding populations with adequate housing, services, and amenities are not bright. Their situation is made worse by such other factors as the uneven distribution of income and ethnic, caste, and religious differences.

Housing construction requires a large volume of capital. Possible sources of finance are government aid, international aid, individual private loans, and private housing schemes. However, capital for housing investment is characterized by high capital output ratios so that, in a sense, it is a luxury that the developing countries cannot well afford. Those most in need of housing, having low incomes, are not able to pay a rent that is only a reasonable return on the high capital investment required. This discourages the private sector from investing in housing. One way in which a government can encourage private sector investment in housing is to sell land for housing below market price and to give easy terms for payment. Where the land is not owned by the government, it can acquire it and do the initial development, such as building roads and installing basic utilities, and then sell the land to private developers. However, such efforts cost more than most governments can afford. In addition, the returns from increasing the quality and quantity of housing are not as obvious as returns from investments in agriculture, health, and education.

If the principal housing need is for construction on a massive scale, there are several possible responses. The building of low-cost, low-rent housing in multi-story complexes by the government is one approach. The building cost per unit should be low enough so that the rent charged is acceptable to squatters and other low-income people. Moreover, less land is required per unit in multi-story dwellings. Later, small units can be converted into larger quarters as the standard of living improves and the backlog of housing needs is met. So far, Hong Kong and Singapore are among the few developing countries that have succeeded in such a housing program.

Another approach is to construct large numbers of low-cost individual units, each on a small, separate plot, arranged in complexes around existing urban centers. Pakistan and India employed this approach to resettle the large number of refugees each country received following political disturbances in 1947. This approach requires more land than the high-rise approach but fewer costly imported materials such as steel beams, elevators, and elaborate waste-disposal arrangements.

Yet another approach is to encourage the upgrading of slums by the people themselves. There is a growing body of evidence from Latin America and Africa that slums tend to upgrade themselves when the residents have succeeded in establishing a foothold in the cash economy of the larger urban complex. Such upgrading can be encouraged by low-cost government loans, direct cash subsidies, and, perhaps more importantly, by providing the necessary infrastructure of paved streets, electrical main lines, trunk sewer lines, and a water supply. Such an approach might well be cheaper than supplying the total housing package to the prospective tenants. Governments have been reluctant to pursue this course, however, for fear of giving squatters a basis for permanency or of attracting more such occupants. Moreover, this scheme might create more problems because, once implemented, squatters might tend to occupy more and more land and it would be nearly impossible to maintain the infrastructure system.

The immediate problems to solve are shortages of funds and land. Not only must there be sufficient land for development, but it must be located near centers of employment. Means of communication and transportation between residential and other areas of the urban conglomerate are also essential. Ideally, a public housing development should be accompanied by a full share of what is essential to modern life: medical and educational facilities, police and fire stations, markets and other facilities such as community centers and parks. And these do not come cheaply. Moreover, there should be land available nearby for private commercial development. Apart from the financial difficulties of achieving all this, there are problems of building technology and housing management to solve.

Even if a government obtains the necessary funds and land for a public housing complex, problems may be encountered in relocating large numbers of people. Some people might not want to move away from relatives or places of employment. Others might fear the loss of freedom consequent on entering the more disciplined and structured environment of a government controlled housing complex. For many, even a marginal rent increase will be a severe disincentive. Some might be frightened of the idea of living in a high-rise structure.

The long-range consequences of housing development plans should be carefully considered. Any plan that adds to the stock of housing in large cities and neglects the smaller urban centers and rural areas will, in the end, only encourage rural-urban migration and intensify the shortages in facilities and services that already exist. Thus, a more effective solution to the current economic-demographic imbalances of most developing countries might be the creation of satellite towns around urban centers and the improvement of rural housing and amenities. But each country must formulate a policy on the basis of its individual circumstances.

SINGAPORE AND HONG KONG: CASE STUDIES

Singapore's housing problem was the result of extremely rapid population growth, which began in the latter half of the nineteenth century. A great influx of migrants from India, China, and neighboring countries gave rise to large slums in and around the city. Only 2,112 public housing units were built in the prewar years and 20,907 units from 1947 to 1959. The Housing and Development Board was formed in February 1960 to improve the housing situation; under their supervision, over 50,000 public housing units were built in the next five years, giving accommodation to 400,000 persons or just under 23 percent of the total population. By the end of 1970, more than 100,000 units had been completed, bringing the total number of occupants to about one-third of the entire population. The special features of these flats are that they are self-contained and are let at rentals of S.$20–60 per month, or within 15 percent of the income of each family. Single individuals with a monthly income of less than S.$500 and families with an income below S.$800 are eligible for application as residents. In 1964, favorable terms were introduced whereby occupants may buy their own flats from the Board. The 1970–1975 Third Five-Year Building Program calls for the construction of another 100,000 units.[9]

Hong Kong is an example of a city in which a large amount of low-cost housing has been provided for both economic and social reasons. The population of Hong Kong grew rapidly during the 1930s, largely because of migration, and in 1941 was estimated at 1,640,000. Much of Hong Kong's housing was destroyed or damaged during World War II, and in 1946 it was estimated that existing accommodations were adequate for some 640,000 persons, about one-third of the population. As a result of the political changes in China in 1949, a large number of immigrants entered Hong Kong. By 1951, the population was estimated to be 2.24 million, whereas adequate housing was available for perhaps half that number. The overcrowding of prewar Chinese-style tenements created serious social and health problems. The renewal and rebuilding of the original central urban areas was left largely to private enterprise; however, renovation was speeded by legislation that allowed existing tenants to be moved out on payment of suitable compensation.[10]

The government authorities were much more concerned with the large concentrations of squatter huts, which in the early 1950s housed about a quarter of a million persons, since these constituted a considerable fire risk and threat to public health and order. In addition, however, they also occupied public land and a certain amount of private agricultural land on the then outskirts of the city, which was required for further urban development.[11] On Christmas eve 1953, a fire at Shek Kip Mei, Kowloon, left 50,000 squatters homeless and led directly to the start of the government building program. Over the period 1954–1964, simple seven-story resettlement blocks were built at the rate of 10,000 units a year, and some 10,000 households a year were moved from squatter areas and rehoused.

The government was able to undertake this ambitious program largely because of the buoyant state of the economy, which provided increasing yields of government revenue. The land system of Hong Kong, whereby possession of all land was vested in the Crown, together with a relatively simple system for acquiring private land for public purposes, were also aiding factors. Because the terrain around Hong Kong is rocky, making site formation and the construction of roads, sewage systems, and water supply systems expensive, the buildings were constructed in a strictly utilitarian, standardized design, with little expenditure on finishings. Washing and toilet facilities were communal and, in the early blocks, residents had to provide their own electric wiring. However, low building costs, together with the fact that both land values and the rate of return of development and building capital were arrived at on a very low noneconomic basis, enabled the government to charge extremely low rents. The original rent of a standard resettlement room was fixed at HK$14 per month, which was found to be within the means of almost all squatter families who were moved and rehoused. With the subsequent enormous rise in household incomes, the present rental of HK$19 for these rooms is very low compared with private accommodations in Hong Kong or public housing rents in Singapore.[12]

The estates were built at a density of 2,000 persons per acre, and the space standard was fixed at 24 square feet per adult and 12 square feet for children under age 10.[13] In the early blocks built from 1954 to 1964, the standard room is 120 square feet and was originally intended for five adults or a married couple with up to six children.

In 1964, 16-story blocks were introduced with individual rooms opening off corridors, each unit with its own balcony, lavatory, and water tap. At about the same time, similar estates were built for which overcrowded families living in private accommodations who had incomes under HK$500 a month could apply. These units were allocated at a limit of 35 square feet per adult. Rents were about one-quarter of market prices.

By the end of 1971, 25 resettlement estates had been built at a total cost of about HK$898 million. In addition to the resettlement estates, there is other government-aided housing that accommodates another half a million people. In March 1972, it was estimated that 1,667,000 persons, or 41 percent of the population of Hong Kong, were living in public housing.[14] In 1970, the government began renovating the Shek Kip Mei estate, the oldest multi-story resettlement estate, by converting the units into self-contained flats, each with its own lavatory and water supply.

With the changing age structure of Hong Kong's population and the rise in incomes and expectations, it appears that present housing standards will require adjustment. Although little information is available about Hong Kong's population in the 1950s, the 1961 census showed that over 40 percent of the population were under age 15, the result of high fertility in the 1950s. By 1971, the large numbers of persons who were aged 10–15 ten years before were approaching marriageable age. In addition, it is estimated that Hong Kong gained more than 100,000 persons from illegal immigration in the last 10–12 years, about two-thirds of whom were in the age group 15–34. As a result of these factors, the population aged 20–24 increased from 200,000 in 1961 to 340,000 in 1971, an increase of 70 percent. These young people are no longer willing to share small, cramped living quarters with their parents, especially couples, who wish to set up their own households upon marriage. At the same time, due to declining mortality, the population aged 60 and over has increased considerably —from 152,000 in 1961 to 293,000 in 1971. Thus, more small living units are needed to accommodate both of these segments of the population. In addition, the estimates of gross domestic product recently published by the Hong Kong Government for the period 1966–1971 show that per capita income is increasing at a rapid rate. Young couples, who are having fewer children than their elders did, now have the financial means to satisfy their expectations for better living standards.

In October 1972, the Hong Kong Government announced a ten-year housing program with a target of housing 180,000 people a year or a total of 1.8 million people in the next ten years.[15] The estimated total cost (allowing 35 square feet per person) is HK$3,340 million. The objectives of this ten-year plan are: (1) to eliminate overcrowding and the sharing of accommodations in both private and public housing; (2) to eliminate the squatter areas; (3) to rehouse persons who have lost their homes as a result of development schemes or disasters; and (4) to keep pace with the natural expansion of the population.

The 1.8 million housing target was arrived at by summing the net population growth for the next ten years and the present population requiring rehousing. The latter figure was obtained by multiplying the average household size by the excess of households over housing units for shared apartment flats and old tenements and adding to this the population in temporary accommodations, the known population in overcrowded public housing, and the marine population that could be expected to come ashore. Although this method tends to give a slight overestimation in that households presently having densities below the maximum desirable level can accommodate future increases in household members, this will be partially offset by the creation of new households from existing households (for example, through children leaving their parents' home).

SUMMARY

Housing the population of the developing countries will be increasingly difficult in the decades to come. While mortality has declined by about half since the 1940s and promises to continue, fertility remains relatively high. The population of the developing countries is currently growing at an average rate of 2.5 percent per year, and this high growth rate is expected to continue in the next 10–20 years. It is estimated that by the end of the century the population of these countries will have almost doubled—from 2,544 to 5,061 million. Proportionately, housing needs increase more rapidly than population as a result of changes in demographic components such as age structure and as a result of social and economic development. Generally, households become smaller in average size and increase rapidly in number.

Both urban and rural areas suffer from a serious shortage of adequate housing. In most developing countries, a large proportion of the population live in rural areas. Governments usually give lower priority to rural housing development, and private investors are reluctant to invest in housing units because of the low capital return ratio. Moreover, rural housing usually needs to be replaced more often than urban housing.[16]

The housing situation in urban areas is no better. Although housing is being constructed at a greater rate in urban than rural areas, the urban population is increasing at a faster rate than the total population as a result of rural migration. Because of capital and land shortages, the governments of these countries have not been able to replace old housing or build new at the rate it is needed. In Asia, for example, no more than 25 percent of the estimated housing requirements were met in the last decade. Some countries have already indicated that they will be able to build only a small proportion of the required housing units in their next national development planning period.

When resources are limited, governments face the difficult task of choosing between many pressing needs. Thus far, more often than not the decision has been to invest in more directly and immediately productive programs and projects that will accelerate economic development or improve educational or medical services. Hong Kong and Singapore stand alone in meeting their housing development targets, and they are atypical of the developing countries in that both have experienced a significant decline in the rate of population growth (through family planning and controlled immigration) and expansion of the economy. In addition, they do not face the dilemma that cities such as Calcutta and Djakarta do: that a successful public housing program in urban areas may defeat itself by encouraging migration from rural areas. Yet it does not seem that alternative policies designed to retain agricultural workers in the countryside or to build new residential centers in rural areas will command the popular support necessary for their success. It may well be that the current trend of migration to large urban centers cannot be reversed and that permanent housing, whatever the side effects, must be provided.

REFERENCES

1. ECAFE Secretariat, "Demographic situation in relation to factors affecting population change" (Paper presented at the Second Asian Population Conference), POP/APC2/BP/1, p. 28.
2. See ref. 1.
3. United Nations, Department of Economic and Social Affairs, *1970 Report on the World Social Situation,* no. 71.IV.13 (New York: United Nations, 1971).
4. United Nations, Department of Economic and Social Affairs, *World Housing Conditions and Estimates of Housing Requirements,* no. 65.IV.8 (New York: United Nations, 1965), Tables 1 and 2.
5. United Nations, Department of Economic and Social Affairs, *1967 Report on the World Social Situation* (New York: United Nations, 1969).
6. See ref. 3, p. 185.
7. United Nations, Department of Economic and Social Affairs, *Asia and the Far East Seminar on Housing Through Non-Profit Organizations,* no. 58.II.H3 (New York: United Nations, 1958), p. 47.
8. United Nations, *Population Aspects of Social Development,* Asian Population Studies Series no. 11 (New York: United Nations), p. 42.
9. Government of Singapore, *1971 Annual Report.*
10. L. F. Goodstadt, "Urban housing in Hong Kong," in Ian C. Jarvie and Joseph Agassi, eds., *Hong Kong: A Society in Transition* (New York: Praeger, 1969).
11. Commissioner for Resettlement, *Annual Report,* 1954–1955 and 1955–1956 (Hong Kong).
12. "Housing the poor," in Keith Hopkins, ed., *Hong Kong: The Industrial Colony* (New York: Oxford University Press, 1971).
13. Commissioner for Resettlement, *Annual Report, 1954–1955* (Hong Kong).
14. Hong Kong Housing Board, *1972 Report.*
15. Speech by His Excellency the Governor, Sir Murray Maclehose, at Legislative Council meeting, 18 October 1972.
16. United Nations, *World Housing Conditions and Estimates of Housing Requirements,* no. 65.IV.8 (New York: United Nations, 1965).

SIX

Population Growth and Health and Family Planning

GAVIN W. JONES

The World Health Organization defines health as complete physical, mental, and social well-being. Since it is impossible to define what services are required to ensure this blissful state, we will settle here for Corsa and Oakley's more limited definition of health services as "organized activities intended to decrease the level of human disease and disability."[1] They classify health services into four major types of activity:

1. Personal health services—those provided for individuals by doctors, nurses, and health technicians to treat illness, prevent disease or disability, and facilitate such normal processes as human reproduction;

2. Environmental health activities—those provided on a mass basis by engineers, sanitarians, and others to minimize disease and discomfort by controlling the quality of such environmental elements as water, food, air, and housing;

3. Public information and education—those provided by individual and mass means to increase public knowledge of health and of conditions affecting it; and

4. Vital registration and health surveillance.

A slightly different classification of health services is used by Stewart: treatment, prevention, information, and research. He notes that treatment and prevention are, on the whole, competitive; they are alternative means to the same objectives.[2]

The effect of population growth on each of these kinds of services is not identical. For example, for personal health services, an increase in numbers requires a more or less direct increase in services. If the service is a mass approach to sanitation or information, however, an increase in numbers may call for little extra service effort; in fact, a minimum population size or population density may even be necessary before the service can be started.

Personal health services are the largest and most expensive component of a nation's health services. The discussion that follows will therefore focus primarily on these services.

HEALTH EXPENDITURES AND RAPID POPULATION GROWTH

We must beware of attributing too strong an influence on mortality and fertility to public health measures. It is generally agreed that the long decline of mortality in the West up to the 1930s was not related to medical measures nor, before the late nineteenth century, to improved sanitation.[3] The more recent, and sharper, decline in mortality in most developing countries is generally believed to have been strongly associated with medical technology through the transfer of public health and vaccination measures developed in the West.[4] But there are those who question whether such measures were the predominant cause of the post-World War II mortality decline,[5] and there is little doubt that improved nutrition, education, and living standards have played a stronger role in mortality decline than is generally recognized.

Moreover, although evidence on this is scarce, it seems unlikely that morbidity has been lowered to the same extent as mortality. To some degree it was possible to lower mortality in the face of continuing poor health conditions through relatively cheap public health and vaccination campaigns that did not require a high degree of public response and participation, but the causes of malnutrition, gastroenteritis, and pneumonia are imbedded in the way people live and cannot be dealt with by teams carrying vaccination syringes. Nor can the incidence of such diseases as typhoid fever, yaws, venereal disease, and tuberculosis be reduced easily, even though effective treatments are available.[1]

To achieve the same reduction of morbidity that has been achieved for mortality will require better nutrition, better sanitation and hygiene, better health surveillance, better health education, and a far higher ratio of health personnel to population than presently exists, organized so that services are readily available where they are most needed.

The role of family planning in lowering fertility is also commonly exaggerated. There is as yet no clear evidence that a family planning program has initiated a decline in fertility in any country. In those countries where family planning programs appear to have had their greatest success—Korea, Taiwan,

---

[1] Vaccines for typhoid, although available, are usually effective for only short periods and therefore mass inoculations would serve little purpose; active cases can be cured, but there is the problem of inadequate health facilities. Adequate control of yaws and venereal disease is almost impossible because the sources of infection are always present. Finding and treating all tuberculosis cases would be prohibitively expensive for almost all developing countries, but a program of vaccinating all children with BCG in order to gradually develop a tuberculosis-free population would not.

Hong Kong, and Singapore—fertility was already declining before the family planning program was introduced. Family planning served to reinforce an established trend.[6]

On the basis of the evidence, therefore, we can say that public health expenditures played a definite role, albeit one that is sometimes exaggerated, in both the postwar mortality decline and the more recent fertility decline in many countries. In neither case, however, is the effect on population growth as clearcut and unidimensional as it may appear at first sight, for the following reasons:

1. Expenditures on health services may raise fertility while lowering mortality because of the improved health and fecundity of couples; at the same time, reduced infant and child mortality sets the scene for a reduction in desired family size, which may be a precondition of any substantial decline in birth rates.

2. Spending on family planning, in leading to a reduction in the number of births to older women, improved spacing of births, and a smaller number of children to be cared for in the home, may lower maternal and infant mortality rates caused by excessive childbearing.[2]

Clearly, there are important interrelationships between fertility and mortality, and any narrowly conceived investment in health or family planning services may give rise to unplanned consequences. To a certain extent, the enormous population growth in the developing countries during the past 30 years was an unplanned consequence of the postwar drive to improve health conditions.

Examination of the unplanned deleterious consequences of the public health programs of the post-World War II period points to some lessons relevant to health planning at the present time. Barlow has conducted a pioneering study of the economic effects of malaria eradication in Sri Lanka by simulating the growth of the economy with and without the malaria eradication program, using an economic growth model of the Coale-Hoover variety. His conclusion is that malaria eradication raised per capita income in the short run but lowered it in the longer run, as the negative effects of the accelerated rate of population growth began to outweigh the positive effects arising, in the main, from enhanced labor productivity. This conclusion held for a wide range of assumptions as to the effect of malaria eradication on the quality of skilled and unskilled labor.[8]

This somewhat unpalatable result should not be interpreted to mean that the anti-malaria campaign should not have been conducted. For one thing, many aspects of human welfare (such as the greater enjoyment of life by those who

---

[2] The evidence presented by Wray indicates that older, high parity women constitute a "high risk" group. Surveys in Thailand show that 85 percent of women over 35 years of age, regardless of parity and number of living children, state that they want no more children. If these women could achieve their desire, Wray estimates that we could expect to eliminate around one-third of maternal deaths.[7]

avoided contracting malaria as a result of the program) could not be incorporated in Barlow's equations. But the clear implication of the study is that it is unwise to interfere with the mortality side of the growth rate equation without taking some steps to keep the fertility side in balance. Barlow concludes that it would have been better to initiate a family planning program concurrently with the malaria eradication program.

The postwar public health drives were conducted at a time when such programs were seen as unquestionably good and humane, but government support of family planning was unthinkable because of the battery of religious, traditional, and cultural objections it would face. Thus, open support was given to "interference" with the death rate side of the growth rate equation, but interference with the birth rate side was opposed. The delay between the onset of sharp declines in mortality in many developing countries (in the late 1940s) and the introduction of family planning programs in most countries of Asia (in the late 1960s) was almost two decades. Even today, the majority of African and Latin American countries have yet to adopt national family planning programs.

Governmental efforts to lower fertility rates may have had little effect if implemented as long ago as the late 1940s. One could expect some delay before the pressure of increased numbers of surviving children would be translated by couples into a downward revision of the number of births desired. By the same token, some degree of "natural" downward adjustment of fertility rates could eventually be expected to occur. The main questions at issue are how long such adjustments take and whether the rapid growth of population in itself hinders the very processes of socioeconomic development that can be expected to slow that growth.

In many developing countries (including large countries such as Indonesia, Nigeria, Pakistan, Bangladesh, and Ethiopia) mortality is still quite high (crude death rates around 20 per thousand or more) and the speed of future mortality decline will have an important bearing on population growth rates. Although all governments are committed to doing all that can reasonably be done to lower mortality and combat disease, there is still the question, "How fast?" It may sound callous to talk of weighing human life against dams and feeder roads, but the government of any country with a relatively high death rate must inevitably weigh alternative levels of health expenditures against other pressing demands on the national budget; with less or greater expenditure in other areas such as housing, education, transport, and power supplies, a larger or smaller number of premature deaths will be prevented.

In most developing countries, political realities and accepted national goals allow only a narrow range of possible choices in this matter. It is in developing more effective health care delivery systems and in balancing family planning expenditures with other areas of the health budget, thereby developing a health system that appropriately balances goals for the reduction of mortality, morbidity, and fertility that the main possibility of imaginative planning lies.

STRATEGIES FOR DEVELOPING HEALTH SERVICES

The gap in health services between the developed and developing countries is wide, and it will clearly take a long time to bridge it. To begin the long process of narrowing the gap is a reasonable objective for most developing countries to pursue, because shortages of trained personnel and facilities are a bottleneck to the improvement of public health care. At the same time, however, it is a dangerous objective because it focuses attention far into the future and may divert attention from the many innovative approaches that could be taken here and now to achieve better health care with limited resources.

For example, when doctors are in short supply, as they are throughout the developing countries, the simplest of logic suggests that any functions for which their high level of training is not absolutely necessary should be taken out of their hands and given to nurses or paramedical staff to perform. Yet all too often, conventions unthinkingly transferred from a Western setting (and sometimes of doubtful wisdom even there) are allowed to prevent this. The "barefoot doctor" system in China shows an approach to community health care radically different from what most developing countries have been willing to try, although other countries have also been searching for health care systems more attuned to their needs.[9] It is certain that without such innovative approaches elsewhere, massive rural populations will be left essentially without the benefit of modern medicine, either preventive or curative.

In addition, a balance between the public and private sectors in the overall medical and health care delivery system is important to ensure widespread coverage. The weight of evidence suggests that completely private systems do not result in health care reaching the rural areas unless subsidy or public conscription (for example, the "health workers" in Iran) are employed. In any event, the countryside usually ends up with public clinics and the urban centers with private doctors.

As for the division of effort between preventive and curative services, re-thinking is also needed. On the basis of an analysis of factors related to increased expectation of life at birth, one health economist concludes that, for the time being, all health resources in developing countries should be concentrated on prevention, none on treatment.[10]

In the sections that follow, we will look at the prospects for improving the ratios of health personnel and health facilities to potential user population. The justification for this emphasis is that medical manpower and facilities are still in short enough supply in most countries to seriously hinder the development of adequate health services. Nevertheless, we must constantly bear in mind that considerable improvements in community health care could be achieved in most countries by innovative strategies designed to deploy the existing personnel more effectively.

PROJECTING HEALTH CARE NEEDS AND COSTS

Let us assume that health planners in a country have developed a set of long-term goals for the development of health services, beginning very simply by looking at the current ratios of health personnel to population and deciding what they would like these ratios to be in the year 2000. We can assume that in deciding on these ratios, the planners will also have given some thought to the structure of health services they want to produce, for example, to what extent curative services would be hospital-centered (which, in turn, would have a bearing on the ratio of nurses to auxiliary personnel).

Let us assume that this country has ratios of health personnel and facilities per 10,000 population as given below and that the aim is to double these ratios by the year 2000.

Personnel and facilities	Number per 10,000 population	
	1965	2000
Physicians	5	10
Dentists	1	2
Pharmacists	1	2
Midwives	2	4
Hospital beds	23	46

These data are, in fact, taken from a study of Turkey.[11] When applied to two alternative population projections, the requirements for health personnel and facilities in the year 2000 were estimated as shown in Table 6.1.

Table 6.1   Projected Demand for Health Personnel and Facilities: Turkey, 2000 (in thousands)

Personnel and facilities	1965	2000		2 as a percent of 1
		Constant fertility (1)	Declining fertility (2)	
Physicians	15.7	93.6	64.1	68
Dentists	3.1	18.7	12.8	68
Pharmacists	3.1	18.7	12.8	68
Midwives	6.3	37.5	25.7	68
Hospital beds	72.2	430.7	295.1	68

This table shows clearly the greater requirements for health personnel and facilities resulting from a rapidly growing population. By applying attrition rates (rates at which the stock of personnel is depleted through death, retirement, or leaving the profession), it is possible to estimate the number of personnel who would have to be trained to ensure the required stock of health personnel in the different years considered. Investment costs (including the cost of training health personnel) can also be calculated.[12] Total costs can then be related to expected trends in government budgets to discover whether in fact the assumed improvement in health service ratios is feasible. Clearly, any given improvement is more likely to be feasible if the fertility rate is declining than if it remains high.

The example just given is the simplest possible case. In practice, it is normally necessary to assume that some fraction of the total population is not "eligible" to use government health services because they are already covered by private medical schemes (for example, those operated by factories and estates and those catering to the wealthy segment of the population). Usually, the fraction of the total population not eligible can be expected to change over time.

Moreover, it is often more realistic to plan for differential improvement in service ratios for different kinds of health personnel, depending on relative strengths and weaknesses in the stock of personnel in the base year and the future personnel needs based on the health strategies adopted.

Finally, the resources required by some health programs are little affected by the size of the population concerned. Therefore, planning the resources needed for such health services (particularly those devoted to certain preventive health measures and sanitation schemes) can be considered independently of population growth. Of course, the resources available for such activities will still be heavily influenced by the effect of population growth on needs for other health services.

All these refinements can fairly readily be incorporated into the simple model.

THE EFFECT OF CHANGING POPULATION COMPOSITION ON HEALTH SERVICE REQUIREMENTS

In seeking a more comprehensive picture of the effect of different population trends on health service requirements, it is necessary to go beyond crude personnel/population ratios and examine the effect of changing population composition on health needs. Two aspects of population composition are particularly likely to have a bearing on health service requirements: the age-sex structure of the population and its regional (especially rural-urban) distribution.

Different age and sex groups in the population have widely differing probabilities of sickness and recourse to medical attention. In both developed and developing countries the general pattern is much the same. As shown in Figure

6.1, infants and old people are the groups with the highest incidence of sickness and hospitalization. At ages above 50, rates of sickness and hospitalization tend to be higher than in the 0–5 age group, and above age 60 they are substantially higher. Nevertheless, illness among young children constitutes a very significant proportion of the total health service demand because in a high fertility population the number of children aged five and under exceeds the total number of people aged 45 and over.

Figure 6.1   Incidence of Sickness by Age Group, Hypothetical Developing Country (Index: Rate at ages 5–9 = 1)

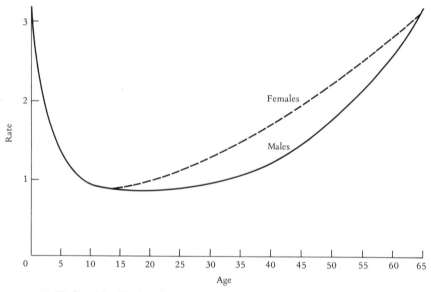

NOTE: This figure is based largely on data on age-incidence of sickness measured in the Survey of Medical Care Utilization and Expenditures on Health conducted by the Ministry of Public Health in Thailand in 1970. The differential between males and females at ages 15-44 would be wider if the measure showed incidence of recourse to medical care or of hospitalization, because maternity cases would show up more in the latter measures. See also data in US Department of Health, Education and Welfare, *Persons Hospitalized*, NCHS Series 10, no. 50, February 1969; US Department of Health, Education and Welfare, *Volume of Physician Visits*, NCHS Series 10 no. 49, November 1968.

Children aged 10–19 normally have the lowest incidence of sickness; thereafter the rates climb gradually. Rates for women in the childbearing age groups and into the 50s are substantially higher than those for men. This presumably is due to health care related to pregnancy and childbearing and, at the later ages, health problems linked with earlier reproductive activities.

When these age and sex differentials are taken into account, will it alter the effect of a decline in fertility on the total needs for health services as measured by the simple reduction in total population growth? Will the age structure effect compound the savings in total health service requirements resulting from a decline in fertility, or will it operate to partly offset those savings? These questions have been examined in two studies, the results of which are shown in Table 6.2.

Table 6.2 Ratio of Growth of Equivalent User Population to Total Population: Thailand and Sri Lanka, 1970–2000

	Thailand			Sri Lanka		
Year	Index of population growth (1)	Index of growth of equivalent user population (2)	Ratio of 2 to 1 (3)	Index of population growth (4)	Index of growth of inpatient cases (non-maternity) (5)	Ratio of 5 to 4 (6)
1970	100	100	1.00	100	100	1.00
1975	115.3	114.3	.99	110.9	111.5	1.01
1980	129.9	127.6	.98	120.7	122.2	1.01
1985	145.5	143.3	.99	129.8	132.9	1.02
1990	160.7	160.4	1.00	138.7	143.8	1.04
1995	177.6	178.8	1.01	147.5	155.2	1.05
2000	193.8	197.6	1.02	156.2	166.7	1.07

NOTE: Population projections assume substantial declines in fertility.
SOURCES: Gavin W. Jones and S. Selvaratnam, Population Growth and Economic Development in Ceylon (Colombo: Hansa Publishers, 1972), chap. 5; Gavin W. Jones and Chet Boonpratuang, The Effect of Population Growth and Urbanization on the Attainment of Public Health Goals in Thailand (Bangkok: Manpower Planning Division, National Economic Development Board, 1973).

This table indicates that, when fertility declines, the sharp differences in the rates of growth of different age groups have very little effect on total health requirements. The growth of health service requirements diverges by less than 2 percent from total population growth in Thailand, and by a maximum of only 7 percent (at the end of the projection period) in Sri Lanka. This is because the decline in the proportion of young children (with their high health service requirements) is counterbalanced by a rise in the share of old persons (also with high health service requirements) and, after a time, by a decline in the proportion of teenage children, who have especially low health service requirements. In both Sri Lanka and Thailand, eventually the age structure is weighted slightly more heavily toward use of health services than it was in the basic year. This is no doubt because the rising proportion of old people and the declining proportion of teenage children more than counterbalance the declining proportion of young children.

The figures shown in Table 6.2 for Sri Lanka and Thailand do not take into account the lower health care requirements for childbirth that would result from lowered fertility. For Sri Lanka, maternity care needs were calculated separately, and the lower maternity requirements counterbalanced the growth in the propor- tion of those age groups with greater health needs. In Thailand, the vast major- ity of deliveries are at home, attended by traditional midwives, but to the extent that the aim is to raise the proportion of births receiving professional care, it would be necessary to take the maternity factor into account.

Nevertheless, from the data in Table 6.2 and with due allowance for the maternity factor, we can conclude that when the birth rate falls steadily over a period of a decade or two, the big savings in health needs results from the smaller growth of total population; the additional effect of the altered age struc- ture is very slight. Therefore, a model that does not apply an age-weighting system will not greatly distort the actual picture of trends in total health service requirements, especially if the number of maternity cases is separately calculated.

The changing geographic distribution of the population also needs to be taken into account in examining the implications of population trends for health needs. If some areas are growing faster than others due to more rapid natural increase or net immigration, this will clearly affect the geographic distribution of health services requirements and should be taken into account in health planning. Increasing population density in previously sparsely settled rural areas (for example, as the result of establishing an irrigation scheme) may facilitate the provision of minimal health care.

Even more important for health planning strategy is the universal tendency to urbanization. In the developing countries, health service ratios are normally much higher in the cities than in the rest of the country. In most countries, attention is being given to the possibility of narrowing the gap between rural and urban areas in the availability of health services. The current wide dis- crepancy in availability and the growth of urban areas make it absolutely essential that health services be planned separately for rural and urban areas. The goal of simply holding health service ratios constant in the country as a whole will mean a decline in health service ratios in urban areas, or in rural areas, or in both. We will return to this point in the following section.

THAILAND CASE STUDY

Methodology

To illustrate some of the points made thus far, we will present briefly the methodology and some of the results of a case study of Thailand.[13] In this study, personnel and budgetary requirements of the nation's public health ser- vices were estimated under four alternative sets of population projections.[3] Four

---

[3] Private sector provision of health services is not considered in this study. The number of doctors and nurses working full-time in the private sector is rather low.

different assumptions as to desired service ratios (that is, ratios of doctors, nurses, hospital beds, and so forth, per 10,000 population) were made for each of the four population projections.

The methodology used in the study is very simple, but it did take into account two important variables that are often neglected in studies of this kind —the differential needs for health services among different age and sex groups in the population and the additional need for health services caused by urbanization when large differentials exist between urban and rural areas in the provision of health services. The population projections, summarized in Table 6.3, indicate that even if the birth rate declines substantially from its 1970 level of around 40 per thousand to about 23 per thousand in the year 2000[4] (see low projection), the 1970 population will almost double during the 30-year period. Nevertheless, the importance of such a decline in fertility can be understood by comparing the total population resulting in the year 2000 with that resulting from a continuation of current fertility levels. The difference is 27.7 million, a number larger than the total population of Thailand in 1960.

The age structure of the population will also be greatly affected by the trend

---

[4] Trends in general fertility rates underlying this decline are from 184.1 in the 1965–1970 period to 91.3 in the 1995–2000 period.

Table 6.3 Population Size and Age Structure, Alternative Projections: Thailand, 1970–2000

Projection	1970	1980	1990	2000
	Population Size (in millions)			
Constant fertility	36.261	50.090	69.895	98.472
High projection	36.180	49.220	66.050	86.803
Medium projection	36.180	48.921	62.898	76.770
Low projection	36.180	47.170	58.805	70.812
	Percentage Age Distribution			
High projection				
0–4	17.4	16.8	15.9	14.7
5–14	26.7	26.7	26.0	25.1
15–44	41.7	42.2	43.8	44.4
45–64	10.6	10.6	10.5	11.8
65 and over	3.5	3.6	3.8	4.0
Low projection				
0–4	17.4	14.2	13.1	11.0
5–14	26.7	26.8	23.4	21.1
14–44	41.7	44.1	47.1	48.6
45–64	10.6	11.1	12.1	14.4
65 and over	3.5	3.8	4.3	4.9

in fertility. A decline in fertility will immediately slow the increase in the numbers of infants and children; after about 15 years, it will begin to affect the numbers in the reproductive age groups. But it will not affect the numbers of old people for generations. Therefore, when fertility declines, the proportion of infants will fall and the proportion of old people will rise. Even so, by the year 2000 the proportion of the population aged 65 and over will be less than 5 percent, whereas it is as high as 12 percent in many Western countries.

Projections of the Bangkok metropolitan population were derived from projections of the urban proportion of the total population and further assumptions about Bangkok's share of the total urban population. The Bangkok metropolitan population will grow from almost 3 million in 1970 to about 10.5–11.5 million in the year 2000, even with substantial declines in the birth rate. A slower decline in the birth rate would result in a Bangkok population of 12 or 13 million. The population of Bangkok as a proportion of the total population of Thailand will continue to increase, growing from 7.5 percent in 1970 to 15 percent in the year 2000. The effect of this increase on requirements for health services is highlighted in the study.

Assumed Trends in Service Ratios, Attrition Rates, and Costs

Table 6.4 shows three alternative trends in service ratios for Thailand between 1970 and the year 2000. In none of them are service ratios in Bangkok assumed to rise. (Any tendency toward further gravitation of health services toward Bangkok should clearly be resisted by the government.) Only in the rest of Thailand, where service ratios are very low, especially for highly trained medical personnel, are improvements in service ratios assumed—namely, a trebling between 1970 and the year 2000. This would still leave the rest of Thailand with more than 10,000 people per doctor, 3,600 people per nurse, and 77,500 people per dentist, ratios considerably worse than they were in 1970 in Bangkok. Ideally, then, the aim should be to more than treble health service ratios in the provinces, but as we shall see later, budgetary constraints would render this an unrealistic aim unless health services are given greater priority than other public services.

Estimates of attrition rates are also shown in Table 6.4. According to these estimates, attrition rates are much higher for doctors (6.5 percent) and nurses (8 percent) than for the other categories of health personnel considered. This is mainly because of the ready availability of alternative jobs for these categories of personnel, both in the private sector in Thailand and in other countries. As we shall see, these high attrition rates, together with improved service ratios that require a rapid increase in the supply of health personnel, will necessitate a very large output from training institutions each year.

Estimation of unit operating and capital costs involved some judicious guesswork because of the paucity of reliable data. In projecting costs after 1970, it was assumed that unit costs in real terms increase at the rate of 3 percent per

Table 6.4 Projected Service Ratios per 10,000 Population and Attrition Rates: Thailand, 1970–2000

| Personnel and facilities | Constant service ratios in Thailand as a whole (1970–2000) | Constant service ratios in Bangkok and rest of Thailand separately | | Service ratios trebled in rest of Thailand, 2000 | Annual rate of attrition[a] (percent) |
		Bangkok (1970–2000)	Rest of Thailand (1970–2000)		
Hospital beds	9.14	41.55	5.86	17.6	5.0
Physicians	0.90	7.27	0.32	0.96	6.5
Nurses	2.03	14.24	0.92	2.76	8.0
Practical nurses	1.29	3.76	1.01	3.03	4.0
Midwives	0.88	0.57	0.91	2.73	4.0
Sanitarians	0.70	0.71	0.66	1.98	4.0
Dentists	0.098	0.71	0.043	0.129	3.0

[a] Rather crude estimates had to be employed because of the paucity of accurate data.

year. This is to allow for increases in wages of health personnel, building costs, and so forth, which over the long run can be expected to increase at about the same rate as labor productivity in the economy. This rate may well be about 3 percent per year if output increases by about 6 percent per year and the labor force by about 3 percent per year.

Constant Service Ratios

First, we will present a brief comparison of the results of the projection assuming constant service ratios in Thailand as a whole with the projection assuming constant service ratios separately for Bangkok and the rest of Thailand (see Table 6.5). The aim of holding service ratios constant separately for Bangkok and the rest of Thailand unfortunately leads to substantially higher costs than does the less realistic aim of merely holding the rates constant in Thailand as a whole. In the projection that distinguishes between Bangkok and the rest of Thailand, total costs over the thirty-year period—Bt. 120.838 million in the high projection—are Bt. 21.437 million or 21.6 percent higher. Costs in the final five-year period are 25.3 percent higher. These figures can be seen as a measure of the cost of urbanization and of meeting it adequately in terms of health services. As column 3 shows, the relative increase in costs builds up over time, as compared with the projection that assumes constant service ratios in Thailand as a whole. By the final five-year period, costs in the high projection are 8.5 times higher than in the 1965-1970 period, as compared with 5.6 times higher when service rates are held constant in Thailand as a whole.

Improving Service Ratios

It is worth presenting in more detail the results of the projection that assumes a trebling of service ratios in provincial Thailand (that is, excluding Bangkok), because it deals with what might be considered a reasonable set of objectives for Thailand to pursue over the long run: a substantial, overall improvement in health service ratios, occasioned partly by the growth of Bangkok's population, with its high health service ratios, and partly by the emphasis on a significant improvement in health service ratios in the rest of the country. It could be argued that a trebling of health service ratios outside of Bangkok in 30 years is not enough, given the existing low ratios. Certainly, this assumption implies that about 57 percent of all the doctors and 28 percent of all hospital beds in the country will still be in Bangkok in the year 2000. Nevertheless, it does represent a substantial improvement over the present situation,[5] and the cost implications are of special interest.

---

[5] Bangkok will have a greater share of Thailand's total population by that time than it does at the moment, so the fall in percentage of doctors living in Bangkok from 67 percent to 57 percent understates the extent to which the rural-urban difference in doctor/population ratio would be narrowed.

Table 6.5 Comparison of Projected Operating Costs for Public Health Services When Holding Service Ratios Constant for Bangkok and Rest of Thailand Separately, and for Thailand as a Whole: 1970–2000 (in millions of bahts)

Year	High population projection			Low population projection		
	Service ratios constant for:			Service ratios constant for:		
	Thailand as a whole (1)	Bangkok and rest of Thailand separately (2)	2 as a percent of 1 (3)	Thailand as a whole (1)	Bangkok and rest of Thailand separately (2)	2 as a percent of 1 (3)
1965–1970 (base)	3.483	3.469	99.6	3.483	3.469	99.6
1970–1975	5.239	5.331	101.8	5.175	5.265	101.7
1975–1980	7.065	7.480	105.9	6.760	7.156	105.9
1980–1985	9.496	10.474	110.3	8.778	9.681	110.3
1985–1990	12.738	14.652	115.0	11.416	13.130	115.0
1990–1995	17.035	20.447	120.0	14.784	17.743	120.0
1995–2000	22.641	28.371	125.3	18.987	23.789	125.3

NOTE: All costs are in 1962 prices: one baht = US$0.0481.

Table 6.6 Number of Health Personnel and Hospital Beds Required with Trebling of Service Ratios Outside Bangkok: Thailand, 1970 and 2000 (in thousands)

Personnel and facilities	1970	2000				Ratio of				
		Constant fertility (C)	High (H)	Medium (M)	Low (L)	L/C	M/C	L/M	M/H	L/H
Physicians	3.23	18.58	16.31	14.38	13.49	.73	.77	.93	.88	.83
Registered nurses	7.31	43.70	38.35	33.83	31.74	.73	.77	.93	.88	.83
Practical nurses	4.48	30.82	27.04	23.85	22.38	.73	.77	.93	.88	.83
Health workers	2.40	17.58	15.43	13.60	12.77	.73	.77	.93	.88	.83
Midwives	3.19	23.68	20.78	18.33	17.20	.73	.77	.93	.88	.83
Dentists	0.36	2.45	1.86	1.63	1.54	.73	.77	.93	.88	.83
Hospital beds	33.01	216.38	189.89	167.47	157.15	.73	.77	.93	.88	.83

Table 6.6 shows the number of medical personnel and hospital beds that would be required, under four different fertility assumptions, in the year 2000 if service ratios were trebled. The growth over the 30-year period is spectacular: if fertility remains constant, almost a sixfold increase in the number of doctors and nurses, a sixfold increase in hospital beds, and a sevenfold increase in midwives and practical nurses would be needed. In the more realistic medium population projection, the required increase would still be 4.5-fold in the case of midwives and practical nurses. The training requirements during the period would be even larger because of attrition. Whether these substantial requirements can be successfully met will depend on both the capacity of the training institutions to produce sufficient trained personnel quickly enough and the cost of training and employing such large numbers of health personnel.

The final columns in Table 6.6 show the relative savings in requirements for health personnel that result from different speeds of fertility decline. For example, requirements in the year 2000 in the low projection are 17 percent below those in the high projection.

It should be noted that the relative savings in requirements for health personnel is exactly the same whether health service ratios are raised rapidly, slowly, or not at all. Rapid increases in health service ratios do not cancel the benefit of fertility reduction.

Improving health service ratios during a period of rapid population growth raises both the number of new personnel needed as additions to the present stock and the number needed as replacements. Replacement needs increase more rapidly when service ratios are improved than when they are held constant, because the stock from which replacement needs are calculated is growing more rapidly. However, the effect on net additions is sharper than the effect on replacements, because the number of additions needed is immediately dependent on the increment needed in the stock of health personnel. The result of this differential effect is that the addition/replacement ratio is higher in the improving service ratio case than in the constant service ratio case.

Nevertheless, the addition/replacement ratio for physicians does not quite reach 1.0 even in the constant fertility projection (see Figure 6.2). In other words, if the estimate of attrition rates is correct, more than half of the doctors trained will be replacements rather than additions to the net stock of doctors available. In the case of registered nurses, because the attrition rate is higher than for doctors, the addition/replacement rate is lower than for doctors. The addition/replacement ratio in the 1970–1985 period is in the range of .70 to .80, depending on fertility trends, but thereafter declines somewhat. For midwives, because the attrition rate is much lower, the addition/replacement ratio remains above 1.0 throughout the projection period, even in the low population projection.

As Figure 6.2 indicates, the more rapidly the population is growing, the higher the ratio of additions to replacements.

Tables 6.7 and 6.8 show the trends in health costs according to the present

Figure 6.2   Physicians: Ratio of Additions to Replacements Needed To Meet Targets of Improving Service Ratios under Alternative Population Projections: Thailand, 1960–2000

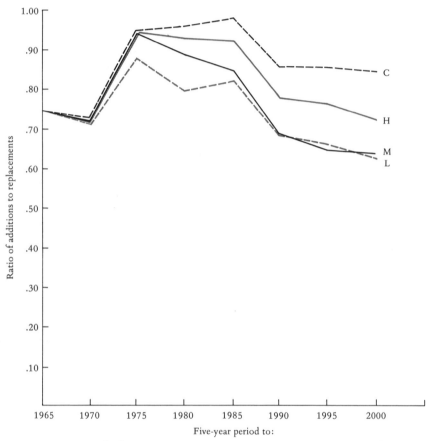

C = Constant fertility projection
H = High projection
M = Medium projection
L = Low projection

assumptions. Comparison of Table 6.7 with Table 6.5 will show the extra costs resulting from the trebling of health service ratios in the provincial areas. The increase in costs in the present projection are spectacular, but the crucial question is how heavy a burden they imply when compared with trends in the GDP and government budgets; we will return to this in the following section. Comparison of Table 6.8 with similar calculations for the example where health service ratios are held constant in Bangkok and the rest of Thailand separately indicates that, according to our assumptions about factors affecting health costs, the rela-

Table 6.7 Costs of Health Services with Trebling of Service Ratios Outside Bangkok: Thailand, 1965–2000 (in millions of babts)

Five-year period to:	High projection			Medium projection			Low projection		
	Investment	Operating	Total	Investment	Operating	Total	Investment	Operating	Total
1965	1.080	1.972	3.052	1.079	1.972	3.051	1.080	1.972	3.052
1970	1.840	3.469	5.309	1.839	3.469	5.308	1.840	3.469	5.309
1975	2.721	5.807	8.528	2.723	5.807	8.530	2.603	5.734	8.337
1980	4.312	9.327	13.639	4.214	9.267	13.481	3.873	8.920	12.792
1985	6.835	14.959	21.793	6.436	14.596	21.032	6.000	13.821	19.821
1990	9.491	23.011	32.502	8.596	21.890	30.485	8.051	20.617	28.668
1995	14.029	34.435	48.464	12.168	31.751	43.919	11.454	29.876	41.329
2000	20.438	51.136	71.574	17.183	45.639	62.822	16.053	42.870	58.923

NOTE: All costs are in 1962 prices: one baht = US$0.0481.

Table 6.8   Ratios of Low and Medium Projection to High and Constant Fertility Projection, Improving Service Ratios: Thailand, 1995–2000 and 1970–2000

Costs	1995–2000					1970–2000				
	L/M	L/H	M/H	L/C	M/C	L/M	L/H	M/H	L/C	M/C
Investment	.93	.79	.84	.65	.70	.94	.84	.89	.84	.79
Operating	.94	.84	.89	.75	.79	.95	.88	.93	.82	.86
Total	.94	.82	.87	.72	.77	.94	.87	.92	.79	.84

tive savings in the health expenditures resulting from a decline in the birth rate is almost the same whether or not health service ratios are raised.

Feasibility of Meeting Rising Costs

We have seen that, by virtue of population growth, health costs will rise sharply in Thailand whether or not health service ratios are increased. How likely is it that such cost increases can be sustained? One way to examine this question is to compare the trends in costs with the expected growth of the GDP during the period 1970–2000. If it is assumed that government budgets will continue to constitute the same share of GDP, the trends shown would also apply to the share of health costs in government budgets. The relation of health costs to GDP is shown in Table 6.9. The assumption that GDP in Thailand will grow at the rate of 6 percent per annum is consistent with our assumptions about trends in health costs.

It would appear that only if the low population projection is followed will health costs remain a more or less constant share of GDP when service ratios in Bangkok and the rest of the country are held constant. If the high population projection obtains, the share of GDP required will rise gradually from 1.1 percent in 1970–1975 to 1.3 percent in 1995–2000.

In the improving service ratio projection, the share of GDP required rises substantially even if the low population projection is followed, but the rise is much sharper if fertility declines slowly, as in the high population projection. The share of GDP required rises 64 percent during the 30-year period when the low population projection is followed, but the increase is 96 percent if the high population projection obtains. In either case, realization of the goal of improving health service ratios would require that a substantially larger share of GDP (and, presumably, also of government revenues) be channelled into health services.

Implications

A number of important conclusions emerge from this case study. One is that there is very little chance that Thailand can reach health personnel/population

Table 6.9 *Total Cost of Health Services as a Percentage of GDP, Alternative Assumptions: Thailand, 1965–1970 to 1995–2000*

Assumption	1965–70	1970–75	1975–80	1980–85	1985–90	1990–95	1995–2000
1. GDP grows at 5% per annum							
Constant service ratios[a]							
High projection	.83	1.11	1.21	1.34	1.47	1.60	1.74
Medium projection	.83	1.11	1.20	1.28	1.38	1.46	1.53
Low projection	.83	1.08	1.14	1.21	1.29	1.36	1.44
Improving service ratios							
High projection	.83	1.27	1.60	2.00	2.33	2.73	3.15
Medium projection	.83	1.27	1.58	1.93	2.19	2.47	2.76
Low projection	.83	1.06	1.49	1.81	2.06	2.33	2.60
2. GDP grows at 6% per annum							
Constant service ratios[a]							
High projection	.83	1.07	1.13	1.00	1.24	1.29	1.33
Medium projection	.83	1.07	1.12	1.14	1.15	1.16	1.16
Low projection	.83	1.05	1.06	1.07	1.09	1.09	1.09
Improving service ratios							
High projection	.83	1.24	1.48	1.76	1.96	2.19	2.42
Medium projection	.83	1.24	1.46	1.71	1.85	1.99	2.12
Low projection	.83	1.21	1.39	1.60	1.73	1.87	1.99
3. GDP grows at 7% per annum							
Constant service ratios[a]							
High projection	.83	1.04	1.05	1.05	1.05	1.04	1.02
Medium projection	.83	1.05	1.05	1.00	0.98	0.94	0.89
Low projection	.83	1.01	0.98	0.95	0.92	0.88	0.85
Improving service ratios[b]							
High projection	.83	1.20	1.36	1.56	1.66	1.76	1.86
Medium projection	.83	1.20	1.35	1.51	1.55	1.60	1.64
Low projection	.83	1.18	1.28	1.42	1.46	1.51	1.53

[a] In Bangkok and rest of Thailand separately.

[b] Improving service ratios outside Bangkok but constant service ratios in Bangkok.

ratios that are even close to international standards before the end of this century
unless: (a) larger proportions of government revenues are channelled into health
care, particularly in the rural areas; (b) attrition rates (caused especially by
doctors and nurses being attracted overseas) can be lowered; and (c) rates of
population growth can be reduced. Probably all three of these changes would
need to occur simultaneously.

Even in the low population projection, the aim of trebling health service
ratios in the provincial areas (to levels still well below those already existing in
Bangkok) would require a rapidly rising share of GDP and government revenues.
If population grows as fast in the high projection, costs would rise so rapidly
that the aim appears quite unrealistic: from 1.2 percent of GDP in 1970–1975
to 2.4 percent in 1995–2000.

Even if holding health service ratios constant in Bangkok and the rest of
Thailand is the goal, the proportion of GDP going to health services will still
rise because of the expected rapid growth of Bangkok, with its much higher
service ratios.

If health service ratios in developing countries are to be rapidly improved,
a decline in population growth is essential, and so too is a decline in attrition
rates. At present, the main function of Thailand's schools of nursing is to supply
a cheap source of nurses to the United States and West Germany: a striking
example, at the international level, of the poor being taxed to subsidize the
rich. The solution is not easy to discover, because marked wage differentials will
continue to exist between Thailand and the Western countries. But the situation
would be ameliorated if the United States and West Germany were to ensure
that an adequate supply of nurses was being trained locally; and there is no
question that developing countries must make every effort to retain a higher
proportion of their trained nurses. This would lead to substantial savings in
the costs of meeting health service goals.

The "brain drain" problem also applies to doctors. It is easy to argue on
the basis of doctor/population ratios that Thailand needs many more doctors
and that the training of doctors should be expanded, since doctor/population
ratios will not reach desirable levels for decades. However, it would be most
dangerous to base irreversible decisions to expand medical schools on such a
crude yardstick as overall doctor/population ratios. Slightly more subtle reasoning suggests that there could soon be an oversupply of doctors according to
some criteria. The doctor/population ratio in Bangkok is already up to Western
levels, and in the largest provincial towns it is rapidly approaching Western levels. It is at the *amphur* (district) level that the ratios are extremely low. But
it is precisely in these areas that the average doctor does not want to work. Moreover, it is expensive to post doctors in these areas, since to work effectively they
need well-equipped facilities, which entail extra costs in support staff, transport,
and so forth. Thus, unless health budgets can be substantially raised and working
conditions for doctors in rural areas made more attractive, there is a distinct
possibility that any increase in doctors would not be absorbed by the rural areas,

where they are needed, but would flow into Bangkok, thus creating an over-supply, or out of the country.

The crude measures used in the Thailand study do not lend themselves to in-depth exploration of important issues such as this. But they can provide a general framework within which such issues can be studied.

Finally, it might be noted that the uphill task facing the health planners in Thailand, as in many developing countries, suggests the need for innovative approaches to community health care. Ready access to a trained doctor will remain a luxury of the urban population for some time to come. The challenge to health planners is to devise ways of improving the efficiency of existing facilities and personnel and of supplementing this with the services of paramedical personnel so that the health care available to the rural population can be improved in a reasonably short time without impossibly high expenditures.

FAMILY PLANNING AS A HEALTH INVESTMENT

We have seen clearly in the case study of Thailand that substantial savings in health expenditures would result from a decline in fertility. This knowledge, in itself, is of little value to planners unless the government can affect the level of fertility by adopting various policy measures. As discussed elsewhere in this book, many government policies do have implications for fertility levels, but the most direct effect is likely to result from adoption of a family planning program. A family planning program should be considered an integral and necessary part of any adequate public health program because it not only lowers fertility levels and, as a result, the cost of providing health services, but it also can be expected to lower morbidity and mortality levels.

Although the contribution of a family planning program to the effective health care of the population may be considerable, and should certainly be weighed in judging the appropriate level of expenditure on the program, improvement of the nation's health is only one aim of a family planning program and, in most cases, not the aim on which most emphasis is placed by the nation's economic planners. Whatever may be the emphasis given in official statements, the major aim of most family planning programs is the reduction of birth rates and population growth.

Just as the health implications of a family planning program are only part of the reason for investing in such a program, so too are the savings in health costs resulting from a decline in the birth rate only a small part of the benefits likely to result from a family planning program.[14] Of course, it is natural that the health authorities, who have responsibility for running the family planning program, will be very interested in knowing the savings accruing to their own budgets as a result of the program. Therefore, the findings of case studies on this question will be of particular interest.

A vigorous and, so far, successful family planning program is being conducted in Thailand by the Ministry of Public Health, assisted by other agencies.

The stated aim of the nation's population policy is to lower the rate of population growth from about 3.0 percent per annum to about 2.5 percent per annum by the end of the Third Five-Year Plan period (1976). The low population projection used in the Thailand case study is consistent with this goal and assumes a continuation of the fertility decline after 1976.

So far, the national family planning program is running ahead of targets. Numbers of new acceptors in the program have increased as follows, exceeding targets in all five years:

1969	130,219
1970	225,439
1971	404,187
1972	451,000
1973	411,000

The total number of acceptors in 1971 and 1972 constituted approximately 16 percent of all married women in the reproductive age groups. Limited available data on continuation rates indicate that these compare favorably with those in other countries having national family planning programs. Calculations of the demographic impact of the program so far indicate that Thailand should be well on the way toward its goal of a 2.5 percent growth rate by the end of 1976.

Government budgets required for attaining improved levels of health care in Thailand have already been calculated. What will be the savings to the government budget resulting from the fertility reduction brought about by the national family planning program? And how will these savings compare with the cost of the family planning program?

Estimates of these variables can only be very crude, but they can give an indication of the general order of magnitude involved. First, let us assume that the national family planning program will be successful in lowering fertility according to the path followed in the low population projection. To calculate the independent effect of the family planning program, it is necessary to know what the trend in fertility would have been in the absence of the program. This is impossible to know, but for the sake of the argument, we can assume that it would have followed the medium population projection. (Certainly a reasonably substantial decline in fertility could be expected before the end of the century, even without any government intervention.)

The costs of Thailand's family planning program (including the indirect costs not specifically included in family planning budgets and the currently very large foreign aid component) have been projected from their actual 1970 and 1971 levels and their planned 1972–1977 levels on the assumption that total costs (in real terms) will continue to grow at 3 percent per annum after 1977. The assumptions underlying this rather slow increase are that the program will be highly developed by 1977 and relatively little expansion will be needed and that foreign aid, which tends to be an expensive way of financing family planning activities, will gradually become a smaller part of the total. These projections indicate that the total costs of family planning in the 1970–2000 period would be Bt. 4.161 million, compared with a savings in public health expenditures of Bt. 6.350 million in the projection assuming constant service ratios in Bangkok and the rest of Thailand, and Bt. 10.399 million in the projection assuming improving service ratios.[6] In other words, the savings in health costs would be more than double the cost of the family planning program designed to bring them about, if a reasonable attempt were made to improve health service ratios in rural areas.

This estimate can be varied widely by altering the assumption about trends in family planning program costs after 1977. If, instead of an increase of 3 percent per annum, an increase of 6 percent per annum is assumed, based on continued expansion of the program as well as steady increases in salary and other cost levels, then the 30-year costs of the family planning program would rise to Bt. 6.030 million, a sum that is still less than the savings in health costs in the constant service ratios example and little more than half the savings in the improving service ratios example.

It should not be expected that the difference between the medium and low population projections will correspond precisely with the demographic effect of the national family planning program. But one fact is clear: even if the effect of the family planning program on fertility were somewhat less than the difference between the low and medium population projections, the savings in health service costs resulting from the family planning program would still exceed the costs of the program. Indeed, in the case of the improving service ratios projection, the impact on fertility could be substantially less (or the cost of the family planning program substantially higher) without reducing the savings in health costs if population growth follows the low rather than the medium projection. Improving health service ratios were assumed in this comparison. It was found that the projected savings in health costs over a 30-year period were three times as great as the projected costs of the family planning program.

The assumptions used in these two case studies were necessarily very crude, and it is possible that estimates of future family planning costs were on the low side, especially for Sri Lanka, where the family planning program has been rather limited in scope up to the present. A new plan for bringing family planning services to the bulk of the rural population, if implemented, would sharply raise family planning costs, although the extent to which the costs should be imputed to family planning is debatable, since it is a comprehensive health plan with family planning as only one component.[15]

The implication of these two case studies is that a large-scale family planning program would need to have only a relatively small independent effect on fertility rates to lead to savings in health costs that would exceed the cost of the family planning program itself. This finding is somewhat unexpected, be-

---

[6] Figures for both costs of family planning and savings in health expenditures are expressed in 1962 prices.

cause savings in health costs are only a small part of the total benefits resulting from a reduction in fertility. This finding serves to reinforce the case for investment in family planning as an integral part of any program for social and economic development.

CONCLUSION

Provision of adequate health care is of vital importance to the welfare of the population of the developing countries, and its effect on productivity is probably greater than is generally recognized. There are reasons for believing that increased investment on health services would yield high returns, if returns are measured in ways reflecting the real welfare of people rather than the more usual measures of output.

Whatever the level of expenditures decided on, returns from health investments will be greater if health services are planned imaginatively to suit the conditions prevailing in the country. Other things being equal, the adequacy of the care provided by a given level of expenditure will also be greater if the population is growing more slowly.

In two decades following World War II, mortality fell spectacularly, partly because of health investments. Unfortunately, not enough foresight was exercised to plan ahead for fertility reduction, which requires a longer lead-time because it requires greater cultural and attitudinal changes. As a result, rapidly expanding populations have compounded the problem of development.

It is now much more widely realized that the introduction of highly effective health measures should be accompanied by effective population control programs to sustain the gains from health development. This is true not only from the standpoint of broad macroeconomic considerations, but also from the standpoint of health planning itself. Excessive numbers and close spacing of children makes for a health syndrome in which the welfare of both mother and children suffers.

General health services and family planning services should promote and sustain each other, especially if they are set in the context of socioeconomic development. A reduction in fertility levels would not only help directly to ameliorate health problems, but would also make for substantial savings in the cost of providing an adequate level of health care. Family planning programs are not expensive, normally using, at a maximum, 1.5 percent of total development funds from both local and foreign sources spent in the developing countries. Considering the evidence, it would not be too harsh to accuse of myopia the planners and policy-makers of any developing country that has not incorporated family planning services into its health program.

REFERENCES

1. Leslie Corsa, Jr. and Deborah Oakley, "Consequences of population growth for health services in less developed countries—An initial appraisal," in National Academy of Sciences, *Rapid Population Growth: Consequences and Policy Implications* (Baltimore: Johns Hopkins Press, 1971), p. 371.

2. Charles T. Stewart, Jr., "Allocation of resources to health," *Journal of Human Resources* 6, no. 1 (Winter 1971).

3. See T. McKeown, R. G. Brown, and R. G. Record, "An interpretation of the modern rise of population in Europe," *Population Studies* 27, no. 3 (November 1972).

4. George J. Stolniz, "A century of international mortality trends," pts. 1, 2, *Population Studies* 9 (July 1955) and 10 (July 1956).

5. See, for example, Harald Fredericksen, "Determinants and consequences of mortality trends in Ceylon," *Public Health Reports* 71 (August 1961); and S. A. Meegema, "Malaria eradication and its effect on mortality levels," *Population Studies* 21 (November 1967).

6. For a review of the evidence concerning the effect of family planning programs on fertility rates, see Robert J. Lapham and W. Parker Mauldin, "National family planning programs: Review and evaluation," *Studies in Family Planning* 3, no. 3 (March 1972); and John A. Ross et al., "Findings from family planning research," *Reports on Population/Family Planning,* no. 12 (October 1972): 2–9.

7. Joe D. Wray, "Population pressure on families: Family size and child spacing," in National Academy of Sciences, *Rapid Population Growth: Consequences and Policy Implications* (Baltimore: Johns Hopkins Press, 1971).

8. Robin Barlow, *The Economic Effect of Malaria Eradication* (Ann Arbor: University of Michigan, School of Public Health, 1968).

9. See N. R. E. Fendall, "The medical assistant in Africa," *Journal of Tropical Medicine and Hygiene* 71 (April 1968).

10. See ref. 2, p. 122.

11. TEMPO Technical Information Center, "Turkey: The effects of falling fertility," vol. 1 (Santa Barbara: General Electric Company, Center for Advanced Studies, 1969).

12. For a simple explanation of the methods of calculation, see TEMPO Technical Information Center, "Manual for calculation of government expenditures for selected social services" (Santa Barbara: General Electric Company, Center for Advanced Studies, 1968), chap. 4.

13. Gavin W. Jones and Chet Boonpratuang, *The Effect of Population Growth and Urbanization on the Attainment of Public Health Goals in Thailand* (Bangkok: Manpower Planning Division, National Economic Development Board, May 1973).

14. Cost-benefit analysis of family planning programs is very complex. For a good summary of the issues, see Warren C. Robinson and David E. Horlacher, "Population growth and economic welfare," *Reports on Population/Family Planning,* no. 6 (February 1971).

15. Howard C. Taylor, Jr. and Bernard Berelson, "Comprehensive family planning based on maternal/child health services: A feasibility study for a world program," *Studies in Family Planning* 2, no. 2 (February 1971).

SEVEN

Population Distribution and Migration

GHAZI M. FAROOQ

Interregional population redistribution during a specified period is the net effect of three components: internal migration[1], interregional differentials in the rate of natural increase, and interregional differentials in the gain or loss by international migration—in most cases, in this order of importance. All these components interact with the economic processes of development.

In the developed countries, long-term internal migratory streams have been particularly important as a mechanism for obtaining efficient population distribution in response to structural changes in the production system accompanying the modern economic growth process. Many developing countries are currently experiencing large-scale population movements from rural to urban areas. In most cases, international migration is almost negligible; in some cases, regional differences in the rates of natural increase are significant; internal migration is the major cause, as it was in the developed countries. Beside being a response to regional variations in social and economic opportunities, rural-urban migration in the final analysis can be attributed to its real source—excessive fertility. In many industrialized countries, rural areas have continued to display fertility rates well above those of urban areas long after industrialization has occurred. The rural areas thus function as a kind of "demographic reserve" from which migration streams pour to the cities in response to improving economic prospects there. This process continues at least as long as excess rural fertility continues. In some developed nations, it has continued well into the last decades.

Unlike the movement in the developed countries, however, this process of

ACKNOWLEDGMENTS: The author is indebted to Vincent H. Whitney for his invaluable criticisms and suggested improvements of an earlier draft. He would also like to thank Chelik Kurdoglu for his suggestions and help in reviewing the literature on the subject.

population redistribution to urban areas in developing countries, particularly to the large metropolises, has been very rapid, often leading to multitudinous social, economic, administrative, and political problems. Government agencies in developing countries are becoming increasingly conscious of this rural-urban shift and the problems associated with it. In response to the UN Secretary-General's enquiry, approximately a dozen governments reported having taken specific measures to influence internal migration, particularly from rural to uban areas, and to achieve a more satisfactory geographical distribution of their population.[2]

In this chapter, we will first discuss the more important types of migration streams, their relative magnitudes and significance, and the problems associated with them. The second part will deal with policies designed to handle the problems of current migrant populations and with the role of policies in achieving economically efficient and desirable settlement patterns.

RURAL-URBAN MIGRATION

There is a vast literature on historical population redistribution patterns in developed countries.[3] In case after case, population redistribution (and especially internal migration) was related to the manpower requirements of the industrialization process and was largely a response to the relative increase in economic opportunities in urban centers. Also, as suggested by Kuznets, in cases where a population is settled in only part of a country's territory, increasing population numbers, even if there are no structural economic changes, can alter regional differentials in economic opportunities and induce migration. Examples are the opening of unsettled areas through frontier expansion in North America and Oceania and the exploitation of unused internal frontiers in the Soviet Union.[4] Among the developing countries, only a few Latin American and African countries still have "frontiers" left.

In the last two decades, the urban population in much of the developing world has grown at a significantly higher rate than the rural population. As a result, the urban population as a proportion of the total population has steadily increased. The migration of people from rural to urban areas is largely responsible for this growth. This factor remains important even for some of the countries in Southwest Asia and North Africa where, due to relatively higher mortality levels in rural areas, the rural-urban natural increase differential may account for a sizable part of urban growth.[5]

Table 7.1 provides average annual growth rates during 1950–1960 for the rural and urban populations of the three major developing regions of the world and selected countries in these areas. Bearing in mind the problems of variations in definitions of urban status and of biases in reporting across countries, the overall picture is quite clear. The reported urban growth rates are significantly higher than the rural—two times higher in South Asia and three times higher in Latin America and Africa. Thailand, Colombia, and Zaïre reported urban growth rates four times larger than rural, and Mexico and Nigeria reported rates five times larger. Chile seems to be experiencing an absolute decline in its rural population. The rapidity of this net transfer of population from rural to urban locations is further evident in Table 7.2, which shows the urban proportion of total population in 1950 and 1960 for the countries in Table 7.1. Given the magnitude of the change involved, it would seem that, even in those countries where the rate of natural increase is higher in urban than in rural areas, only part of the increase in the proportion of the population urbanized can be attributed to this differential.[1]

As Tables 7.1 and 7.2 suggest, it is important to look not only at overall urban population growth but also at the relative growth of different size-class localities. This is essential for evaluating the nature and characteristics of the process of population redistribution to urban areas. For example, India, with an overall urban growth rate only slightly larger than the rural rate (2.3 percent compared with 1.8 percent), has been frequently cited as a country undergoing a significant reduction in rural-urban migration. However, as Table 7.1 shows, during 1950–1960, the population of large metropolitan cities (100,000 or more and 500,000 or more inhabitants) grew remarkably—at more than twice the rates of rural population and total population growth.[2] It was actually the net absolute decline of more than 2 million in urban localities of less than 20,000 inhabitants (from 20.09 million in 1950 to 18.06 million in 1960) that dampened the overall urban growth rate.[3] This evidence suggests the possibility of three kinds of migration streams operating in India: (1) some urban to urban migration, with people moving from small towns to large towns and metropolitan cities; (2) urban to rural migration, with some people moving from small towns to rural areas; and (3) rural to urban migration, with people

---

[1] This is because, mathematically, the differential in rural and urban natural increase, given the empirically observed upper limits of the natural increase rates and the small base of the urban population, cannot alone significantly increase the proportion of urban population in a relatively short period of time. For example, assuming that the present proportion of urban population is 25 percent and the urban natural increase rate is 3.5 percent per annum as compared to 2.5 percent for the total population (implying a rural rate of 2.2 percent), the proportion of urban population will increase to only 30.3 percent in 20 years with no rural-urban migration. On the other hand, in some other regions, Latin America for example, there is not any appreciable difference between rural and urban rates of natural increase. Some of the gaining urban regions are even found to have lower fertility rates. And, in at least these regions, although mortality conditions are possibly relatively better in urban than rural areas, this cannot overcompensate for the lower urban fertility rates and result in significantly higher urban rates of natural increase.[6]

[2] The population gain of cities of 100,000–499,999 inhabitants was 4.2 million, and the gain of cities of 500,000 or more inhabitants was 6.7 million. Together these gains accounted for about 70 percent of the overall urban growth.

[3] However, according to C. Chandrasekaran and K. C. Zachariah, the definition of urban population was modified in the 1961 census. If the 1951 definition had been adopted, an additional 4.4 million would have been enumerated as urban in 1961, presumably all in localities of less than 20,000. Still, this warrants only a low growth rate (1.1 percent) for small-sized urban communities.[7]

Table 7.1   Average Annual Growth Rates in Total, Urban, and Rural Populations: Selected Countries, 1950–1960

Major area and country	Total population	Reported rural population	Reported urban population[a]	Urban population in localities of		
				20,000 or more	100,000 or more	500,000 or more
South Asia	2.1	1.8	3.4	4.3	4.6	4.8
India	1.9	1.8	2.3	3.5	3.9	4.0
Turkey	2.8	2.3	4.7	6.8	6.6	7.4
Philippines	3.0	2.2	5.1	4.0	4.1	3.8
Thailand	3.0	2.2	8.3	6.9	5.3	4.9
Iraq	2.9	2.0	4.3	6.6	6.9	n.a.
Latin America	2.8	1.3	4.5	5.5	5.5	5.8
Brazil	3.0	1.5	5.2	6.3	5.8	6.8
Mexico	3.0	1.5	7.8	6.9	7.8	7.3
Colombia	2.8	1.2	5.0	6.6	7.5	9.4
Chile	2.3	−0.2	3.7	4.7	4.1	5.1
Peru	2.3	1.2	3.7	6.0	5.3	4.7
Africa	2.1	1.6	4.5	5.4	6.5	5.3
Egypt[b]	2.4	1.5	4.1	4.1	4.9	3.5
Nigeria	2.6	2.1	5.4	7.6	11.6	n.a.
Algeria	2.3	1.1	5.5	7.1	6.3	3.4
Zaïre	1.9	1.1	4.9	10.8	6.9	n.a.

n.a. = Not applicable.
[a] According to the national definition of an urban area.
[b] United Arab Republic.
SOURCE: United Nations, Department of Economic and Social Affairs, *Growth of the World's Urban and Rural Population, 1920–2000*, Population Studies, no. 44 (New York: United Nations, 1969), tables 1, 8, 11, 13, 16, and 41–44.

moving directly to large towns (20,000 or more) and cities from rural areas. This third kind of migration had to be substantial in magnitude to warrant the high growth rate in large cities.

In almost every country listed in Tables 7.1 and 7.2, the population gains of large towns and cities were proportionately much larger than those of smaller-sized towns and urban communities and were mainly responsible for the accelerated rural-urban shifts during the 1950–1960 decade. In the majority of countries, large metropolitan cities grew faster than even large towns or medium-sized cities (20,000–99,999 inhabitants). More striking is the fact that, on the average, in South Asia and Latin America, cities of half a million or more inhabitants showed the largest growth rates. Particularly in Latin America, the

Table 7.2 Urban Population as Proportion of Total Population: Selected Countries, 1950 and 1960 (In Percents)

Major area and country	Total urban population		Urban population in localities of					
			20,000 or more		100,000 or more		500,000 or more	
	1950 (1)	1960 (2)	1950 (3)	1960 (4)	1950 (5)	1960 (6)	1950 (7)	1960 (8)
South Asia	15.9	18.2	11.1	13.7	6.7	8.7	3.8	5.0
India	17.2	17.9	11.6	13.7	6.4	7.9	3.8	4.7
Turkey	21.7	26.0	14.3	21.3	8.1	11.9	4.8	7.6
Philippines	24.3	30.0	15.1	16.7	8.9	9.9	7.4	8.0
Thailand	10.8	18.2	6.0	8.9	5.1	6.4	4.1	4.9
Iraq	35.1	40.5	21.9	31.8	15.2	22.9	n.a.	10.0
Latin America	40.7	48.6	25.1	32.8	17.2	22.6	12.1	16.1
Brazil	36.2	45.0	20.6	28.8	14.5	19.3	11.5	16.7
Mexico	42.6	50.7	23.6	34.7	14.7	23.7	11.6	17.7
Colombia	37.3	46.5	21.4	31.4	13.7	21.9	6.0	11.6
Chile	58.6	67.8	41.6	52.8	26.2	31.6	19.7	26.3
Peru	40.5	46.6	17.9	26.0	12.3	16.7	12.3	15.7
Africa	14.4	18.3	9.7	13.4	5.7	8.9	2.7	3.7
Egypt[a]	31.9	37.8	30.6	36.4	21.1	27.0	16.7	18.5
Nigeria	12.4	16.5	6.4	10.6	2.5	6.2	n.a.	2.1
Algeria	23.4	32.3	15.1	24.5	9.1	13.6	5.7	6.4
Zaïre	17.6	23.8	3.6	8.8	2.6	4.3	n.a.	n.a.

n.a. = Not applicable.
[a] United Arab Republic.
SOURCE: See Table 7.1.

growth of these large cities was phenomenal. For example, if the 1950–1960 growth rates are maintained (and these trends continued during the 1960–1970 decade[8]), the number of people living in cities of half a million or more will double every ten years in Brazil, in less than ten years in Mexico, and in less than eight years in Colombia.

The continuing accelerated growth of metropolises in developing countries has led to a wide array of serious problems in these centers. The most difficult one to tackle is associated with the huge settlements that have sprung up on the periphery of these cities. This problem is more acute in Latin America, which, despite its already high level of urbanization, shows one of the highest growth rates for large cities. Shanty towns and squatter settlements are becoming an almost permanent characteristic of the urbanization process in Latin America. These settlements account for one-quarter to one-half of the total population in many metropolitan areas, and are growing at phenomenal rates of 12 to 15 percent annually.[9] Nearly all countries in Asia and some in Africa (particularly tropical Africa) also face similar problems. Apparently, no effort at constructing new urban housing could be sufficient, particularly given the limited availability of funds, to meet the housing demands of the multiplying numbers of people in metropolises.[10] And large numbers of persons in these cities are deprived of such basic social services as electricity, running water, sanitation, adequate transport, education, and health care.[4]

CAUSES OF RURAL-URBAN MIGRATION

An understanding of rural-urban migration and its determinants is essential to the formulation of regional policies and programs.

Generally, economic factors have been emphasized as the primary motivation for internal migration and particularly for rural-urban migration. Recent works by Todaro, Harris, and López Toro, among others, have attempted to explain rural-urban migration flows in terms of economic behavioral models.[12] Formulating his model on the lines of permanent income theories[5] (rather than wage differential theories), Todaro employs as the decision variable rural-urban *expected* income differential, that is, the income differential adjusted for the probability of finding an urban job. The crucial assumption in all these analytical migration models is that "rural-urban migration will continue so long as the *expected* urban real income at the margin exceeds real agricultural product—*i.e.,* prospective rural migrants behave as maximizers of expected utility."[14]

---

[4] According to one estimate, in Turkey a per capita investment of more than US$1,000 would be required to meet the housing and social infrastructure needs of urbanization.[11]

[5] The concept of "permanent" income was first introduced by Milton Friedman. It is the normal, usual, or expected average income of consumers "to which consumers adapt their behavior." This income is the "planning income" to which consumers adjust their expenditure decisions and plans, and presumably it is also the relevant income for determining fertility, migration, and other demographic decisions.[13]

"Marginalization" of large urban centers, or the development of shanty towns and squatter settlements, can be explained by what Todaro calls a "two-stage migration phenomenon." Initially, the rural unskilled migrant worker can only be absorbed into the traditional urban sector; only after some time will he be able to obtain a more permanent job in the modern sector.[15] However, as López Toro suggests, rural-urban migration is motivated not only by the expected income differential between the rural sector and the modern urban sector, but also by the expected income differential between the rural sector and the traditional urban sector. Actually, real incomes of workers in the traditional urban sector are substantially higher if we include in their average earnings the subsidies that the urban community provides in terms of education, health, other public services, and cultural amenities, which persons in rural areas do not normally receive.[16] Hence, paradoxically, although there may exist positive marginal productivity of labor in agriculture—even a relatively high marginal product, as in the case of some African and Latin American frontier regions—continuing rural-urban migration in the face of substantial overt unemployment in urban areas probably does represent an economically rational decision on the part of migrants.

A substantial flow of remittances from urban to rural areas also occurs as migrants send part of their earnings back to their families. This has the effect of reducing to some extent the apparent urban-rural income differential and is more efficient in some ways than moving more people. This transfer process also has the effect of raising the real utility or consumption value of the money so transferred: because prices are likely to be lower in the rural areas and because money income is more scarce, the marginal utility of money income is likely to be greater there than in the cities.

Income differentials and unemployment are actually only intermediate variables. The more fundamental factors, as already noted, are the rate of natural increase (supply factors) and the economic growth rate (demand factors), and hence the basic variable to consider is the population increase rate relative to the economic growth rate. Even if the rural natural increase rate is below or equal to the urban rate, the usual bias in the economic development process in favor of the urban economy will generate net rural-urban migration. Unfortunately, many contemporary development plans, in their attempt to foster rapid economic growth, continue to give priority to development of urban infrastructure and public services while neglecting the need for these services in the rural areas. This fosters the flow of rural migrants to the cities. For example, one study of Brazil mentions as a main cause of large internal migration, "the imbalance resulting from the development of industry and the complete abandonment of agriculture."[17] This is, perhaps, too strong a generalization, but in Latin America as a whole it seems that agriculture is in a depressed state. Techniques of production in this sector are still backward and there is a general lack of infrastructure needed to foster agricultural and rural development. The traditional land tenure system, based on *latifundia* in many regions of Latin

America, did in its best forms provide some minimal services to the cultivators, as did also the church. But these old forms, unjust as they often were, are under attack and are breaking down before there are adequate public social services to replace them.[18] Needless to say, if these conditions are not remedied, the present high rural-urban migration rates will continue and further aggravate the situation in Latin American cities. These conditions, of course, are not restricted to Latin America.

Urbanization may be a necessary condition (although not a sufficient one) for industrialization; the two may tend to reinforce each other. It is important here to point out that it is difficult through policy to reduce rural-urban migration flows. For example, in spite of conscious efforts by the governments of the United Arab Republic and Tunisia to check rural-urban migration by developing underdeveloped areas, the growing concentration of population in cities and regions of denser population continued.[19] Nevertheless, government policies have frequently led to what amount to distortions in the price of public services between urban and rural areas, encouraging migration.

OTHER TYPES OF MIGRATION

Urban-Rural Migration

Usually migration streams are not exclusively from rural to urban areas. In Sri Lanka, for example, a survey by the International Labour Organization (ILO) estimated that during 1960 about 40,000 persons moved from rural to urban areas and about 30,000 from urban to rural areas.[20] Sometimes an adverse economic and employment situation in the urban economy may generate a significant flow back to rural areas. In the United States, a small net urban-to-rural migration was observed in 1932. Schultz ascribed this reversal of the historical flow of rural workers to the city to severe unemployment in depressed city establishments and a greater likelihood of finding agricultural jobs, even though there still existed a significant rural-urban wage differential.[21] A contemporary example is India: with an already sizable urban labor force and high urban unemployment rates, push-back factors are operating in both rural and urban areas and, as a result, there is a high rate of turnover migration, indicating a push to and fro.[22]

Seasonal Migration

Seasonal migration, which is quite prevalent in developing countries, is usually economically motivated and occurs in response to an increased demand for labor at times of peak agricultural activity, for example, at harvest. The need for extra hands may be met, to a large extent, by rural migrants to urban areas returning for short periods to their family farms.

A recent study indicates that in West Africa, because of regional variations in the seasonality of crops, seasonal or temporary migration has been more economically efficient and much larger than permanent migration. This study found a significant north-to-south seasonal migration flow in Ghana. (The north is a subsistence agricultural area and has only one growing season. The south has comparatively richer farm land with multiple food crops and tree crops, including exportable cocoa. The south also contains all the industrial activity of the country.) With this migration, the combined income from the north and the south is larger than it would be with either full-time employment in the north or permanent migration to the south.[23]

Rural-Rural Migration

With the opening of new lands in Africa and Latin America, particularly in the latter, there have been substantial permanent population transfers, largely from rural areas, to these new agricultural lands. For example, with extensive road development and widespread application of insecticides, many tropical areas in Colombia have become habitable since World War II. Between 1951 and 1964, almost 400,000 people moved into these newly opened areas.[24] A substantial rural-to-rural movement, in search of new land, has also occurred in Thailand and other parts of Southeast Asia.[25]

As mentioned above, seasonal migration in West Africa involves primarily a movement between rural areas. In India and Pakistan there is also a substantial flow of people, especially women, among rural areas. This is mainly the result of a marriage tradition that dictates that the bride move to the bridegroom's village.[26]

Two-Step Migration

Overall, large cities have been growing relatively faster than small cities or towns, and in a number of cases, rural-urban migration alone was not responsible for that part of their growth attributable to migration; migration from small urban communities was also a significant contributor. It has been suggested that there is a two-step migration process involved: first a movement from rural area to town (rural-urban migration), and then from town to large city (urban-urban migration). This process is said to be operating in Chile.[27]

Fill-in Migration

The fill-in migration process involves the migration of rural inhabitants to towns to fill in the gaps left by residents of these towns who have migrated to large cities. Although involving similar kinds of migration streams, two-step migration is different from fill-in migration in that the former type involves the same people making two moves. An ILO report suggests the possibility of substantial fill-in migration in Colombia.[28]

It is probable that in most cases the growth of metropolises is the combined result of all three types of migration flows—rural-urban, two-step, and fill-in—and, of course, natural increase.

POLICIES

Patterns of population distribution and redistribution are not uniform across developing countries. There is also a great deal of diversity in economic, social, demographic, and geographical characteristics. Hence, the problems involved may be different and the solutions and policies required may be unique to each case. The aim here is to give only a broad outline of policies that may influence internal migration.

The discussion is divided between policies that deal with existing migrant populations and ones that serve as tools for obtaining a more efficient population distribution. Policies of the first kind can be referred to as "remedial" and policies of the second kind as "redirectional."

Remedial Policies

Migrants increase the pressure on the local job market and on the social service facilities of a community. A major problem especially associated with rural-urban migration, and one with sometimes grave social and political repercussions, is that of unemployment. In most countries, urban unemployment rates are quite substantial. As a solution to this problem, an ILO study recommended that governments induce private enterprises (through taxes and subsidies) to hire more workers than warranted by wage and productivity conditions.[29] Such a policy, however, may prove to be futile. For example, the Kenyan government adopted such a policy in 1964 for the greater Nairobi area. Private employers hired additional workers. The response to the prospect of more jobs being available was a sizable increase in the existing labor supply through increased migration, with the consequence that the unemployment rate probably increased rather than decreased.[30]

The example of Kenya demonstrates that manpower and employment policies should be consistent with the existence of rural-urban migration. The guidelines for employment creation discussed at the end of Chapter Three are relevant here. Also, in cases where the quality of migrant labor is not at par with the standards required by urban jobs or where there are problems of adaptability to new jobs, it is essential to organize special education and training programs for migrants.

Perhaps equally important as the provision of jobs for migrant populations is the provision of basic facilities and services, as well as decent housing. Provision of new housing and other social service facilities, however, will add further to the real rural-urban income differential and will help to perpetuate rural-urban migration, particularly to metropolitan areas. Perhaps the most practical policy for meeting housing needs in urban centers, as noted in Chapter Five, is one of self-help, with basic services and facilities provided by the government.[31]

The general policy should be to provide, concurrently, social infrastructure and more job opportunities in both rural and urban areas, thereby bringing the real income differential toward parity. Therefore, while remedial policies for accommodating existing migrant populations may be necessary, more essential in the long term are policies dealing with the redirection or the reduction of excessive migration flows.[6]

Redirectional Policies

Redirectional policies are generally directed at stemming the flow of people to metropolises. Sometimes even compulsory measures and direct controls such as residence permits, food ration cards, and persuasive propaganda are used to regulate this flow in particular, and rural-urban migration in general. Direct controls have recently been adopted in Tanzania, for example, and are under serious consideration in Kenya, among other countries. Such policies raise serious questions of equity and economic efficiency.[7] Their actual enforcement is often almost impossible. Moreover, it should not be forgotten that a degree of urbanization is an inevitable and essential counterpart to the process of modern economic growth.[34]

The appropriate measures are ones that influence migration flows by means of positive incentives and that involve long-term planning policies based on the underlying causes of population shifts. The specification of these policies is largely based on the resolution of a basic and often controversial issue confronting the planners—the choice between one (or a few) large urban agglomerations and numerous moderate-sized urban centers.

Concentrated or Dispersed Urbanization

Obviously, the choice between singular concentration and dispersed centers will largely be determined by certain specific conditions in a country: land area, geography, and financial resources. A small country may need and be able to afford only one large metropolitan area.

Theoretically, there are arguments in favor of both. The proponents of one

---

[6] The flow of rural migrants to large urban centers is sometimes claimed to be one of the factors responsible for the serious social and political unrest prevailing there, mainly because of inadequate job opportunities and housing.[32] However, this position implies that rural unemployment and underemployment is less undesirable than urban unemployment and underemployment, and therefore involves a value judgment.

[7] Thus, if direct controls are applied to restrict rural-urban migration, "substantial compensation to the rural sector will be required if it is not to be made worse off by removing the opportunity for free migration."[33]

or a few large cities point out the externalities already present in these centers. These externalities include the availability of infrastructure facilities, social services, commercial and financial systems, industrial activity, and the proximity of both labor and consumer markets. If the development program favors heavy, modern industry and rapid industrialization, it is generally claimed that the policy should be one favoring only a few concentrated settlements. Also, the very size of large urban settlements allows for a certain amount of incremental growth without proportional increases in social service facilities. If the social overhead capital, one of the scarcest production factors in developing countries, is spread over numerous growth poles, there is little probability of acquiring any real external economies in any one of them. Such a dispersion policy would no doubt be unsuitable for the stimulation of long-term sustained economic growth. On the other hand, as observed earlier, in most Latin American and Asian countries, concentrated metropolitan areas seem to have reached or exceeded the point where additional population can be absorbed without providing additional and generally costly social services. In such singularly concentrated population centers, the economies of scale and external economies should be compared with the high and rising social costs and internal diseconomies associated with high and increasing population density.

This can be put into a useful policy perspective by thinking in terms of public versus private externalities; that is, the agglomeration effects are favorable from the viewpoint of private firms. Their costs are lower, markets wider, and so forth. However, the diseconomies or negative externalities may accrue to the public sector in the form of increased expenses of pollution, sanitation, and other infrastructure. Thus, the agglomeration effects are a composite of public and private and ought so to be viewed.

The optimal choice for planners may fall somewhere between the two extremes of complete dispersion and singular urban concentration. In cases where it is deemed essential to develop alternate urban concentrations away from the main centers, the guiding principle should be one of equating marginal economic and social benefits to marginal economic and social costs. The cumulative net benefits over a reasonable planning period should be at least as great as the benefits foregone in the alternative situation of investing in the existing centers.[35]

Moreover, each urban center, however large or small, forms part of an urban hierarchy, and it is the optimality of the hierarchy that planners presumably should be working toward.

Alternate growth poles can be developed in two ways. One is to promote the growth of existing small cities and medium-sized towns. In a number of developing countries, many of these smaller urban settlements (along with rural areas) have been losing their populations to metropolitan cities and are in a more or less stagnant socioeconomic condition. Moreover, it is plausible, in some cases at least, that the population lost by these communities is of relatively better quality in terms of education, training, skills, and initiative. Even if these communities receive compensatory migration inflows from rural areas, the quality of most of these rural migrants may not be at par with that of the people leaving these settlements.[36] If true, this situation itself is sufficient reason for a careful regional planning effort.

The second way is to establish entirely new centers, although it should be realized that more often than not the overall social infrastructure cost for building a viable new town is much larger than that for improving an existing one. One example of such a new urban center, and supposedly a worthy one, is the city of Tema in Ghana. Tema is a comprehensively planned urban complex and is an example of a regional approach to the problem of urbanization.

> The town is being built on the construction schedule of the Volta River project and will eventually become the chief industrial and commercial centre as well as the outlet of the Volta development region. A key feature of the urban plan is the neighbourhood unit, each one to contain between 3,000 and 5,000 people, a number which represents the average size of a typical Ghanaian village, but also justifies the provision of basic social services. The units will be grouped together to form communities of between 12,000 and 15,000, the population necessary to provide for the more advanced community needs which should result in a compact new town.[37]

Carefully planned endeavors along these lines will be almost a necessity for optimal exploitation of sparsely populated areas or previously uninhabited areas, as in Africa and Latin America, and for attracting the desired migration flows to them. Such cities will provide the administrative, commercial, and financial functions necessary for potent agricultural development programs in such areas.

Regional Planning Policies

Regional planning within the framework of a national development policy is now being recognized as a fundamental method for obtaining desirable settlement patterns. Increasingly, policy-makers and planners are realizing the significance of the interdependence between the economic, social, administrative, political, and physical aspects of development planning at both the regional and national levels.

Industrial Location Policies

Policies that govern the geographical location of industry are known to be potentially one of the most effective ways of influencing population distribution and of redirecting population movements. The most direct policy is that of the geographical licensing of investments. Such direct measures can be instrumental in scaling down undesirably high growth rates in already congested regions. Governments can adopt the policy of refusing to license new enterprises and new investments in these centers. Another measure, and a more positive one, is to use monetary and fiscal tools. For example, additional taxes can be levied upon establishments in large urban centers equivalent in amount to the external economies they gain by being there. Conversely, subsidies in the form of tax exemptions and depreciation allowances, along with favorable credit policies, will encourage investors to establish enterprises in other, less developed regions.

In determining the best location for different types of industries and investments, private or public, it is of vital importance to take into account the type of local labor and raw materials available, as well as the probability of expanding the absorptive capacity of the region, and perhaps more importantly, the probability of generating new complementary and secondary investments and industries. Again, the conclusions of Chapter Three regarding policy measures (for example, choices of techniques of production and technology) are relevant here, particularly with respect to the generation of employment opportunities in these otherwise economically depressed areas of out-migration.

Infrastructure Location Policies

It is increasingly being recommended that the desired dispersal of social and economic development may be achieved more efficiently by policies controlling the location of infrastructure and social service facilities than by attempting to locate or relocate industry itself. Also, the locating of social infrastructure is relatively more easily controlled than is the locating of industry under a free or semipublic enterprise system, since infrastructure investments are basically public and regulated by central authorities. Needless to say, an efficient social infrastructure within an area is a necessary, although not sufficient, condition for attracting industry over time.

Among infrastructure investments, the most important for attracting industry are transportation and communication systems and administrative, financial, and commercial facilities. The provision of the usual social services is obviously essential for the general development of an area.

Rural Development Policies

Given the force of rural-urban population shifts and associated problems, the general development of rural areas should be a specific planning goal. Any attempt to improve the social and economic conditions of rural areas is simultaneously an attempt to blunt the "push" factors operating in these areas. The foregoing explanation of factors responsible for rural-urban migration suggests the kind of measures to be taken. The overall policy should include measures aimed at improving the existing land tenure and land settlement systems, improving techniques of production, introducing agricultural extension and development services, introducing irrigation systems, and allocating more resources for infrastructural investment in rural areas—the latter being crucial to agricultural and rural development. In the following we will discuss a few important specific policy measures not discussed before.

The rural-urban real income differentials in most developing countries are significantly large and in many cases are widening. This is an important immediate factor contributing to rural-urban migration. The problem should be tackled at two levels. First, there should be a strict check on the common tendency of many governments to establish an institutionally determined urban wage, often at a level much higher than free market interplay would allow.[38] In other words, urban wages should be kept in line with shadow or opportunity cost criteria. Restraints on urban wages, as suggested by Frank, "must not be viewed so much as a stimulus to demand as a retardant operating on the supply of workers to the urban areas, especially if accompanied by policies which might raise rural real incomes."[39] Second, the earning level of rural workers should itself be improved. One way (besides the obvious, essential improvement in production itself) is through a pricing policy designed by the national government or marketing boards to reset the internal terms of trade in favor of agricultural and rural goods. It is generally contended that the terms of trade continue to be unfavorable to these products.

Besides improving the general social infrastructure and rural amenities (which also add to real rural income), efforts should be made to bring the typical urban functions and the advantages of urban life closer to rural areas in the form of service centers, or rural-urban townships, or, as sometimes termed, "rurban centers":

> The idea is that a group of villages should be serviced by its own industrial and middle-sized urban centre. These service/market centres would include processing industries and various social, cultural, economic, recreational, and administrative services (such as secondary schools, hospitals, larger dispensaries) which would not be practicable in each small village. The service villages would be selected from among the natural trade and communication centres, and be connected in turn to larger urban centres within the framework of an over-all network. In many cases, these centres would use as a nucleus the traditional market towns, established centres of trade, capital and enterprise to which artisans move spontaneously from nearby villages as the villages become more homogeneous agricultural units in the process of growth. These service villages or town centres would be the basis of agricultural co-operatives, which are proving unworkable on an individual village basis. These settlements of perhaps 20,000/50,000 population may not be attractive to large-scale industry, but they would be crucial for rural and agricultural development and serve as the centralizing point for agricultural marketing, co-operatives, services, and village industries.[40]

Such rurban centers are said to be models for efficient settlement patterns and the means for achieving balanced agricultural and industrial development.

Among the social services provided to rural areas, special attention should be paid to education. The problem is that, in general, migration occurs selectively with respect to education and age. Rural areas lose a large proportion of their relatively limited number of educated persons, usually those in prime working ages. Often the enterprising operators of medium-sized commercial and family-run farms move to cities due to the lack of adequate education facilities for their children in rural areas. Or at least they send their children to cities, and these children, after completing their education, seldom return to the more backward rural life. It is this high-quality human capital that is most urgently required, particularly in countries with high illiteracy levels, to provide leadership for agricultural and community development programs. Expansion and improvement of educational facilities in rural areas in conjunction with expanded and ambitious agricultural development programs, and effective land reforms where required, may stimulate these groups to stay in rural areas.[8] An education program, besides including formal education, should place emphasis on an understanding of the basic problems of rural life and the structural obstacles to its improvement. Also, improved education by itself would help the rural migrant to assimilate more rapidly and efficiently into the urban environment.[41]

Overall, besides the obvious need for deflating the force of push factors operating in rural areas, the very fact that in most developing countries 60 to more than 90 percent of the total population still live in mostly backward rural and semi-rural areas and earn their living from agriculture, is sufficient reason for generating social and economic development in these areas.[42]

CONCLUSION

It is pertinent to conclude by reemphasizing the need for long-term redirectional policies rather than short-term remedial ones. Any short-term measure for increasing the volume of urban services and urban employment in order to cope with the needs of existing migrant populations will only serve as an additional attraction for the rural population. Also, population redirectional and settlement policies should to the largest extent possible be framed with the real cause of the excessive growth and movement—fertility—in mind. Policies for the distribution and redistribution of both population and economic resources should be consistent with those designed to deal with manpower and employment, technological choice and methods of production, education, and other aspects of socioeconomic development.

---

[8] Note that providing education without improving local economic opportunities in rural areas would accentuate rural-urban migration.

REFERENCES

1. For direct and indirect methods of measuring internal migration and population redistribution or the population displacement rate, see United Nations, Department of Economic and Social Affairs, *Methods of Measuring Internal
   Migration,* Manual 4, ST/SOA/Series A/47 (New York: United Nations,
   1970).
2. United Nations, *Official Records of the Economic and Social Council, Thirty-
   Seventh Session, Annexes,* E/3895/Rev. 1, agenda item 21.
3. A few of these studies are: Phyllis Deane and W. A. Coale, *British Economic
   Growth, 1688–1959* (Cambridge: Cambridge University Press, 1964); Dorothy
   S. Thomas, *Social and Economic Aspects of Swedish Population Movements,
   1750–1933* (New York: Macmillan Co., 1941); Simon Kuznets and Dorothy S.
   Thomas, comps., *Population Redistribution and Economic Growth: United
   States, 1870–1950,* 3 vols., (Philadelphia: American Philosophical Society, 1957,
   1960, and 1964); and Irene B. Taeuber, *The Population of Japan* (Princeton,
   N.J.: Princeton University Press, 1958).
4. Simon Kuznets and Dorothy S. Thomas, comps., *Population Redistribution and
   Economic Growth* (Philadelphia: American Philosophical Society, 1964), vol.
   3, p. xxiii.
5. J. I. Clarke and W. B. Fisher, eds., *Populations of the Middle East and North
   Africa: A Geographical Approach* (New York: Africana Publishing Corp.,
   1972), pp. 24–25.
6. See Robert O. Carleton, "Fertility trends and differentials in Latin America,"
   and Louis J. Ducoff, "The role of migration in the demographic development
   of Latin America," *Milbank Memorial Fund Quarterly* 43, pt. 2 (October
   1965): pp. 17ff. and 202–203.
7. C. Chandrasekaran and K. C. Zachariah, "Concepts used in defining urban population and data available on its characteristics in countries of Southern Asia,"
   in UNESCO Research Centre on Social and Economic Development in Southern Asia, *Urban-Rural Differences in Southern Asia* (New Delhi: United India
   Press, 1964), pp. 55–56.
8. Kingsley Davis, *World Urbanization, 1950–1970: Basic Data for Cities, Coun-
   ties, and Regions* (Berkeley: University of California, Institute of International
   Studies, 1969), vol. 1, table C.
9. Ernest Weissman, "Population, urban growth and regional development," *Proceedings of the World Population Conference, 1965* (New York: United Nations, 1967), vol. 4, p. 452. See also H. L. Browning, "The demography of the
   city," in Glenn H. Beyer, ed., *The Urban Explosion in Latin America* (Ithaca,
   N.Y.: Cornell University Press, 1967); United Nations, Department of Economic and Social Affairs, "Recent changes in urban and rural settlement patterns in Latin America," *International Social Development Review,* no. 1 (New
   York, 1968), pp. 55–62.
10. For a review of the actions taken by different governments to solve this housing
    problem in their metropolises, see United Nations, "Uncontrolled urban settle-
    ment: Problems and policies," *International Social Development Review,* no. 1
    (New York, 1968), pp. 122–128.
11. Republic of Turkey, State Planning Organisation, *Second Five Year Develop-*

ment Plan, 1968–1972 (Ankara: The Central Bank of the Republic of Turkey, 1969), p. 295.

12. Michael P. Todaro, "A model of labor migration and urban unemployment in less developed countries," *American Economic Review* 59, no. 1 (March 1969): 138–148; John R. Harris and Michael P. Todaro, "Migration, unemployment and development: A two-sector analysis," *American Economic Review* 60, no. 1 (March 1970): 126–142; Álvaro López Toro, "Migración y marginalidad urbana en paises subdesarrollados," *Demografía y Economica* 4, no. 2 (1970): 192–209.

13. Milton Friedman, *A Theory of the Consumption Function* (Princeton, N.J.: Princeton University Press, 1957).

14. See ref. 12, Harris and Todaro, p. 127.

15. See ref. 12, Todaro, p. 139.

16. See ref. 12, Toro, pp. 196–199. The available evidence shows that, generally, in Asian, African, and Latin American countries, the distribution of facilities between city and country is radically uneven. See, for example, United Nations, Department of Economic and Social Affairs, "Population movements and the distribution of social services," *International Social Development Review*, no. 1 (New York, 1968), pp. 92–94.

17. Manuel Diégues, Jr., "Internal migration in Brazil," *Proceedings of the World Population Conference, 1965* (New York: United Nations, 1967), vol. 4, p. 492.

18. See Giorgio Mortara, "Factors affecting rural-urban migration in Latin America: Influence of economic and social conditions in these two areas," *Proceedings of the World Population Conference, 1965* (New York: United Nations, 1967), vol. 4, pp. 509–512.

19. See ref. 5, pp. 5, 301–303.

20. ILO Reports and Inquiries, "A survey of employment, unemployment and underemployment in Ceylon," *International Labour Review* 87, no. 3 (March 1963): 257.

21. T. W. Schultz, *Agriculture in an Unstable Economy* (New York: McGraw-Hill, 1945), pp. 90–99.

22. Ashish Bose, "Internal migration in India, Pakistan and Ceylon," *Proceedings of the World Population Conference, 1965* (New York: United Nations, 1967), vol. 4, pp. 483–484. See also D. J. Bogue and K. C. Zachariah, "Urbanization and migration in India," in Roy Turner, ed., *India's Urban Future* (Berkeley: University of California Press, 1962).

23. Ralph E. Beals and Carmen F. Menezes, "Migrant labour and agricultural output in Ghana," *Oxford Economic Papers* 22, no. 1 (March 1970): 109–127.

24. Dale W. Adams, "Rural migration and agricultural development in Colombia," *Economic Development and Cultural Change* 17, no. 4 (July 1969): 528.

25. See Ronald C. Y. Ng, "Recent internal population movement in Thailand," *Annals of the Association of American Geographers* 59, no. 4 (December 1969).

26. For example, see Bose, ref. 22, p. 485.

27. Bruce H. Herrick, *Urban Migration and Economic Development in Chile* (Cambridge, Mass.: M.I.T. Press, 1965).

28. ILO, *Towards Full Employment: A Programme for Colombia* (Prepared by an

inter-agency team organized by the International Labour Office (Geneva, 1970), p. 97.

29. ILO, *Employment and Economic Growth* (Geneva, 1964).

30. F. Harbison, "The generation of employment in newly developing countries," in James R. Sheffield, ed., *Education, Employment and Rural Development* (Nairobi: East African Publishing House, 1967). See also C. R. Frank, Jr., "Urban unemployment and economic growth in Africa," *Oxford Economic Papers* 20, no. 2 (July 1968): 266–268.

31. See United Nations, Department of Economic and Social Affairs, "Community planning in marginal urban settlements" and "Techniques for improvement of marginal areas," *International Social Development Review*, no. 2 (New York, 1970): pp. 7–12, 19–23.

32. See, for example, Ulla Olin, "Population growth and problems of employment in Asia and the Far East," *Proceedings of the World Population Conference, 1965*, vol. 4, pp. 314–317.

33. See ref. 12, Harris and Todaro, p. 137.

34. See Richard A. Easterlin, "Economic growth: An overview," *International Encyclopedia of the Social Sciences* (New York: Macmillan Co., 1968), vol. 4, pp. 395–401; Simon Kuznets, *Modern Economic Growth: Rate, Structure and Spread* (New Haven: Yale University Press, 1967): pp. 490–497.

35. United Nations, "Economic aspects of urbanization," *International Social Development Review*, no. 1 (New York, 1968), pp. 71–78.

36. This has been suggested to be the case in Colombia. See ref. 28.

37. United Nations, "Urban growth and social development in Africa," *International Social Development Review*, no. 1 (New York, 1968), p. 42.

38. For an example of minimum wage legislation practices in Africa and the rapid growth of urban wage rates, see ref. 30, Frank, pp. 262–266.

39. See ref. 30, Frank, p. 270.

40. United Nations, "Urban-rural population distribution and settlement patterns in Asia," *International Social Development Review*, no. 1 (New York, 1968), p. 53; see also J. A. Ponsioen, "An analysis of—and a policy regarding—rural migration in developing countries," *Proceedings of the World Population Conference, 1965* (New York: United Nations, 1967), vol. 4, pp. 519–522.

41. For further elaboration of the role of education, see ref. 24, pp. 534–536.

42. See also, United Nations, "Rural community development and planning: Promise and reality," *International Social Development Review*, no. 2 (New York, 1970), pp. 28–33.

EIGHT

The Demographic Aspects
of Income Distribution

ISMAIL A. SIRAGELDIN

In recent years concern has arisen about the social consequences of the distribution of the costs and benefits of socioeconomic development. An equitable distribution of income and wealth among individuals and households in a given country is being recognized as central to that country's social and economic welfare goals. The recognition of the important role in social planning of the distributive effects of growth is further reinforced by the growing evidence that, at least in the early stages of development, the lower income groups, relative to the higher income groups, pay more of the costs and receive less of the benefits of development. This process is evidently self-defeating. Increased economic inequality and social injustice could threaten the achievements of economic development by leading society into a costly collapse of social and political stability.[1]

Understanding the determinants and consequences of population growth and structure in the process of socioeconomic growth and its distribution is becoming an important element in development planning.[2] Accordingly, development strategies must deal explicitly with the problems of achieving a balance among a desired rate of economic growth, a desired level of social and economic equality, and a rate (and structure) of population growth that is compatible with these two desired social goals. The balance must be achieved within the constraints of the existing national and international sociopolitical systems.

Consideration of the consequences of population growth and structure, as well as consideration of social and economic inequality in the context of socioeconomic development, is clearly an important departure from conventional development strategies, which are usually expressed almost entirely in pure economic growth terms. Whenever the population factor was mentioned, it was usually taken as an exogeneous element in the planning model. Whenever social justice was mentioned, it was usually expressed in general, non-quantifiable terms.[3] The conventional development orientation is partly a result of the bias of the economist toward goals that are well-defined in terms of measured output and its rate of growth as compared to the relative lack of acceptable indexes of equity and social justice. More seriously, however, is the lack of an adequate body of theory that explains the interrelations and interactions among the processes of population growth, economic growth, and economic inequality; and the lack of reliable data that can adequately begin to describe the extent and dimensions of inequality in most countries of the world.

This chapter will examine the role of demographic factors in the process of income and wealth distribution—its allocation among individuals and families and its functional shares. A basic premise of this chapter is that population policies will not achieve their desired objectives if they are not an integral part of a package that includes social and economic reforms designed to change the entire social structure. In order to participate actively in a national program of social engineering, people seem to need some sense of living in a dynamic society where there is hope for change and for sharing the fruits of that change.

The content of the chapter is divided into three parts. The first part presents an "accounting frame" of the forces that influence the shape of income distribution and examines how these forces are related to the various dimensions of population growth and structure. No attempt is made to develop or synthesize theories; rather, a modest attempt is made to develop a general frame that encompasses the relevant dimensions of the problem. The second part examines the relation of population growth to the personal distribution of income and probes problems related to issues of adequacy, equity, and intergenerational mobility of income and wealth. The third part examines the relationship between population growth and the functional distribution of income, that is, factor shares, in the context of the process of economic efficiency and growth.

GENERAL ANALYTICAL FRAME

In general, the distribution of income is the final output of the social system (that is, an outgrowth of social inequality) at a particular point of time. It may mean, however, different things, for instance, distribution among persons (personal), among factors of production (functional), or among social groups. The nature of the theoretical approach depends on the subject but usually examines the market forces that determine the rate of factor incomes—wages, interest, rent, and profit—and the forces that influence the individual allocation of these returns among society's stock of physical and human capital. In a dynamic frame, the present distribution is an outgrowth of its past structural history and will affect its future path, given the nature of society's legal, political, and social institutions. These latter noneconomic factors can have a significant effect on the shape of the income distribution and serve as policy tools to alter its shape. Their relative importance could lead to the conclusion that "economics does not give a clear-cut and single answer to the question of what really determines the distribution of income."[4]

The influence of the rate of population growth on income distribution can be traced through the effects of its basic components—fertility, mortality, and net migration rates, and accordingly, dependency ratio and family size—on the rate of capital accumulation in the case of examining functional shares and on the factors that influence individuals' potential economic opportunities in the case of examining personal shares. There are certain demographic realities, however, that are relevant to this discussion of income distribution and population growth, which need not be diffused.

First, current high rates of population growth in developing countries are a recent phenomenon. They are basically a result of a sharp decline in mortality rates without a parallel decline in fertility rates.

Second, the current gap between mortality and fertility rates is an aggregate of individual family decisions and experiences. It is the sum of individual disequilibrium situations in which the various family parameters of procreation (that is, of parents' supply and demand for a given quality of children) have changed.[5] For example, lower infant mortality rates have resulted in an increase in the average number of surviving children. But the direct and indirect costs of raising children have also been increasing, both as a result of the process of modernization and economic growth (for example, through increased opportunities for women in education and employment) and as a result of an increase in the social pressure to educate children, which probably reduces children's early contribution to their families' productive capacity.

Third, families adjust to improved socioeconomic conditions either through a change in their perceived value of children (derived satisfaction or psychic utility), which could be conceptualized as a shift in demand, or through the voluntary control of their fertility, including the use of modern and more efficient methods of contraception. The latter adjustment seems to be a more difficult one for many individuals since it implies a change from a natural adjustment mechanism (that is, through high enough mortality) to a purposive adjustment mechanism based on deliberate individual fertility decisions. This adjustment process is not necessarily uniform among various socioeconomic groups.

Fourth, the sudden and widening gap between aggregate mortality and fertility rates has created a parallel widening gap between the supply and demand for various social goods and services, as discussed elsewhere in this book (for example, health, education, and housing). The result is a chain reaction of policy measures and counter-measures designed both to ration limited supplies and to speed up the adjustment mechanism. The social costs and benefits of these policy measures are not necessarily equally distributed among population groups.

Fifth, the relevant question at the micro level is whether the poor are poor in part because they have too many children and/or because their parents had too many children. Alternatively, it is not only the level of exposed or realized fertility that will influence parents' and children's potential for economic advancement, but also the circumstances and intergenerational dynamics under which procreation took place. We shall give this matter major attention in our discussion.

Figure 8.1 is a schematic presentation of an accounting frame for the various factors that are relevant to our discussion. There are three types of demographic forces that have short- and long-term influences on the shape of income distribution. The first could be called the *pure demographic effect*. It is the result primarily of the effects of changes in the age distribution on the age-earning profile, the dependency ratio, and family size. For example, an older age distribution, which results in an increased proportion of the young (and the old) who are in their early (and late) low-income earning years, could result in increased inequality in the "apparent" current income distribution, given no changes in the age-earning patterns, family structure, and other socioeconomic parameters. (These effects can be traced through the first loop in the right-hand side of Figure 8.1.) Adjusting for family size and composition (for example, on an equivalent adult basis) could have an indeterminate effect on inequality, depending on the relation between changes in income and reproductive behavior.

The second kind of demographic force could be called the *social demographic effect*. It is the result of the interaction of demographic variables with changing social, institutional, and political forces, such as changes in marriage, retirement age, family structure, the pattern of inter-family transfers, inheritance laws, or attitudes toward work and life. For example, in periods of rapid economic growth that are associated with an energetic labor market mobility, to the extent that young family members seek different jobs in different places, there could be an increase in the relative number of nuclear families as well as changes in the pattern of inter-family transfers, resulting in greater "apparent" income inequality, as illustrated by the second loop in Figure 8.1.

The third type of demographic force could be called the *economic demographic effect*. It is the result of the effects of demographic changes on the potential labor supply (its quality, composition, and distribution), on potential aggregate savings, on the market structure (the share of agriculture in total output), and on the distribution of functional shares (the share of wages in total incomes). For example, it is hypothesized that income inequality decreases in the later phases of economic growth when, through the favorable demographic effect of reduced fertility and mortality, agricultural productivity increases through increased aggregate savings and investment and when urban inequality declines and the share of labor income increases.

This discussion is only meant to indicate the complexity and interdisciplinary nature of the relationships. We shall now attempt to examine these factors within a frame of policy criteria that are relevant to planning activities.

Figure 8.1 Relationship Between Population Growth and Income Distribution: A Schematic Presentation

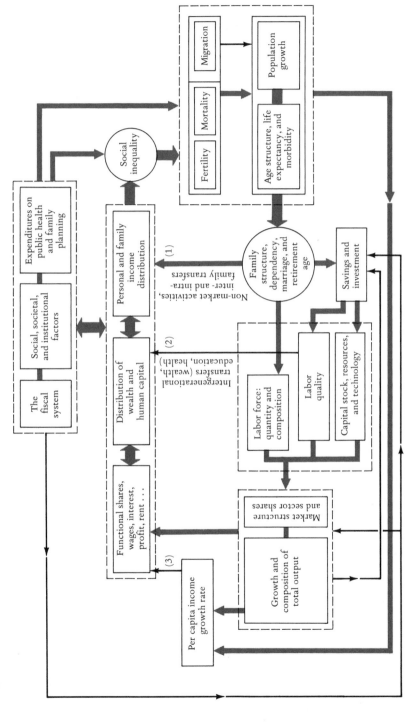

POPULATION GROWTH AND THE PERSONAL
DISTRIBUTION OF INCOME

Income distribution statistics can be presented in different ways to draw attention to different properties of the statistical facts.[1] Such presentations are closely related to the sociodemographic characteristics of a population and could cause confusion when interpreting changes in the basic parameters of income distribution. We shall examine some of these measurement problems in the context of estimating a poverty gap. This will also serve as a basis for the more substantive discussion of the demographic aspects of equity that will follow.

The Demographic Aspects of Adequacy

As a first step, one needs to define operationally what an adequate income[2] is for a given society at a given time in order to estimate the number of poor families and assess the social dimension of the problem for planning purposes. It is possible to define adequacy in terms of a poverty line or threshold that is a function of household size.[3] The poverty gap at a given time period (t) could then be estimated using the following simple definition:

[aggregate poverty gap] = [aggregate poverty threshold] − [aggregate pre-welfare income]

(1) $G_t = [H_t \cdot K_t \cdot Q_t] - [Y_t \cdot L_t]$
where: G = Aggregate poverty gap

---

[1] A review of available data and reported findings suggests that the distribution of income and wealth is, and will continue to be extremely unequal in developing countries. We must be careful, however, in interpreting international differences in income distribution data. Such data are extremely unreliable and, in many respects, may be misleading, especially for comparative analysis.[6] A discussion of some of these methodological problems is presented in the appendix to this chapter.

[2] The problem of adequacy in social planning arises because, theoretically, income shares cannot be negative; that is, for each individual there is an absolute minimum income. But members of a society, for reasons that may be beyond their control, can fail to earn the minimum share.

[3] For example, the national average poverty threshold at time t may be calculated as follows:

$Q_t = \Sigma \ (h_t^i \cdot q_t^i)$, where $\Sigma \ h_t^i = 1$ and $h_t^i =$ the fractions of all poor households with i persons.

$q_t^i =$ poverty line for poor households with i persons.

If poverty lines are constant, then we have $q_t^i = q_{t+n}^i$; but if poverty lines are relative, then we have $q_t^i = q_{t-n}^i (k_t/k_{t-n})$, where k_t is income per capita.

Adequacy, however, is related to consumption needs and requires careful definition of equivalent consumers. First, the definition will depend on the unit of analysis (e.g., individuals or families), the demographic characteristics of the population, and the cost of living. Second, we need to evaluate adequacy in terms of the income unit life cycle, and accordingly the definition of income used (e.g., current or permanent) becomes equally important.

H = Total number of households

K = Fraction of households below the poverty threshold

Q = Average value of poverty threshold (either constant or relative)

Y = Total national income

L = Fraction of national income (excluding welfare) received by poor.

But such an apparently simple approach could be difficult to estimate and could give misleading guidelines for planning policies. For example, it is tempting to examine the change in G_t over time:

$$(2) \quad dG_t/dt = K_t \cdot Q_t \left[\frac{dH_t}{d_t}\right] + K_t \cdot H_t \left[\frac{dQ_t}{d_t}\right] + H_t \cdot Q_t \left[\frac{dK_t}{d_t}\right]$$
$$- Y_t \left[\frac{dL_t}{d_t}\right] - L_t \left[\frac{dY_t}{d_t}\right]$$

and conclude that the poverty gap, G_t, could be reduced either by increasing the rate of growth of the income shares of the poor or by reducing the rate of growth of household number and/or size.[4] This "gross" conclusion, however, ignores both the case of income mobility and the effect of the sociodemographic structure of poverty and the poor on the future path of the poverty gap, and it could have other shortcomings when applied to less developed economies.

In order to illustrate some difficulties that arise when estimating a poverty gap, a hypothetical example is presented in Table 8.1. The data were selected to approximate the case of a less developed economy. They represent a country with six million people, a per capita income of $100, and an average family (or household) size of six. The distribution of income is typical: the lowest 20 percent of families have 6 percent of the total income and the top 5 percent have 40 percent of the income. Families, as usual, are ordered according to the level of their personal income, but the ordering is made according to the family's per equivalent adult income. Equivalent adults (EQV) are calculated simply by giving adults a weight of 1.0, children (under age 15) a weight of 0.50, and people 65 and over a weight of 0.75, and adding the weights for each family.[5] It is assumed in the illustration that average family size is larger for low income people and that the latter have a higher dependency ratio (see lines 2 and 10 of the table).[6] Based on these assumptions, the average family income of the lowest quintile (lowest 20 percent) is 30 percent of the country's average ($180

---

[4] However, assuming that the rate of growth of H equals that of population; that K and L are constants (i.e., a constant income distribution); and the Q is relative (see preceding footnote), then it could be shown that $\frac{dG}{dt} / G = \frac{dY}{dt} / Y$, that is, the poverty gap will grow as fast as income.[7]

[5] For further discussion and references, see the appendix to this chapter.

[6] This assumption seems justifiable based on scattered evidence, although adequate documentation appears to be lacking. See, however, the discussion below.

Table 8.1 Share of Ordinal Groups of Per Equivalent Adult (EQV) Personal Income for Family Units: A Hypothetical Case

Characteristics	Shares of ordinal groups					All	Notes
	0–20	21–60	61–80	81–95	96–100		
Demographic Data							
1. Number of families ('000)	200	400	200	150	50	1,000	
2. Average number of people per family	6.50	6.30	6.00	5.00	4.50	6.00	
3. Total number of people ('000)	1,300	2,520	1,200	750	225	6,000	= (1) × (2)
4. Average number of living children	3.20	2.90	2.70	2.10	1.60	2.74	(under age 15, per family)
5. Total number of living children ('000)	640	1,160	540	315	80	2,735	= (1) × (4)
6. Average number 65+ per family[a]	0.20	0.22	0.24	0.23	0.27	0.22	(estimate)
7. Total number 65+ ('000)	39.0	88.2	48.0	33.8	13.5	222.5	= (1) × (6)
8. Total number of EQV units ('000)[b]	970	1,918	918	584	182	4,577	
9. Average number of EQV per family	4.85	4.79	4.59	3.89	3.63	4.58	= (8) ÷ (1)
10. Dependency ratio	0.52	0.50	0.49	0.47	0.42	0.49	= [(5) + (7)] ÷ [(1)]
11. Percent of family	20	40	20	15	5	100	from (1)

Table 8.1 Continued

Characteristics	Shares of ordinal groups					All	Notes
	0–20	21–60	61–80	81–95	96–100		
Income Data							
12. Income shares (percents)	6	17	15	22	40	100	
13. Aggregate personal income ($'000)	36,000	102,000	90,000	132,000	240,000	600,000	
14. Average income per family ($)	180	225	450	880	4,800	600	= (13) ÷ (1)
15. Average income per person ($)	28	41	75	176	1,067	100	= (13) ÷ (3)
16. Average income per EQV ($)	37	53	98	226	1,132	131	= (13) ÷ (8)
17. EQV income range ($)	10–43	46–64	70–207	210–800	890–3,000	10–3,000	(estimate)
18. EQV income as percent of national average	28	40	75	173	864	100	

[a] It is assumed in the calculation that the percent 65 and older are 3, 3.5, 4, and 4.5 within income groups starting from the lowest quintile, respectively, and 3.7 percent for the population as a whole (it was 3.47 for the Arab Republic of Egypt, 3.32 for Mexico, 5.64 for Puerto Rico, and 9.58 for the US in 1968/1969 (UN, *Demographic Yearbook*, 1969).

[b] It is assumed, to simplify the calculation, that a child equals 0.50 of an adult and an elderly person equals 0.75 of an adult (i.e., EQV = [(5) × 0.5] + [(7) × 0.75] + [(3) − (5) − (7)]. For more refined weights, see E. Kleiman, "Age composition, size of households and the interpretation of per capita income," *Economic Development and Cultural Change* 15 (1966) : 37–58.

compared to $600) and is less than 4 percent of the income of the top 5 percent of the population ($180 compared to $4,800). On a per equivalent adult basis, the average income of the lowest quintile is about $37 (about 28 percent of the country's average). If we assume that $45 is the poverty line, then all families in the lowest quintile (lowest 20 percent) are defined as poor and the poverty gap is estimated to equal $8.1 million. This calculation is sensitive to the shape of income distribution. For example, increasing the poverty line by 40 percent would increase the poverty gap more than six fold.

It is evident that a systematic analysis of those below the poverty line in a given year (say, those in the lowest family income quintile) requires data that differentiate between at least three poverty groups: (1) those who are transitionally poor, reflecting the income life-cycle pattern expected for that particular society, for example, the low income young who have just started working and whose current income is below their permanent income, or those who are retired. Although this group will affect the shape of the aggregate income distribution, it has a "warranted reflection in income differentials and inequalities."[8] The relative weight of these two groups on the age distribution of those in the lowest quintile should be determined by the aggregate age distribution of that society and its average earning life-cycle pattern; (2) those who are poor because of such accidental misfortunes as sickness, unemployment, or death of a main family supporter. This group may or may not be randomly distributed over the working-age distribution, since short-term income instability could vary systematically with age; and (3) people who are in the poverty trap—those who continue to be poor over their life-cycle and across generations.

Such a classification would greatly enhance the understanding of the anatomy and dynamics of poverty, especially if the analysis is done for families on an age-specific income-cohort basis in which the income behavior of families in various income groups (for example, the lowest two quintiles) is examined over time to determine the pattern of upward and downward mobility. Available income data for developing countries (mainly cross-sectional), unfortunately, are not designed for such analysis.

The Demographic Aspects of Equity and Income Mobility

Development or growth is not an equilibrium state. It implies continuous response to new opportunities for investment in both physical capital and human capital. Investment in human capital includes formal education, on-the-job training and experience, and health care. In an equitable distribution of earnings, investment in human capital is expected to be strongly correlated with earnings, which implies equality of social and economic opportunities, allowing for differences in individuals' human abilities and capacities.

This would be the case because the concept of equity implies equal opportunities and the absence of discrimination in rates of returns to similar goods and services. It does not follow, however, that equal opportunities imply greater income equality, partly because of the dispersion of native talents. Indeed, perfect equality of opportunities does not imply equality of earnings as long as there are differences in abilities. Health (and nutrition) and education are two major factors that determine ability. Both factors interact in their effect on ability. For example, a child's ability to acquire the full benefit of schooling depends on his health status and physical and mental fitness; the same is true for an adult. Therefore, the distribution of abilities in a population depends on, among other things, the distribution of health and educational facilities—their quantities and qualities.

Population dynamics affect the distribution of abilities on three levels. On the aggregate level, the capacity of a society to provide adequate health and educational facilities is limited by the relative growth of its total output, the growth of its population, the opportunity costs of other competing investments, and the existing level of health and education in that society (that is, how far the society lags behind adequacy). Furthermore, given the low level of resources in most developing countries, increasing numbers of health and educational facilities usually results in lower quality. However, high income groups, because of both their relatively higher income and lower fertility, can afford to purchase high quality (private) services, thus increasing (personal) intergenerational income inequality.[7]

On the regional level, within countries, there is evidence of uneven distribution of health and educational facilities. For example, in rural areas, health and educational facilities are usually reported as less adequate than in urban areas. This is also reflected in some health indicators, for example, the higher reported infant mortality rates in rural than in urban areas.[8]

On the individual level, inequality in education and health could be a result of voluntary decisions or a result of constraints that limit individual choices (including the lack of knowledge and motivation). For example, whether a child continues in school depends largely on parental decisions and circumstances. The choice between school and work is usually made without the complete consent of the child. But this decision determines the child's future options in career advancement and mobility. As Table 8.2 indicates, in 1960 the proportions of children aged 10–14 who were economically active were 24 percent for boys and 10 percent for girls in agricultural societies compared to 4 and 2 percent, respectively, for industrial societies. The opportunity cost of work at

---

[7] A study in the United States demonstrated that there are substantial returns to the quality of early education.[9]

[8] There is some evidence that infant mortality rates are higher in rural than in urban areas. In Taiwan, Sullivan reports an infant mortality rate of 43.8 for rural townships compared to 37.7 for cities. S. L. N. Rao found in Latin America a high positive zero-order correlation between the level of urbanization (percent urban) and life expectancy within age groups and for both sexes. John Cassel reports evidence in the United States of higher death and morbidity rates in rural than in urban areas. This, however, seems to have been the reverse before the 1950s.[10]

school age is mainly the potential loss in future ability through lack of adequate education, which can reduce a worker's ability to acquire and decode information about costs and productive characteristics of other inputs. This recently has been labeled "allocative benefits."[11] Some studies in India indicate educational differentials among farmers in accepting and utilizing new agricultural techniques.[12]

Table 8.2 Labor Force Participation Rates of Children Aged 10–14 by Degree of Industrialization of Economy and for Selected Countries

	Year	Number of countries	Percent economically active	
			Males (10–14)	Females (10–14)
Degree of industrialization				
1. Industrial	1960	18	4.1	2.4
2. Semi-industrial	1960	28	13.2	—
3. Agricultural	1960	18	23.9	10.2
Selected countries				
4. Japan	1920	1	20.6	25.2
5. Japan	1950	1	5.2	4.0
6. USA	1920	1	10.3	3.9
7. USA	1950	1	2.6	0.8
8. India	1962	1	33.1	25.1
9. Indonesia	1962	1	22.6	15.6
10. Venezuela	1962	1	16.6	3.7

SOURCES: Lines 1–3, 4–5, 8–10: "Age patterns of participation in economic activities," *Demographic Aspects of Manpower,* Report 1, Population Studies, no. 33 (New York: United Nations, 1962), pp. 12–22; and U.N., *Demographic Yearbook,* various issues.

Lines 6–7: United States, Bureau of Census, *U.S. Census of Population,* 1950, Vol. II, Characteristic of the Population, Part 1, U.S. Summary, Washington, Government Printing Office, 1953, p. 259.

See also, Moni Nag, "Economic value of children in agricultural societies: Evaluation of existing knowledge and an anthropological approach for studying it" (Paper presented to the Workshop on Assessment of the Satisfactions and Costs of Children, East-West Population Institute, Honolulu, 27–29 April and 1–2 May 1972).

As mentioned earlier, low levels of education and health can interact and have a cumulative negative effect on individual abilities. One example is nutrition. Evidence indicates that malnutrition during pregnancy can have an adverse effect on the child's intelligence by permanently impairing brain functions. Malnutrition in either the mother while pregnant or the child during infancy may also result in defective growth of the child and less resistance to disease in general. Belli, after a survey of evidence, concludes that

> poverty and ignorance are the most likely causes of malnutrition. People do not have enough money to buy the foods that would nourish them well.... But ... even moderately well-to-do families do not know the elements of good nutrition.[13]

Differentials in the various components of equity—health, education, social and economic opportunity—affect more than a single generation. Lack of equity affects not only an individual's social mobility and economic opportunity during his life, but also intergenerational mobility.

The Demographic Aspects of Income Mobility

Planners, in dealing with impoverished people, must find ways to help them without making them more dependent on help. From this point of view, the targets of a redistribution policy are children and youth. Accordingly, the factors of concern to planners are the rate and circumstances of reproduction, and the distribution of property income, savings, and wealth. It is also useful to distinguish between factors affecting socioeconomic mobility over the life cycle and factors affecting intergenerational mobility (for example, the transmission of poverty from parents to their children).

Income Mobility and Reproduction: As a first approximation, data on age-specific fertility behavior within family income groups could be examined. Although the data presented in Table 8.3 are for the United States, they are

Table 8.3   Age-Specific Excess Fertility for US Families with Incomes Below US$2,000 in 1959, by Various Characteristics

Age of mother	Percent by which poverty group exceeds average of all income classes in children ever born				
	All mothers	Not in labor force		In labor force	
		White	Non-white	White	Non-white
20–24	7.4	5.9	8.4	10.4	15.9
25–29	17.5	15.6	15.2	20.9	15.1
30–34	23.1	21.8	22.1	20.6	35.5
35–39	25.0	23.3	23.3	18.8	32.6

SOURCE: Based on Kingsley Davis, "Some demographic aspects of poverty in the United States," in Margaret S. Gordon, ed., *Poverty in America* (San Francisco: Chandler Publishing Company, 1965), pp. 303–307.

nevertheless illustrative of both the main points of the analysis and the type of data required. The table indicates that, age for age, mothers in poor families (incomes less than US$2,000 per year) have higher birth rates than mothers with higher incomes. This relation holds true regardless of employment status and race, although the extent of excess fertility generally varies according to these characteristics. One obvious and immediate effect of this above-average reproduction rate is to make the poor poorer. But, in terms of future generations, the major concern of social planners should be on the children of these already poor families.

It could be estimated from Table 8.1, for example, that 24 percent of the children in our hypothetical developing country—or one out of every four—are raised in the lowest quintile of families who have 6 percent of the income (and who could be defined as below the poverty line), while 3 percent of the children are raised in the top 5 percent of families who have 40 percent of all income. This is based on the assumption that the average number of living children is larger for low income families (see Table 8.1, line 4). These assumptions are not far from reality. For example, it has been estimated that in Brazil, "a typical upper-class (or middle-class) completed family has about four surviving children, while a typical lower-class completed family has about eight." As a consequence, if "lower- and upper-class total incomes both increased by 6.5 percent, the *lower-class per capita income* (a mean, which is a good approximation to the mode and thus representative of central tendency) would stay about the same."[14] We do not mean, however, to suggest that the problem of children in poor families is one only of maintenance in the sense of being only concerned with providing minimum basic needs. This view is clearly oversimplified. First, it is an underestimate of the extent of inequality among children, because in poor families, the extent of investment in human capital is probably much lower than in higher income families; education, training, and health levels and habits invested in poor parents will be transmitted at least partly to their children and will affect their overall ability and motivation to achieve. Second, this view frames the problem of children in quantitative terms, as if

> ... it were a matter of a given family income divided by the number of members in the family. It seems quite possible that the demographic problem of the poor is not solely the number of children they have but also the circumstances under which they have them.[15][9]

It is probable that the high fertility levels of the poor and associated high mortality and morbidity levels are largely responsible for reducing the ability of poor families to reach their potential economic capacity and for reducing opportunities

---

[9] For example, the incidence of illegitimacy and abortion and their socioeconomic burden might be larger among the poor. Also, since the number of total pregnancies and of surviving children is larger among the poor, the burden and duration of dependency, measured, for example, in terms of total child-year-dependency, is also greater among the poor.

for both parents and children.[10] Third, this view does not consider the problem of family planning—the differentials in demand and supply conditions for birth control methods among the parents and potential parents in the various income groups.

Income Mobility and Property Income: Property income is probably an important source of income inequality in developing countries. The two main sources of such income are inheritance and savings. It is not evident which one of these sources is the major source of property income inequality, although such knowledge could enhance the effectiveness of policies aimed at reducing such inequality. For example, if saving is only a temporary postponement of consumption (that is, if no inheritance is involved), and if labor earnings, saving behavior, and the rate of return on investment are the same for everyone, then the distribution of property income will be a direct function of the age distribution of the population. If differentials in saving behavior (for example, people saving different proportions of their wages) were based on voluntary choices, then it would be arguable that lifetime real earnings are equal (although money incomes are not). But, as mentioned earlier, there could be serious imperfections in wage levels and rates of return; and, to the extent that saving behavior is related to desired family size, realized family size could be based on imperfect knowledge about contraceptive behavior.[16]

Introducing inheritance probably tends to increase inequality. Its importance as a component of property income in a given society is related to the rate of increase of wage income, the average working life, the rate of return on investment, the rate of saving from income,[11] and inheritance laws and systems (for example, primogeniture systems). A full discussion of the possible relationships is beyond the purpose of this chapter; the discussion will be limited to a few issues related to land ownership, since it is an important form of holding wealth in developing countries and raises many issues relevant to the demographic aspects of wealth and income distribution.

1. In places where the expansion of cultivated areas is not keeping pace with population growth, the effect on the distribution of land ownership appears to be a cumulative subdivision and fragmentation of the cultivated area.[12]

---

[10] It is sometimes argued that the micro benefits of more efficient reproduction (i.e., lower infant mortality) could outweigh the cost of raising additional children. This argument, however, ignores, among other things, the limited alternatives available for many families to alter their reproductive behavior, mainly because of ignorance and economic constraints to acquire knowledge or try new techniques of birth control. These constraints set severe limitations on the social meaning of decisions and their rationality.

[11] It is argued that the higher these three rates, the lower the share of inherited wealth in total wealth.[17]

[12] It has been reported, for example, that in a village in the Poona district of India, near Bombay, the average holding had been 16 hectares in 1770 and was below three hectares in 1919. The rate of population growth has accelerated since.[18]

2. A relatively high rate of population growth tends to worsen the economic position of the peasantry and make them more vulnerable to loss of their lands. Maintaining traditional standards of expenditure (for example, weddings and funerals) in the face of decreasing income further aggravates poverty and may result in additional loss of land. The result of this process is a more unequal distribution of land ownership as reflected in an increase of the landless and a rise of large landowners.[13] Societal factors, such as the type of inheritance laws, play an important role in the process, but it is the rate of population growth relative to land availability that seems to be the major factor.[14]

3. Of relevance to the dynamics of land ownership is the role of moneylenders. The power of moneylenders in a rural structure is derived not only from their role as financial intermediaries but also from their role as traders with monopolistic power (for example, raising the rate of interest and reducing the peasants' selling price of farm products). The relevant point is that the extent of inequality in terms of families' welfare can be underestimated and its causes diffused if no account is taken of the extent of farmers' indebtedness.[15]

POPULATION GROWTH AND THE FUNCTIONAL DISTRIBUTION OF INCOME

A full analysis of the relationship between population growth and the functional distribution of income would require a general equilibrium model that is very complex and beyond the scope of this paper. The discussion in this section is limited to a brief examination of two issues that are important in current planning. The first is the relationship of population growth to the structure of output and the relative growth of the various sectors and their shares in total output and employment. The second is the effect of a more equitable income distribution on aggregate saving.

The Impact of Population Growth on Economic Structure

It is important to know to what extent slowing population growth rates will produce a more developed economic structure in that the agricultural sector is relatively smaller than the industrial, transportation, and communication sectors. Using cross-sectional regression analysis, Chenery estimated sector growth elas-

---

[13] Changes in the size of ownership-holdings may be reflected in an increase in the practice of leasing land without changing the size of the operational units. It is not certain, however, how this affects productivity.[19]

[14] A comparative study of this process in India, Burma, Thailand, and South Vietnam indicates that the degree of land fragmentation and landless peasants is less where populations did not grow as fast.[20]

[15] And it is not only the peasantry who become indebted to the moneylenders but also big landlords.[21]

ticities with respect to per capita income growth and population growth. He found that the per capita income elasticities are more important for all sectors but especially in the industry, transportation, and communication sectors.[22] These findings cast doubt on the argument that rapid population growth is desirable on the ground of enlarging the domestic market in order to achieve economies of size. Using Chenery's elasticity coefficients, Ruprecht and Wahren[23] attempted to examine further the market size argument by disaggregating the economy into developed sectors (industrial, transportation, and communication) and less developed sectors (agriculture and mining), and by assuming two rates of population growth (constant fertility and declining fertility) and two rates of growth of output over a period of 30 years. The result of this simulation is presented in Table 8.4. It presents the ratios of the absolute size of each sector when fertility is declining to the absolute size of the same sector when fertility is constant. The table indicates, given the restrictive assumptions of the projections, that declining fertility is associated with a growth in the industrial and transportation sectors, which are most characterized by economies of size. Also, this structural advantage seems largely independent of the rate of growth of output, especially in the long term (that is, after 20–30 years). This is consistent with Kuznets' conclusion that the rise in productivity amounts to at least eight-tenths of the rise in per capita product in several countries.[24]

A realistic examination, however, of the effect of population growth on sector shares that is more relevant to the problem of income distribution must consider not only the relative growth of sector income, but also the relative growth of sector employment and, accordingly, sector productivity since income growth without employment growth may indicate an undesirable income distribution as well as unwanted leisure. Thus, as Kuznets put it:

> The sectoral structure of production is of interest because active participation in specific sectors imposes specific patterns on the lives of the participants (and those of their dependents), affects the kind of enterprise and occupational status that the participants share, and determines the activity that they engage in. Since active work within the economy plays a dominant role in the lives of the people so engaged (and their dependents), and since the pattern of life and work imposed on the participants (and their dependents) are its most important aspect, the effects of the differentials in production structure among countries are consequently also important.[25]

Although the relationship between changes in income and changes in employment is extremely complex, a first approximation that starts from a simple identity could identify some basic indicators.[26] Thus we could assume three major sectors—agriculture (A), industrial (I), and service (S), and define a sector's value added per equivalent consumers as follows:

$$V_{ij}/N_{ij} = [(E_{ij}/W_j) \div (N_{ij}/W_j)] \times (V_{ij}/E_{ij})$$

where: $V_{ij} =$ The value added originated in the ith sector, in j^{th} year;

Table 8.4 Impact of Population Growth on Sector Size: Ratio of Each Sector, Declining Fertility, to the Same Sector, Constant Fertility

Number of years after fertility decline	Agriculture		Industry		Transportation and communication		Mining		Other services	
	3.5	6.0	3.5	6.0	3.5	6.0	3.5	6.0	3.5	6.0
0	100.0	100.0	100.0	100.0	100.0	100.0	100.0	100.0	100.0	100.0
10	98.2	98.3	101.4	101.1	100.9	100.9	99.1	98.8	100.2	100.1
20	93.6	94.3	104.9	104.5	103.7	103.3	96.5	97.0	100.8	100.6
30	86.7	87.4	110.8	110.1	107.9	107.6	93.8	93.7	101.7	101.5

Annual growth rate of total output in percent

SOURCE: Theodore K. Ruprecht and Carl Wahren, *Population Programmes and Economic and Social Development* (Paris: Development Centre, Organization for Economic Cooperation and Development, 1970), p. 33.

> E_{ij} = Employment in the ith sector, in the jth year (in full-time equivalent);
>
> N_{ij} = Equivalent adult consumers in the ith sector in jth year, arrived at by weighting children roughly by their relative consumption needs as explained earlier; and
>
> W_j = Total working population in jth year

The first term to the right of the equal sign indicates the fraction of total working population employed in the ith sector. Trends in this fraction indicate the "gross" absorptive capacity of the ith sector. The second term indicates the relative dependency in the ith sector to the total working population. The sum of value added originating in each sector, added for all sectors, and appropriately weighted, will give gross domestic product—abstracting from particular problems of data handling and adjustments. Sector employment (E_{ij}), based on full-time man-hour equivalence, could be decomposed further into number of people employed (e_{ij}^n) and hours per worker per year (e_{ij}^h) in order to examine the trade-off between trends of average hours of work per worker and numbers of workers within and among the various sectors. In general, this simple frame permits an examination of individual trends in the main components of sectoral output per equivalent adult. Thus, a sector's relative share in total value added is influenced both by changes in its relative productivity and by changes in its labor absorptive capacity.

In his major study, *The Economic Growth of Nations*, Kuznets concludes that trends in the share of the agricultural sector in gross or net, domestic or national product, and either in current or constant price volumes in the course of the growth experience of the developed countries during the last century and a half have shown a marked decline, from over 40 percent in the initial decades of development to less than 10 percent in recent years; that the share of the industrial sector has almost doubled, from about 25 to 50 percent; and that the share of the service sector has shown a slight but not consistent rise.[27]

Furthermore, in terms of labor force, the share of the agricultural sector declined sharply in the course of growth of the currently developed countries from initial levels of 50 and 60 percent to current levels between 10 and 20 percent, while the shares of the industrial and service sectors rose from levels of about 20 percent to above 40 percent. This large decline in the share of the agricultural sector in labor force over a century, if weighted by the natural growth of labor force (and population), which averaged an annual rate of increase of about one percent, will imply that the relative decline of the labor force in the agricultural sector was about half, while the relative increase of the labor force in the nonagricultural sector was about six fold.

But since the increase in population (and labor force) was not necessarily affected by economic changes alone, the natural rate of increase of the rural population (and its labor supply), during this period of structural change has been higher than the country's average. This, Kuznets argues, made a conflict between the demographic and economic trends of the agricultural and non-agricultural sectors and might have been partly responsible for much of the economic and social mobility during the growth history of the currently developed countries.[28] There is no systematic evidence, however, that this process is being repeated for the developing countries, given their levels of per capita income and the shares of their agricultural sector in output and labor force.

Observations from country cross-sectional data, for example, indicate that the current shares of the agricultural sector in some developing countries are lower than what would have been predicted, based on their relative levels of per capita products; that is, the share of the agricultural sector declined in those countries even when per capita product did not rise, implying that institutional and technological factors could have been responsible for the shift. Because, in the developing countries, the internal dynamic forces of social change are largely independent of the introduction of such factors as imported technology and institutional innovations, predictions about the future path and structure of their economic growth that are based on only historical economic indicators (of the now developed countries' experience) could be very unreliable and could have misleading policy implications—a situation similar to deriving implications from demographic predictions for the developing countries that are based on the historical path of the demographic transition but which ignore that recent developments in public health (responsible for reduced mortality in the developing countries) were largely independent of the level of these countries' socioeconomic development and accordingly might have a different role in the process of social change. As an illustration, it was reported in a recent study of economic growth and changes in the industrial structure of income and labor force in Pakistan during 1951–1961, that there have been significant differences in the industrial structure, in sector labor absorption, and in sector productivity between Bangladesh and Pakistan. Such differences are reflected in the annual rates of growth of output: 2.12 percent for Bangladesh and 3.10 percent for Pakistan as illustrated in Table 8.5.[29] It is evident from the table that the growth of the labor force (and, accordingly, population) was mainly responsible for the modest realized positive rate of total output growth in Bangladesh, because it more than compensated for the combined negative effects of a declining product per worker and an inefficient structural change. The latter is reflected in the low coefficients of labor absorption of the industrial and service sectors. This is in contrast to Pakistan where, although increases in labor supply remained the primary factor accounting for almost 93 percent of the increase in real output, the labor absorptive capacity of the nonagricultural sectors far exceeded that of the agricultural sector, thus allowing for a more favorable industrial structure. It is evident that population (or labor force) growth alone cannot explain the more favorable industrial structure of Pakistan since the total growth rate of labor supply was almost equal in both countries.. The only noticeable difference seems to have been in pro-

Table 8.5 Sectoral Indexes of Growth in Output and Composition: Bangladesh and Pakistan, 1951–1961 (Index: 1951 = 100)

Country and sector	Index of growth of					Output per laborer per year (Rs)	
	Output	Labor supply	Product per worker	Coefficient of absorption[a]	Change in industrial structure	1951	1961
Bangladesh							
Agriculture	115	133	86	1.06	n.a.	769	604
Industry	180	121	149	0.70	n.a.	1,404	2,085
Service	125	119	105	0.64	n.a.	2,355	2,496
Annual rate of growth	2.12	2.69	−0.26[b]	n.a.	−0.30[b]	938	883
Pakistan							
Agriculture	114	120	94	0.61	n.a.	1,088	1,028
Industry	205	185	111	2.14	n.a.	1,539	1,707
Service	142	143	100	1.35	n.a.	1,872	1,864
Annual rate of growth	3.10	2.88	−0.13[b]	n.a.	0.36[b]	1,255	1,296

[a] Coefficient of absorption =

$$\frac{\text{annual growth rate of labor force in the } i^{th} \text{ sector}}{\text{annual growth rate of the total labor force}}$$

[b] These are standardized product per worker and structural changes, estimated by a decomposition of the product per worker index for the whole economy (weighted by relative labor shares of each industry using Paasche and Laspeyres index formulas). See source, p. 303.

n.a. = Not applicable.

SOURCE: Based on Ghazi M. Farooq, "Economic growth and change in the industrial structure of income and labor force in Pakistan," *Economic Development and Cultural Change* 21, no. 2 (January 1973): tables 2, 3, and 4.

ductivity, especially in agriculture, and in the labor absorptive capacity of the nonagricultural sectors.

The declining absolute productivity in the agricultural sectors of both Bangladesh and Pakistan during the 1950s has resulted in a worsening relative position of the "average" agricultural output/labor ratio as compared to that of nonagricultural sectors. For example, the average agricultural output/labor ratio in Bangladesh was 55 percent of that of industry and 33 percent of that of service in 1950–1951, but declined to 32 and 27 percent, respectively, in 1960–1961. The data for Pakistan indicate similar but less extreme patterns, as illustrated in the last two columns of Table 8.5. How much of this worsening position is a result of rural population pressure and how much is a result of inadequate planning requires careful examination. It could be argued, for example, that a combination of these two factors was responsible (among other things) for the apparent worsening relative position in Bangladesh. For example, the decline in agricultural output per worker was partly a result of a high rate of increase in the agricultural labor force that could only be absorbed at a lower marginal and average product, coupled with almost stagnant employment opportunities in the nonagricultural sectors, as indicated by their low growth rates compared to the rate of growth of the total labor force.

It seems that planners, within the constraints of availability and adequacy of data, should attempt to answer the following questions:

1. To what extent an apparent increase in sector productivity was a result of improved methods of production as opposed to a relatively stagnant employment situation, that is, low labor absorption capacity, as was the case with the nonagricultural sectors in Bangladesh during the 1950s;

2. To what extent relatively stagnant sector employment was a result of a shortage of supply of the appropriate quality of labor as opposed to the introduction of labor-saving technology;

3. To what extent a change in the distribution of income (output) within a sector was a result of a change in the quality and composition of workers (for example, more technicians) as opposed to shifts in the shares of management and profits in total output with the same composition of workers.

Population Growth, Income Inequality, and Savings

A social policy that promotes the growth of a labor-intensive sector may result in reducing inequalities in the size distribution of incomes and, it is argued, may also reduce aggregate personal savings, thus retarding potential capital formation and economic growth. Such conclusions cannot be accepted theoretically without guarded assumptions and qualifications (for example, the propensity to save out of capitalist profit is higher than from nonprofit incomes), and can be verified only on empirical grounds. One important factor that needs emphasis, however, is that we are dealing with net and not gross savings. Thus, consideration must be given to the extent of dissaving.

The extent of dissaving could be rather sizable in low income countries, especially when low income is combined with sizable income inequalities, as is the case with almost all developing countries. But low income countries will also have a large Engel coefficient (for example, 0.6, which is more than double that of more advanced countries); thus, the presence of sizable inequalities will force significant dissaving among the low income groups. (This is another case in which comparison with developed countries is misleading.) Oshima reviewed income and expenditure data for various Far Eastern countries during the last three decades and concluded that, at least in Japan and Taiwan:

> Probably the more equal distribution of family incomes in postwar Japan compared with prewar decades contributed to the increase in personal savings by eliminating dissavings in the lower-income groups in a distribution of family incomes which was probably highly unequal in prewar Japan (with tenants comprising 40 percent of the farm families compared with the postwar period.[30]

A report on Colombia by the International Labour Office seems to support Oshima's conclusions. Although an extreme degree of economic inequality prevailed in Colombia, total personal savings appear to be quite low—averaging about 2 percent in the period 1961–1967—and a large part of it flows abroad or is not used in the most productive way when it remains in Colombia.

> On balance, then, it does not seem that the consideration of the hypothetically favourable effect on savings of greater economic inequality changes our earlier conclusions (i.e., does not carry a great deal of weight in Colombia) . . . the best way to raise the level of investment . . . is through taxation . . . on the upper rather than the lower income groups.[31]

What are being examined, however, are the interrelationships among population growth, equality, and aggregate savings. It has been argued that both differential rates of population growth (within a country) and a rapid total rate of population growth could reduce aggregate savings as well as increase income inequality. This argument leads to the conclusion that policies directed toward reducing inequality must consider the rate of population growth (total and within sectors and social classes) as an important policy parameter. The final outcome of such policies on distribution and growth, however, will depend not only on changes in the economic structure, but also on the aggregate of individual behavior and motivations—the efficiency and productivity of thousands of small units and the net effect of a redistributional policy on total output through its *net* effects on work incentives. This is an area, however, neglected in both theory and research.

SUMMARY AND CONCLUSIONS

Economic inequality in developing countries is sizable by any measure and is not narrowing. The factors related to inequality are large in number and varied and accordingly the discussion has been both empirical and institutional, that is, country- or region-specific, with awareness of the limitations of broad generalizations.

Two effects of population growth on economic inequality could be labeled the *pure demographic effects*. These can be traced primarily through the effect of the age distribution of the population on (a) the age-earning profile and, given that profile, on the personal income distribution, and (b) the dependency ratio and, given family structure, on the definition of the earning-expenditure units.

The important effects of population growth on economic and social inequality cannot be identified easily. They work their way through the socio-economic and legal structure of the society. An important example is the impact of differential circumstances and rates of reproduction among socioregional and economic groups, which affects income mobility and raises ethical questions about equity and efficiency. It is evident, however, that these differential rates and circumstances tend to increase social inequality over time and make it persistent across generations.[32]

The demographic problems of the poor are not solely the number of children they have but also the circumstances under which they have them. There is strong evidence of an unequal distribution of effective knowledge about ways and means to control fertility; thus, the effective demand for contraception is unequally distributed. This apparent inequality is reflected in realized family size, which is negatively related to level of income (that is, the poor not only have more children but also have fewer means to control their fertility). This pattern of fertility inequality affects the distribution of individual abilities and opportunities and their transmission from parents to children through unequal health and education. It is evident that such differentials in fertility behavior exert a negative pressure on society's efforts to reduce inequality among its population groups and across generations.

Added to the effects of differential fertility and mortality among population groups on the shape of the size distribution of income is the total rate of population growth, which acts as a basic constraint on a society's ability to remedy the increasing demand for existing education and health services without reducing quality or uniformity. Such pressure could increase total inequality since the upper income groups not only have fewer children (having better access to fertility control) but can afford private health and education facilities for themselves and their offspring.

The effect of the apparent negative relationship between fertility and income is also related to property income through inheritance, which could be an important part of total social and economic inequality.

It is evident that policies that may succeed in reducing the rate of population growth (total and differential) are neither a sufficient nor a necessary condition for reducing size income inequality since change in the latter is also a function of society's social and institutional setting, including its value system. Also, the possibility of changing income inequality is limited by the extent of social inequalities and their direction of change.

Population growth alone does not seem to improve the economic structure by increasing the share of the industrial sector; rather, it seems to worsen the relative position of the agricultural sector without reducing its share. This could be a result of a faster rate of rural population growth and a relatively low industrial labor absorptive capacity. Accordingly, total personal income inequality may tend to increase.

There is a strong argument for a positive effect of greater equality on saving in low income countries with an initial high degree of inequality. Rapid population growth, however, may reduce potential savings even further. Such conclusions, although plausible, will depend on other factors, however, and can only be verified by empirical testing.

The demographic aspects of income distribution are both varied and complex. Given the limitations of both knowledge and space, the discussion has been selective and has not included, for example, redistribution policies, the introduction of new technologies, or the important but controversial subject of the ethical meaning of equity and its relation to justice.

APPENDIX: On the Measurement of Income Inequality

The discussion in the previous sections indicates that, aside from being handicapped by the lack of an adequate workable theory of income distribution, there are serious measurement and methodological problems related to the adequacy and interpretation of income distribution data. This is attested to by Turnham, who observes that, "with some small degree of exaggeration, most writings on income distribution in less developed countries which deal in numbers, are nine-tenths description of statistical estimations, pitfalls and approximations, and one-tenth analysis of the end product."[33] Indeed, the validity of any analysis of the various dimensions of income distribution (for example, adequacy, equity, and efficiency) and its policy implications will depend on at least four factors: (1) the measure of income inequality employed; (2) the definition of income-receiving and income-expenditure units used; (3) the concept of family income adopted, including the length of time over which the flow of income is measured; and (4) statistical errors resulting mainly from sampling variability, nonreporting, errors of response, and lack of uniformity. We shall discuss these factors briefly in this section since they influence the conclusions derived from an analysis and since some of these factors are related to, and could be influenced by, the demographic characteristics of the population studied.

THE MEASURE OF INEQUALITY [16]

The distribution of income among a number of income recipients, whether individual wages or total family income, can be described in tabular form. A familiar basis for statistical presentation that highlights degrees of inequality is provided by comparisons between the percentage shares of income received by income units classified by level of income. But for comparing two distributions, one needs a summary measure. Such a measure should be independent of the variate scale, that is, the units for which income is measured; it should be a pure number in order to compare different countries, different regions within the same country, or different time periods. There is no perfect measure of inequality, however. And, since the choice of a particular measure is always to some degree arbitrary, the presentation of the percentage shares distribution seems essential.

Inequality could be viewed as a measure of the distance between perfect inequality and perfect equality. With perfect equality, everyone has the same income and there is zero variance. With perfect inequality, one unit has all the income, but the variance depends on how much that income is, which means that there is a difference between variance and inequality. One can hold inequality constant and vary the variance, at least for some distributions. To be sure, if there is a wide variance of incomes, then some inequality is likely, but the degree of inequality will depend on other characteristics of the distribution, including its mean. Furthermore, although extreme skewedness means some inequality, it is possible to have a symmetrical distribution that has greater inequality than a skewed one that happened, for example, to have more kurtosis and/or smaller variance. A measure of inequality should, then, depend on both the variability of incomes and their mean and should have a lower and upper limit that reflect both perfect equality and perfect inequality. Perhaps the most frequently applied of such measures has been the Lorenz measure or its close relative, the Gini Ratio of Concentration.

The Lorenz curve shows the cumulated fraction of aggregate income plotted against the cumulated proportions of income recipients, when units are arranged in ascending order by income.[34] If all incomes are equal, it is a straight line bisecting a square area. In practice, it is a sagging curve; the more inequality exists, the more it sags (see Figure 8.2). The Gini index can be interpreted as a measure of the divergence of the Lorenz curve from complete equality expressed as a ratio to complete inequality. The Gini Ratio of Concentration, G, may be written as:[17]

$$G = \frac{1}{2} \sum_{j=1}^{n} \sum_{i=1}^{n} \left| w_i y - x_j y_i \right|$$

[16] Discussion with John Bongaarts helped clarify various points in this section.

[17] The Lorenz measure, L, is simply one-half of the Gini Ratio; the latter could also be defined as the coefficient of mean differences divided by twice the arithmetic mean.[35]

Figure 8.2 Lorenz Curve and Coefficient of Inequality

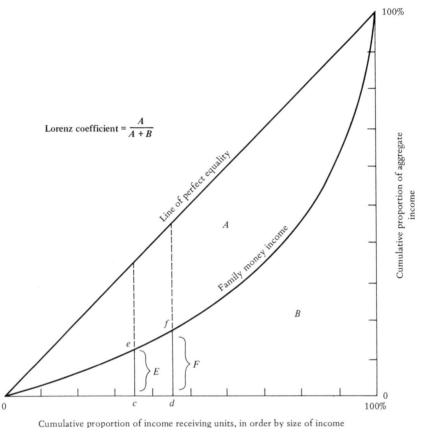

Cumulative proportion of income receiving units, in order by size of income

That is, the Gini Coefficient is one-half the sum of the absolute differences or divergences between all possible pairs of products consisting of population shares and income shares. Equal distribution of incomes is represented by $G = 0$, which occurs when $x_i = y_i$ for all i.[18] A simple method of calculating the coefficient is done by approximating the Lorenz curve by straight lines between plotted points, which gives the following results (with reference to Figure 8.2):

$$G = \frac{\text{area between curve and diagonal}}{\text{area under diagonal}} = A \frac{A}{A + B} = \frac{0.5 - B}{A + B} = 1 - 2B$$

---

[18] One criticism of the Gini Coefficient is that it is expressed in terms of absolute value, thus making it deficient when used to express temporal changes in income distribution. However, the straightforward mathematical properties of the Gini Coefficient and its simple geometric interpretation, combined with the intuitive meaningfulness of the definition even for extreme cases, assures the measure's acceptance.[36]

$G \doteq 1 - \Sigma\, [(D - C)\, (E + F)]$, which could easily be calculated from income group data, and for eight or more groups this approximation should be quite close.[37][19] Also, as a graphical check, the slope of the Lorenz curve is $+1$ at the mean income.

It must be mentioned, however, that the Gini coefficients are very sensitive to a few extreme cases. It is advisable to truncate any cases more than five standard deviations from the mean in order to have substantive comparisons of different income distributions. Also, changes in the definition of income or of the income units make substantial differences in the Gini coefficients.

THE INCOME EXPENDITURE UNIT

The proper unit of analysis depends upon the purpose for which an inequality measure is desired. If the purpose of inequality measures is to assess the justice of the egalitarian ethic with which society's output is distributed, then the basic analysis unit must include members who share decisions concerning search for employment, search for other sources of income, living arrangements, and means of support. Family units are the conventional base for many income statistics and thus are widely used as the basic units in the analysis of the size distribution of income. But this means that differences and changes in the structure of family units will have direct implications for the shape of income distribution. First, the sharing of decisions concerning living arrangements and means of support will usually vary from one society to another, as well as over time for the same society. The extent of extended family units is usually greater in rural than in urban areas and in less developed, traditional than in industrialized regions within or between countries. Second, there could be not only intra- but also inter-family decision sharing, which makes the family boundary obscure and insufficient to understand the micro allocation decisions. Third, size distribution of income becomes more meaningful when related to differences in individual units' needs and not merely to individuals' intrinsic productive properties. Family or household units vary in size and composition and accordingly in their basic needs. These differences could be a result of one or more of the following factors: differences in the phase of the life cycle, living arrangement (for example, doubling up or extended family), and differential fertility and mortality, which is reflected in the size of the family and its dependency ratio.

---

[19] There is an approximate estimate for the sampling error of the Gini Coefficient. Assuming simple random sampling and a lognormal mode, the sampling error of G would be about half the standard deviation of the logarithm of income.[38] In general, the Gini Coefficient of Concentration, G, is equal to the Gini Coefficient of mean difference divided by twice the arithmetic mean, μ_1, i.e., $G = \dfrac{\Delta 1}{2\mu_1}$. Kendall and Stuart derived an estimate for the variance of the sample value of Gini's mean difference for a normal population, $\doteq \sigma^2\, (0.8086)^{2/n}$; for an exponential population, $\doteq 4\sigma^2/(3n)$; and for a rectangular population, $\doteq K^2/(45n)$.[39]

How much difference does it make in the index of inequality and its very meaning whether one uses different units of analysis and whether the structure of units changes spatially or temporally? In general, and for obvious reasons, income distribution among individual income recipients shows wider inequality than the corresponding distribution among family units, because family units may include extra adults with very low incomes. Hence, if income is tabulated separately for each adult couple or unmarried individual, the coefficient of inequality will tend to increase. One way to isolate differences in living arrangements from differences in income shares is to examine separately, over time, the income distributions for various types of families, for example, the young, the retired, those widowed or divorced, and the rest. This will enable examining the relative increase in the number of units of these groups as well as their total share and its distribution. Another possibility, although current data are scarce, is to examine the distribution of income among clusters of families or households who share in making community decisions.

In dealing with differential needs among families, it is possible to examine the distribution of income per equivalent adult, where equivalence is determined by assigning weights to family members according to their relative basic needs. These weights are usually based on the age, working status, and sex of the various family members.[40] The problem of differences in the phase of the life cycle is best handled in the context of a proper definition of the concept of income, which is discussed in the following section.

THE CONCEPT OF INCOME AND ITS PERIOD OF CUMULATION

One obvious question in interpreting measures of income inequality is whether they are not exaggerated since most income data come from cross-sectional surveys of one year's duration and the income of some people could be temporarily high or low for that year. These short-term effects could result from three groups of factors: (1) events that are largely random in their origin and incidence, such as crop failure, sickness, or personal misfortune (not all these events, however, are necessarily unrelated to income levels[20]); (2) systematic "macro" factors that are not a direct outcome of individual decisions, as during business cycles when different income shares may be affected differently (for example, entrepreneurial incomes and profit compared to retired fixed incomes or salaries of government employees or the incidence of unemployment); (3) life cycle events

---

[20] There is some evidence that the incidence of sickness and disability could be selective (i.e., not completely due to chance) for some socioeconomic classes. For example, some occupations, like mining, involve greater hazards and greater likelihood of workers developing special types of illness than other occupations, and the extent of sickness may be related to level of nutrition, living arrangements, and income level. In general, the "chance" factor is essentially a substitute for a large number of obscure reasons that cannot be treated explicitly or systematically.

that account for observed differences in family incomes even after allowing for the first two types of factors. For example, the reported low income of the young (especially students) or the old and retired may not imply the apparent relative impoverishment, but could merely be an outcome of genuine planning to allocate individual resources over the "family" life cycle to produce a desired stream of income given the market structure for human investment.[41]

Inequality should be assessed free from both short-run changes and life cycle differences in income in order to understand more fully how inequalities in family income are related to equity and efficiency considerations or to opportunities and abilities. One way to assess inequality free from short-run changes in income is by averaging income over two or three years for the same unit. Such data are not easy to collect, however. The collection of reliable two- to three-year income data requires either an accurate memory or reinterviews, in which maintaining an acceptable level of accuracy could be costly in many field situations.[42] In dealing with the inequality of lifetime or "long-run" incomes, one needs to do more than examine inequality within age groups since this will not control for the level of education, sex, or patterns of marriage, and since what is included (or excluded) as income is equally important. However, simply controlling for age could reveal how much of the overall inequality in cross-sectional data is due to differences in the incomes of different age groups and how much is due to inequality within age groups. For example, a US study indicates that inequality is lowest in the 25–34 age group but increases subsequently with age and is highest for the 65 and over age group.[43] Differences between age groups in income inequality may be due to various factors, for example, differential rates of advancement in salaries (due to differentials in education or training); accumulation of wealth, which provides income for some; changes in the number of workers in the family unit; differential impact of sickness or unemployment of potential family earners; or differential impact of other short-run fluctuations in income.

These latter points indicate the importance of the coverage and components of the concept of income when assessing the inequality of its distribution. The relevant definition of income, and accordingly the interpretation of its inequality, will depend on the objectives of the analysis, for example, families' economic welfare, families' contribution to the economy's productive capacity, or the impact of families' behavior on the level of economic activity.[44] The study of any objective may involve a balance sheet and an income statement. Without further details, the following observations are made:

1. To the extent there is unequal distribution of nonmarket production, and to the extent that the level and shape of nonmarket production change over time, its exclusion from income measure will probably distort income measure and its distribution as a measure of real welfare. These nonmarket activities include the value of the output of unpaid family and nonfamily workers, imputed returns to households' real assets (for example, houses and other durables), the value of

all transfers (cash and in kind) received by the family, and the value of time spent on education and training.[45]

2. There is a need to examine, separately, the distribution of family units' factor incomes, personal incomes, and disposable incomes in order to assess the extent of private and public transfer payments.

3. There is a need to examine the value of factor incomes for adults and children within the family units in order to understand the differential impact of the dependency burden between families and over time.

4. There is a need to estimate the extent of net saving (including dissaving) for the family unit.

This type of data is usually obtained through special family income-expenditure surveys, which could be repeated every two or three years.

STATISTICAL ERRORS AND INCOME INEQUALITY

An adequate discussion of statistical errors is beyond the scope of this book. But because some kinds of errors could have a striking effect on income distributions, a few words of caution are in order. Errors in income statistics and especially in comparing two distributions could be the result of some or all of the following: (a) the dissimilarity of the populations covered; (b) the extent to which a probability sampling scheme is adhered to; (c) the extent of nonresponse; (d) whether there are adjustments for nonresponse bias; and (e) the questionnaire design, the extent of details about income of all persons and sources, and the care taken in eliciting responses. In general, it appears to be the extremes of the income distribution that suffer the most whenever sampling and interviewing techniques are inadequate, and it is precisely these two extremes that have the most important policy implications.

To summarize, the discussion in this appendix has attempted to caution the reader about interpreting data on income distributions for different regions, population groups, or time periods without giving adequate care to the criteria employed, the limitations of the index of inequality and its interpretation, the definition of income units, the concept of income and its components, and statistical errors.

REFERENCES

1. See, for example, Gustav F. Papanek, *Pakistan's Development: Social Goals and Private Incentives* (Karachi: Oxford University Press, 1968), especially chaps. 7 and 8, pp. 184–225.
2. For a recent illustration, see John H. Adler, "Development and income distribution" and V. C. Nwaneri, "Income distribution and project selection," *Finance and Development* 10, no. 3 (September 1973).
3. See ref. 2, Adler.
4. Jan Pen, *Income Distribution* (New York: Praeger, 1971).
5. For a full discussion of the costs and benefits of children and an extensive review of the literature, see Warren Robinson and David Horlacher, "Population growth and economic welfare," *Reports on Population/Family Planning*, no. 6 (February 1971); and, more recently, Theodore W. Schultz, "New economic approach to fertility," *Journal of Political Economy* 81 (March/April 1973).
6. D. J. Turnham, "Income distribution: Measurement and problems" (Paper presented to the Society for International Development, 12th World Conference, Ottawa, 16–19 May 1971, Document no. 1, Plenary Session).
7. For more details and applications to the US case, see David H. Greenberg, *Population Growth and Poverty,* prepared for the Commission on Population Growth and the American Future, R-1034-CPG (Santa Monica: Rand Corporation, 1972).
8. Simon Kuznets, "Demographic aspects of the distribution of income among families: Recent trends in the United States," Center Discussion Paper no. 165 (New Haven: Economic Growth Center, Yale University, 1972), pp. 35–36.
9. J. N. Morgan and I. Sirageldin, "A note on the quality dimension of education," *Journal of Political Economy* 76 (September 1968).
10. Jeremiah M. Sullivan, "The influence of demographic and socioeconomic factors on infant mortality in Taiwan, 1966–68," *Taiwan Population Studies*, Working Paper no. 18 (Ann Arbor: Population Studies Center, University of Michigan, 1972), tables 9 and 10. S. L. N. Rao, "Socio-economic and public health factors affecting mortality by age in Latin America" (Paper presented at the International Population Meeting, Mexico City, August 1970). John Cassel, "Health consequences of population density and crowding," in *Rapid Population Growth: Consequences and Policy Implications*, Prepared by a Study Committee of the Office of the Foreign Secretary, National Academy of Sciences (Baltimore: Johns Hopkins University Press, 1971), pp. 462–478. See also Leslie Corsa, Jr. and Deborah Oakley, "Consequences of population growth for health services in less developed countries—An initial appraisal," in *Rapid Population Growth*, pp. 368–402; and Pravin Visaria, "Urbanization, migration, and fertility in India," in *The Family in Transition*, A Round Table Conference, Fogerty International Center Proceeding no. 3 (Bethesda, Md.: National Institutes of Health, 1968), pp. 267–271.
11. Finis Welch, "Education in production," *Journal of Political Economy* 78 (January/February 1970): 35–59. Theodore W. Schultz, "Optimal investment in college instruction: Equity and efficiency," *Journal of Political Economy* 80, supplement (May/June 1972): 2–33.

12. P. D. Chaudhri, "Farmers education and productivity: Some empirical results from Indian agriculture," Investment in Human Capital, Paper no. 69:4, mimeographed (Chicago: University of Chicago, 1969). Fawzi M. Al-Haj and Salah M. Yacoub report similar findings for Lebanese farmers. "Factors affecting adoption of new agricultural techniques in Lebanese agriculture," in Charles A. Cooper and Sidney S. Alexander, eds., *Economic Development and Population Growth in the Middle East* (New York: American Elsevier, 1972), pp. 548–549.

13. Pedro Belli, "The economic implications of malnutrition: The dismal science revisited," *Economic Development and Cultural Change* 20, no. 1 (October): 1–23.

14. Herman E. Daly, "The population question in Northern Brazil: Its economic and ideological dimensions," *Economic Development and Cultural Change* 18, no. 4, pt. 1 (July 1970): 545.

15. Kingsley Davis, "Some demographic aspects of poverty in the United States," in Margaret S. Gordon, ed., *Poverty in America* (San Francisco: Chandler, 1965), p. 300.

16. For a discussion of the demographic aspects of saving, see Paul Demeny, "Demographic aspects of saving, investment, employment and productivity" (Background Paper submitted to the United Nations World Population Conference, Belgrade, Yugoslavia, 30 August–10 September 1965), pp. 13–14.

17. George Stigler, *The Theory of Price*, 3rd ed. (London: The Macmillan Company, 1966), p. 289.

18. R. D. Choksey, *Economic Life in the Bombay Decan* (Bombay: Asia Publishing House, 1955), p. 196.

19. See, for example, V. M. Dandekar and G. J. Khudanpur, *Working of Bombay Tenancy Act, 1948, Report of Investigation* (Poona: Gokhale Institute of Politics and Economics, 1957).

20. C. K. Meek, *Land, Law and Customs in the Colonies* (London: Oxford University Press, 1949).

21. For illustrations from Southeast Asia and additional references, see Gunnar Myrdal, *Asian Drama* (Clinton, Mass.: Pelican Books, 1968), pp. 569–572.

22. Hollis Chenery, "Patterns of industrial growth," *American Economic Review* (September 1960).

23. Theodore K. Ruprecht and Carl Wahren, *Population Programmes and Economic and Social Development* (Paris: Development Center of the Organization for Economic Cooperation and Development, 1970), pp. 28–34.

24. Simon Kuznets, *The Economic Growth of Nations* (Cambridge, Mass.: Belknap Press of Harvard University Press, 1971), p. 306.

25. See ref. 24, p. 201.

26. See also Peter Newman, " 'Population pressure' and economic growth: An operational treatment," *Journal of Development Planning*, no. 2 (1970): 31–57.

27. See ref. 24, pp. 174–198.

28. See ref. 24, pp. 303–314.

29. Ghazi M. Farooq, "Economic growth and change in the industrial structure of income and labor force in Pakistan," *Economic Development and Cultural Change* 21, no. 2 (January 1973): 293–308.

30. Harry T. Oshima, "Labor-force 'explosion' and the labor-intensive sector in

Asian growth," *Economic Development and Cultural Change* 19 (January 1971): 173–174.

31. International Labour Office, *Towards Full Employment, A Programme for Colombia* (Geneva: International Labour Office, 1970), pp. 148–150.

32. James E. Kocher, *Rural Development, Income Distribution, and Fertility Decline* (New York: The Population Council, 1973); William Rich, *Smaller Families Through Social and Economic Progress* (Washington, D.C.: Overseas Development Council, 1973).

33. See ref. 6, p. 2.

34. The Lorenz coefficient of inequality has come to be generally accepted as one of the best measures of inequality. See, for example, J. Aitchison and J. A. C. Brown, "On the criteria for description of income distribution," *Metroeconomica* 6 (December 1954): 88–107; Mary Jean Bowman, "A graphical analysis of personal income distribution in the United States," *American Economic Review* 35 (September 1945): 608–628; Maurice E. G. Kendall, *The Advanced Theory of Statistics*, vol. 1 (London: Charles Griffin, 1945), pp. 145–155; I. B. Kravis, *The Structure of Income* (Philadelphia: University of Pennsylvania Press, 1962), pp. 178–191; J. N. Morgan et al., *Income and Welfare in the United States* (New York: McGraw-Hill, 1962), pp. 16–18 and chap. 20; M. O. Lorenz, "Methods for measuring concentration of wealth," *Publication of the American Statistical Association* 9 (1905): 209–219; Dwight B. Yntema, "Measures of inequality in the personal distribution of wealth and income," *Journal of the American Statistical Association* 28 (December 1933): 348–361.

35. Maurice E. Kendall and S. Stuart, *The Advanced Theory of Statistics*, vol. 1 (London: Charles Griffin, 1958), pp. 46–48.

36. See ref. 34, J. N. Morgan et al., p. 311. For a discussion and a proposal of another measure, see J. W. Hooper and H. Theil, "The information approach to the measurement of income inequality," Report no. 6501, Econometric Institute, Netherlands School of Economics, February 1965.

37. James N. Morgan, "The anatomy of income distribution," *The Review of Income and Wealth* 44, no. 3 (August 1962): 276–281.

38. Peter Vandome, "Aspects of dynamics of consumer behavior," *Bulletin of the Oxford University Institute of Statistics* 20 (February 1958): 65–106.

39. See ref. 35, pp. 241–242.

40. See, for example, M. Friedman, "A method of comparing incomes of families differing in composition," in *Studies in Income and Wealth*, vol. 15, Conference on Research in Income and Wealth (New York: National Bureau of Economic Research, 1952), pp. 9–24.

41. For a lucid exposition of a difficult subject that also clarifies some of the normative issues that arise in the context of income distribution, see Jacob Mincer, "The distribution of labor income: A survey with a special reference to the human capital approach," *Journal of Economic Literature* 8, no. 1 (March 1970): 18–20.

42. See ref. 38 and Richard F. Kosobud and J. B. Lansing, "Two year saving relationships," in R. F. Kosobud and J. N. Morgan, eds., *Consumer Behavior of Individual Families Over Two and Three Years* (Ann Arbor: University of Michigan Press, 1964), pp. 71–101.

43. See ref. 37 and Lee Soltow, "The distribution of income related to changes in the distribution of education, age, and occupation," *The Review of Economics and Statistics* 42 (November 1960): 450.
44. John B. Lansing, "Concepts used in surveys," in Lawrence R. Klein, ed., *Contributions of Survey Methods to Economics* (New York: Columbia University Press, 1954), pp. 20–37.
45. For a discussion and empirical estimate, see Ismail Sirageldin, *Non-Market Components of National Income* (Ann Arbor: University of Michigan Press, 1969). For an empirical study of time use and its relation to economic behavior, see James N. Morgan, Ismail Sirageldin, and Nancy Baerwaldt, *Productive Americans: A Study of How Individuals Contribute to Economic Progress* (Ann Arbor: University of Michigan Press, 1966).

NINE

Population and External Economic Balance

Edward K. Hawkins and Roberto Cuca

External economic relationships and their major magnitudes—imports, exports, capital movements—play a crucial role in the economic fortunes of nearly all developing nations. The earlier chapters in this book have argued that population, viewed from several different perspectives, is also a critically important factor for developing states. The present chapter addresses itself to an obviously important yet largely unexplored area: the relationship between a nation's external economic balance and its population size, growth, distribution, and composition. Our effort is tentative and exploratory, but perhaps we can at least identify some of the right questions about this relationship, even if we cannot yet supply definitive answers.

RELATIVE FACTOR ENDOWMENT

The classical theory of international trade holds that trade among nations springs up more or less naturally because of different relative factor endowments. Some countries have an abundant supply of particular raw materials or skill relative to other countries. Given the different factor combinations required to produce different final products, these various factor endowments also imply different specializations in production among nations. Every nation has a comparative advantage in producing some product, and the welfare aspects of classical trade theory attempt to show that international specialization is a good thing since trade increases total output, thus benefiting all concerned.

Although the writers are staff members of the World Bank, the views expressed here do not necessarily represent the opinions of the Bank.

Population and labor force are certainly a factor of production in the most basic sense. Thus, trade theory could be said to argue that, the relative factor endowments being what they are, most developing nations should concentrate on labor-intensive products and techniques in choosing their international specialization. However, as is well known, there are very few international trade products in the modern world that can be produced in a labor-intensive way—certainly not most manufactures (even textiles of any quality) and not the extractive industries, either. Agriculture is about the only remaining sector from which products can be produced labor-intensively so as to compete in world markets.

Thus, classical trade theory explains why most developing nations continue to rely upon agriculture as their chief export source of foreign exchange. Population growth, however, also competes with exports since more people require more domestic foodstuffs. We will consider this aspect shortly when we turn to a more systematic review of the balance of payments, item by item.

TERMS OF TRADE ARGUMENT

It has been widely argued that there exists a secular tendency for the terms of trade of the primary-producing developing countries to decline. The thesis is controversial, to say the least, but in its most simplified form it states that the demand for the output of the primary producers has stagnated or declined through time, while the requirements of these nations for manufactures have risen. The result is alleged to be adverse shifts in the terms of trade.

Without accepting this entire argument or its policy implications, one thing does seem clear. Population growth alone could almost explain such changes in relative demand. One hundred years ago the populations of the developed nations were growing more rapidly than were those of the developing countries. This meant an ever-growing market for primary products and presumably favorable export situations. Beginning some 30 years ago, the relative population growth rates reversed themselves: the developing countries now are growing demographically at unprecedented rates, while the developed countries are leveling off. Thus, the developing countries' need for imports has increased because of growing numbers, while the demand for their exports has suffered from the slower growth of markets in the developed nations. Population almost certainly has been a factor, although not the only factor, in shaping the terms of trade between primary producers and the developed nations. This situation continues today.

BALANCE OF PAYMENTS ASPECTS

Year-to-year external economic relationships are expressed through the balance of payments, and it is through the various items that make up the balance of payments that we would expect the size, rate of growth, and composition of the population to affect such relationships in the short run. These effects do not occur in isolation; the specific consequences of population for foreign economic relationships work through the macroeconomic structure of the economy. The general propositions relating to population and economic development apply *a fortiori*. The additional dimension introduced relates to the possibility that population characteristics will or will not improve or worsen the foreign aspects of development.

The balance of payments summarizes the foreign economic relationships of a country, recording the flow of goods and services received from abroad and those supplied to other countries. In principle, the presentation is always in two parts. The first details the flow of goods, services, and transfers (which are unilateral transactions) in a current account; the second part, or capital account, covers the financing of the transactions in the current account. Table 9.1 shows a sample balance of payments for a developing country for two recent years. In this case, the country had a deficit on current account in the first year that was more than covered by net inflows on capital account, so that the country added to its foreign exchange reserves in that year. In the following year the same thing occurred, but this time there was a surplus on current account, due to a short-term improvement in current receipts.

Year-to-year changes in the balance of payments will be heavily influenced by short-term factors. Nevertheless, it is only through the items in the balance of payments that population factors will impinge upon foreign economic relationships. We should expect, however, that such influences will become apparent only in the longer run (although there may be short-run population effects arising from drought, famine, or other disasters).

One further point of principle is important, however, and this concerns the financing of long-term economic development. Developing countries draw upon resources from abroad for this purpose, and these can be either private capital or official capital in the form of concessionary aid. In both cases these flows will be recorded in the balance of payments. The net support or transfer from abroad will be equal to the difference between imports of goods and services and exports of goods and services. This difference represents the extent to which the total demand for resources exceeds domestic availability. (In the reverse case, there may well be an outflow of resources to the outside world.) This gap between resources and needs is a central feature of the development process. It is particularly important in planning to clarify the manner in which population impinges upon the needs of development and the requirements for resources from abroad.

The key population variables to be considered are population size, rate of growth, geographical location, distribution by age and sex, and the industrial structure of the labor force. The extent to which the various components of the population participate in economic activity as producers is the main element to take into account. It can be assumed that all are consumers, but the extent to which people contribute to production depends on age, sex, and the socioeconomic

Table 9.1 Example of a Balance of Payments for a Developing Country (in US $ millions)

Item			1970	1971
Current Account				
Receipts from:	1.	Exports of goods and services	1,083	1,144
	2.	Freight and insurance, travel and transport services	132	110
	3.	Income from investments	10	15
	4.	Private transfers	95	107
	5.	Public transfers	97	120
	6.	Other services	48	56
		Total Receipts	1,465	1,552
Payments for:	1.	Imports of goods and services	1,090	1,186
	2.	Freight, insurance, travel and transport services	155	149
	3.	Interest and dividends on investments and past debt	140	112
	4.	Private services	88	38
	5.	Public services	16	24
	6.	Transfer payments	5	10
		Total Payments	1,494	1,519
Balance on Current Account			−29	+33
Capital Account (Net)				
Direct investment			− 29	− 6
Private long-term capital			175	−31
Private short-term capital			−147	−76
Official long-term capital			35	70
Allocation of special deposit receipts			18	17
Balance on Capital Account			+ 52	−26
Net change in monetary reserves			+ 23	+ 7

NOTE: This is an actual example for a developing country, which is not identified so as to avoid the need for special explanations of particular items. It should be noted, however, that the item for special deposit receipts occurred only in the years shown.

conditions that govern participation rates. (Since in many cases labor is very abundant, "participation" may also depend upon job opportunities.)

When the modern sector of the economy is relatively small and the traditional sector is still dominant, self-employment will be significant. What is important is the net effect of each member of the population on the demand for and supply of goods and services and the net effect on the foreign earnings of the country. These effects have to be viewed in the broadest perspective so as to include the impact on the capital account of the balance of payments as well. In this connection, a highly important but frequently overlooked demographic phenomenon is international migration, which has a direct effect on the balance of payments through transfers and, perhaps, short-term capital movements.

Let us attempt to consider systematically the impact of population on a series of key macroeconomic variables.

CONSUMPTION AND IMPORTS

Since all members of the population are consumers, the clearest impact on the foreign sector comes via consumption effects. For planning purposes, therefore, one comes back to the familiar determinants of consumption, namely real incomes, with a lower level to consumption related to minimum nutritional standards. This level is not, unfortunately, given by the level of physical requirements for health and survival. The ability to sustain minimally adequate levels of food and shelter depends on real incomes. If they are inadequate, it will ultimately be reflected in the morbidity and mortality of the population, so that the size, rate of growth, and age structure are not independent of the level of real incomes. The effect is most likely to operate demographically through the rate of infant mortality, although the average length of life of adults who survive through childhood is another variable that will reflect this factor.

There are also effects exercised by the age distribution of the population on both the level and the composition of aggregate consumption. There is a relationship between age, body weight, and the intensity of physical exertion and caloric and other nutritional intake. Other things being equal, children eat less than adults, and this is recognized and corrected for in most macro models through the use of "equivalent adult consumer" units, thus correcting for possible extremes in the age distribution.

The composition of aggregate consumption will also depend partly upon the age distribution of the population. Young adults in the early stages of marriage, who are rearing children and equipping a household, are likely to have somewhat different expenditure priorities than old couples approaching retirement. This consumer "life cycle" is the medium through which the sex and age distribution affect the patterns of consumer demand.

From the point of view of the balance of payments, it is the import content (both direct and indirect) of consumption that is relevant. Since this is not given, but can be influenced by economic and other forces, it becomes a planning variable. A full analysis, therefore, requires a breakdown of personal consumption into its component parts and an examination of the various income and price elasticities of demand through which tastes will be reflected. Significant shifts in tastes and preferences may have relatively large impacts upon the demand for imports. In developing countries, these changes in taste may be triggered by goods, services, and information from other countries. In those cases where import substitution is possible, ultimately there may be local production of the desired goods. In some cases, however, this may not be possible.

One example of the latter situation is the growth of the demand for bread made from imported wheat flour in West Africa, where it cannot be produced. The taste for wheat bread displaced that for locally produced cereals, with a permanent effect upon the import bill.

Even when import substitution is possible and takes place, there may still be an import content in the total product in the form of intermediate goods and raw materials. In all these interrelationships, however, actual population numbers are less significant than per capita incomes. Changes in population (and consequently in labor force) do lead to changes in total output and income, leaving aside the extreme case of zero or negative marginal productivity. Indeed, in the aggregate, population changes appear to be closely associated with changes in total output. But, other things being equal, one would expect that the propensity to import would be low at very low levels of per capita income; or, to put the matter another way, the income elasticity of demand for imports would be fairly high. Thus, population numbers are not the crucial determinant of import demand.

The great exception to this rule is the country that must import any substantial portion of its basic requirements of food, fibre, or other natural resources. As population grows, so does the demand for these fundamentals, and if incomes do not grow also, then government will almost certainly step into the breach somehow to provide at least minimum requirements. Providing these minimum requirements will mean resorting to some form of imports. In the short run, some form of accommodating finance may be available. But clearly, even in the intermediate-range future, continued increases in population coupled with inadequate domestic agricultural supplies have a direct implication for the balance of payments.

One other demographic factor bearing on demand should be mentioned, and this is the degree of urbanization. Urban people are, on the whole, likely to have a higher propensity to buy relatively sophisticated imported consumer goods than rural people. To some extent this is probably due to the urban dwellers enjoying, on the average, higher levels of education, income, and health. But there are numerous well-documented examples of a clear-cut "demonstration effect" at work too. That is, simply being in cities and being exposed to the advertisements, the shop windows, and the spectacle of the well-living elite leads urban consumers to demand more of these imported goods than they would otherwise.

Thus, the more urbanized a population, the more pressure there is likely to be for imported consumer goods. This has clear implications in terms of a desirable national population policy, insofar as population distribution as well as size and structure should be part of a well-designed policy. Moreover, as numerous studies have shown, urban growth is likely to be closely associated with population increase and inadequate employment and income opportunities in the rural areas, with consequent migration to the cities. The more rapid the population growth in the countryside, the more likely are the large urban centers to grow, leading to a rising demand for imported consumer goods, with very clear adverse implications for the balance of trade.

EXPORTS

It is also possible for the quantity and composition of exports to be affected by the growth of both population and incomes and for the content of consumption to be competitive with exports. While this can apply to all components of consumption (except non-tradables and services), it has been most noticeable in the case of foodstuffs. There are cases, for example, where countries have been exporters of such basic foodstuffs as rice, wheat, tea, and coffee, but whose exports have declined and finally disappeared as a result of population growth, which increased the domestic demand for the products. Again, it should be noted that it is the combination of population growth and income growth that is important. Countries with rising per capita incomes but with little or no population growth have also seen their exports suffer from the growth of domestic consumption.

Yet cases also exist in which, due to continued population growth, the entire structure and direction of agriculture has changed. Farmers are producers but also consumers. Where the factor proportions are favorable, that is, where the labor/land ratio is low, labor productivity is likely to be high; if material incentives are at all strong, a marketable surplus will emerge. If population continues to grow, factor proportions will become less favorable to labor and labor productivity will begin to decline. The marketable surplus may also decline in proportionate terms, if not at first in absolute terms. The next logical stage will be a situation in which virtually the entire potential ouput is given over to subsistence, labor productivity is low (but yield per acre high) and virtually no marketable surplus exists. In short, it can be shown logically that very dense rural populations are probably inconsistent with any marketable or exportable surplus. Such rural economies will be concerned with subsistence and little else.

Nor does this picture change if in the first instance the exports are not foodstuffs. Where land is scarce and the domestic food supply inadequate, pressure will develop to take land from nonfood export-generating use and put it into food production.

To summarize, most developing nations are principally exporters of primary products, and such products are very often either foodstuffs or competitive for resources that can produce food. Rapid population growth inevitably creates pressure within a country to put more and more of its production and resources into simple subsistence agriculture. One can easily see this occurring through market processes in a decentralized economy or through pure exigency and political expediency in a planned economy. In either case, exports may be virtually wiped out and serious balance of payments consequences follow.

A full analysis is required of the relationships between exports, imports, and the pattern of consumption, especially as it varies with incomes over time. It is not possible, a priori, to state exactly how population will be linked to these magnitudes. But it seems clear that links do exist and that population is a very relevant variable, although possibly not always the most direct and important influence upon imports and exports.

EXCHANGE CONTROLS AND POPULATION DISTRIBUTION

Controls and exchange rate policies are almost always employed as tools of some larger economic planning strategy by developing nations. Thus, "import-substitution" means allowing domestic manufacturers' prices to be above those of potential import competition by using controls and tariffs, a modern adaptation of the old "infant industry" approach. Subsidies or taxes on exports are also frequently employed. These policy manipulations all have effects, indirect and direct, on relative prices within the country and through them on population composition and distribution. For, by affecting relative prices, these policies also affect the sectoral terms of trade, particularly rural-agricultural versus urban-industrial. The general impact of most such policies is to depress the price of agricultural products, thus affecting adversely rural income levels, while raising prices of industrial goods, thus increasing employment and incomes in the urban centers. The effect of this on internal migration is clear, since there is an increasing weight of evidence that high urban income levels do attract rural migrants even though their chances of employment are much less than unity. (See Chapter Seven of this volume.)

Thailand provides an interesting case study of such an effect of export policy on internal migration. An export tax on rice has been an important part of Thai economic policy, off and on, for a hundred years. More particularly, in the post-World War II years, the foreign demand for Thai rice has remained uniformly brisk. Thailand has been one of the major rice exporting countries in the world, in spite of a heavy export tax on rice (the "rice premium," as it is called). The effect of the tax, of course, has been to keep the domestic price of rice well below the world market price. During this same time, the urban population has increased sharply, particularly in Bangkok-Thonburi, the major metropolitan area. One can argue that, given the cheap price of rice and other foodstuffs in the cities, there was an increased incentive for persons to give up growing rice and move to Bangkok to work for money and buy their rice.

The example of Thailand could undoubtedly be extended to other countries. Surplus food grain shipments from the United States and other aid-donor countries have likewise benefited primarily the urban sectors, resulting in lower food prices or greater availability at existing prices, thus encouraging migration to these centers. Neither the "rice premiums" in Thailand nor the PL 480 shipments to India were intended to encourage rural-to-urban migration, but they seem to have had this effect.

PUBLIC INVESTMENT AND SERVICES

So far, the discussion of consumption has been limited to the private sector. Public consumption must also be taken into account. Here the relationships between population, public consumption of goods and services, and the foreign sector are more indirect. They are best considered via an analysis of the effect of population size, rate of growth, and structure on the public services. It is generally recognized that total population size and age structure, which together result in a given dependency ratio, are among the main determinants of the volume of public services required or desired. This applies mostly to the supporting services required to provide the increment to the population with education, health, and other social services.

If it is assumed that governments will always be able and willing to provide an agreed level and quality of such services, there will be an induced demand for them that will depend directly upon the rate of growth of population; the higher the rate of growth, the greater the burden upon available public savings if these needs are to be met.

There are also such investments as housing, roads, public utilities, and the necessary levels of defense and law and order. Such public investments can be financed either from local savings or they can be partly covered by a capital inflow from abroad. The dependency burden aspect of public expenditure (both capital and current—the distinction cannot be precise in the public sector) affects both parts of the balance of payments. For planning purposes, therefore, attention should be focused on the content and nature of public consumption and investment—whether domestically supplied or not—as well as on the way in which the expenditures are financed, by local financial resources or inflows from abroad.

We know relatively little about the import content of many industries and activities. Most of the public service industries—education, health, sanitation, and so forth—are relatively labor-intensive. The main direct resource inputs are personnel, and rather more indirectly, construction, which also makes intensive use of local labor. However, it can be shown that in some areas the way in which the production of public services typically has been organized has required substantial amounts of highly specialized imported equipment, a situation with considerable balance of payments implications. Let us examine urban services as a case in point.

As a city grows, the provision of basic services becomes more difficult. Among these are water supply, sewage, traffic and mass transport, and welfare services. The costs of providing needed water and sewage systems for the large and growing urban centers of the developing world can be staggering. Very often, specialized equipment—electrically controlled traffic light systems, sewage treatment machines, filtration plants, vehicles, and so on—are required. The technology is imported from Europe, Japan, or the United States and some of the needed equipment must be also. Persons trained in the use of this equipment must also be obtained and this means importing foreign advisers or training local people. Both solutions have balance of payment implications.

The point here is simple enough. If the population is growing, whatever level of public services per capita is desired will now require additional resources. To the extent that any of these outputs have an import content, there is a negative item for the balance of payments unmatched by any positive ones.

SAVINGS AND INVESTMENT

As noted in earlier chapters, there is evidence suggesting a clear link between the rate of population growth, the level of per capita income, and the savings rate. Other things being equal, a higher population growth rate means a lower savings rate.

The principles involved in linking population to private investment are similar to those discussed in connection with public investment and service expenditures. They will have varying domestic and import contents and different impacts upon the current and capital accounts of the balance of payments. The impact of population variables on this process will be indirect and is unlikely to be paramount compared with other economic variables, except in special cases.

Much depends upon the links between savings, private investment, and population. If, as has been frequently asserted, population growth is negatively related to domestic savings and positively related to investment (and to the import requirements for investment), higher growth rates are likely to intensify dependence on outside sources of finance for any given development plan.

FOREIGN AID

In the strict terminology of the balance of payments, there is no such thing as "foreign aid." Foreign aid is a composite of accommodating capital movements, transfers, and shipments of goods or commodities at special prices or under special arrangements. The thrust of several of the points suggested earlier in this chapter is that rapid population growth and its likely distributional concomitants will increase a country's need for or dependence on such aid. In view of the great importance attached to aid in all discussions of development, it may be well to spell out these suggested relationships more clearly.

Rapid population growth, other things being equal, tends to:

1. Drive the agricultural sector more and more to subsistence use of all its resources, reducing the potential exportable surplus of primary products;

2. Increase the need for imported foodstuffs, especially if urban areas grow rapidly and domestic agriculture is unable to meet their requirements;

3. Increase the domestic demand for imported consumer goods, especially in the cities;

4. Increase the demand for public services and, in consequence, the import requirements for the intermediate goods and skills associated with such services; and

5. Decrease the domestic savings rate, making it harder to successfully finance a desired level of investment from domestic resources.

SOME TECHNOLOGICAL IMPLICATIONS

Investment has been called the "vehicle" of technical change. But, even more fundamentally, technical change itself is the "vehicle" of development. In common with other aspects of the economy, a nation's balance of payments goes through a kind of cycle as the nation develops. The change from being a primary producing debtor country to being an industrial creditor country reflects, in the main, a change in the structure of the economy; in the proportions in which capital, labor, and natural resources are combined; and in the way in which they are combined.

Rapid population growth and movement tend to "use up" much of the investable social surplus that might otherwise be used to transform the economic structure of the nation. By keeping such pressure on the economy, by denying it any pause to redirect itself, these forces also impede any movement to the next stage. Thus, most fundamentally, rapid population growth tends to perpetuate the nation's balance of payments problems as they exist and thus to perpetuate also its debtor status.

TRANSFERS

There is one category of receipts and payments within the balance of payments that may often be directly linked to population and requires special attention. These are transfer payments made up of gifts and remittances sent across national boundaries by individuals. These remittances are related to population movements and migration. They reflect social, ethnic, and political links in economic and monetary movements, and they can become very significant elements in the balance of payments. In several countries, transfers in the form of gifts are a major source of foreign exchange. Such gifts are linked to population only in the sense that large groups living overseas identify with the national population along racial or cultural lines. Kinship links are another powerful source of such foreign exchange flows, arising out of past population movements that have dispersed distinct population groups throughout the world.

For planning purposes, perhaps the most significant form of such foreign exchange flows arises from the migration of workers across national boundaries. Historically, large population movements have taken place with an economic motivation—seeking better opportunities to make a living. These movements often involved major demographic changes in both the recipient countries and the countries of origin. Although the scope for such large-scale movements has disappeared with the settlement of virtually all the better unutilized land in the world, population movements for economic reasons have not ceased. New forms of population movements have resulted in substantial flows of foreign exchange across national boundaries to an extent that is only now being fully appreciated. These flows originate in the remittances of migrant workers who have left relatively less developed countries to seek work opportunities in more developed countries. They differ from earlier population movements because they are, in principle, short-term in nature; it is not usually the intention of the migrant or of the recipient country that there should be a permanent change of residence. This increases the flow of remittances, because the workers' families often remain behind and are supported by the absentee workers, who feel little need to save or invest their earnings in the country in which they are working.

Although the individual worker may regard such periods of work as temporary, as do national governments, there is some tendency for such employment to become a permanent feature. The individuals concerned may change and circulate but the contribution to the labor force in the recipient country and to the foreign exchange earnings of the supplying country tend to become permanent and may grow over time. In this respect, therefore, such transfers are exactly parallel in the balance of payments to the flow of interest and dividends that result from international movements of capital. While the latter have long been recognized as significant items in the balance of payments, however, the potential importance of migrant workers' remittances has only been widely recognized in the last decade.

This point can be illustrated by the cases of Yugoslavia and Turkey, countries from which large numbers of workers have gone to other countries of Western Europe in the last decade. Between 1963 and 1972, the number of Yugoslav migrants to West Germany (the most common destination) rose from 44,000 to 472,000; from Turkey the increase was from 86,000 to 625,000. Remittances by the migrant workers are calculated to have increased over the same period from $13 million to $600 million (for Yugoslavia) and from $9 million to $800 million (for Turkey).[1] These flows have become the major source of foreign exchange earnings for these two countries, a prospect which nobody foresaw in the early 1960s.

There is also an important qualitative aspect to migration. The type of manpower involved can make a considerable difference to an economy. If significant numbers of well-trained and educated people migrate, the effect on the country of origin can be severe. Any receipts from remittances have to be set against the losses that arise from the costs of training.

INVISIBLES AND CAPITAL FLOWS

Two other important invisibles in the balance of payments have already been referred to above—interest and dividends. These flows relate to past capital movements and cannot, therefore, be directly linked to population factors. Insofar as there are links, they are best traced through the possible relationships with the investments concerned, in a suitable macroeconomic framework. From the point of view of the balance of payments itself, such payments can be significant, either as receipts or debits. As receipts, they add to the disposable free foreign exchange, and as payments they reduce the amount of foreign exchange available. The possible interrelationships with population variables cannot be determined on an a priori basis or with reference to the other items of the balance of payments.

Much the same applies when considering the capital items of the balance of payments. These record the short- and long-term capital flows, indicating the manner in which the surplus or deficit on current account is either disposed of or financed. The economic significance of these movements requires that they be broken down in different ways. Of special importance, for example, is the division between private capital movements and "official," or public, capital flows. Both may be related, in principle, to population variables, but there would be little virtue in trying to define such links outside of the basic macroeconomic framework.

SUMMARY AND CONCLUSIONS

We have pointed to the linkages that can exist between population factors—size, rate of growth, age and sex composition, and geographical dispersion—and the various major items and categories of a nation's balance of payments. We feel there can be no question whatever but that such linkages exist. For the most part they work through the macroeconomic framework in the longer run, although some shorter-run (five years or less) effects may be important. Not only is population a factor in determining the overall payments balance, but it structures many of the individual items within the export, import, and capital accounts as well. Accidental (or incidental) effects on internal migration because of effects on relative prices in the rural and urban sectors may also be important. In practice, the likely size and significance of the influence of population on the balance of payments must be estimated through a macroeconomic planning model. These effects will vary so much from country to country that there is little worth in hypothetical calculations; a model suitable to the circumstances of a particular country must be used.

One final word should be said. Very often, in discussing population with practical economic planners, one confronts the argument that, while population undoubtedly "matters" in the long run, it does not affect the balance of payments next year. And this is correct, for very few things markedly affect the balance of payments next year. The examples that spring to mind—a sudden collapse of export prices, a sharp change in international currency values, a newly imposed tariff or quota—are memorable precisely because they are infrequent events. If this were not the case, no consistent balance of payments planning would be possible.

The changes likely to occur in population size, growth rate, structure, or location in any one calendar year are, in fact, not likely to have more than a marginal impact on the balance of payments. Nor are similar changes occurring in foreign demand for exports, in international competition, and so forth. Yet all of these factors will matter within a very few years because their impacts are cumulative. If they are ignored each year because they do not matter that year, then all at once, and not in Keynes' "very long-run" when we are dead, they will matter and we will have lost our option for taking any measures to deal with them. Unrestricted population growth in the primary producing developing countries is almost a guarantee that these countries will remain, in comparative advantage terms, exactly where they are. And this is not where they want to be.

REFERENCES

1. Estimates made by I. M. Hume in an unpublished study. See also I. M. Hume, "Migrant workers in Europe," *Finance and Development* 10, no. 1 (March 1973).

TEN

Resources, Environment, and Population

RONALD G. RIDKER AND PIERRE R. CROSSON

World population growth has now acquired a tremendous momentum, as Chapter Two of this volume demonstrates. It seems almost inevitable (so long as death rates do not rise), that the population of virtually every developing country will more than double in size within the lifetime of the majority of those alive today.

The prospective increase in population should be of major concern to planners for two reasons. First, it will have profound resource, environmental, and economic consequences, consequences that will determine how much or little progress can be made in terms of improving the standard of living. Second, these consequences will in turn affect a number of important demographic variables. More specifically, changes in the socioeconomic, resource, and ecological environments within which an individual finds himself can have a strong influence on the age at which he decides to marry, the number of children he has, his life expectancy, and where he decides to live. For example, attempts to improve environmental sanitation and housing in urban areas may result in even faster rates of rural-to-urban migration. This example is not meant to suggest that such attempts are futile or ill-considered, but rather that the planner who wishes to improve the urban environment must consider more than urban environmental problems; he must also consider the reasons why people move and the possibility that improvements in the rural environment might slow down migration and hence improve the urban environment more than an equivalent investment in urban infrastructure.

But these linkages are poorly understood and can vary greatly from one country or even region of a country to another. So too can problems of resource depletion and pollution. The best that we can do in this short essay is to suggest a perspective that may be helpful in guiding thinking and analysis by those on the scene. Most of our comments will be on issues associated with resource and environmental consequences of the population growth that seems more or less inevitable during the next half century or more. We will begin by discussing some general issues and then illustrate them in two areas of special concern for developing countries—agriculture and urbanization. A third area of special concern to developing countries is the effects on their international trade situation of growing environmental problems elsewhere; these will not be discussed except peripherally since they do not result from domestic population pressures within the developing countries.

SOME GENERAL CONSIDERATIONS

In recent years a number of thoughtful Western writers have voiced concern about the effects of population and economic growth on world-wide resource adequacy and the earth's ecological systems. Are we, as these writers suggest, in danger of overtaxing the earth's carrying capacity? Or are pollution problems mainly a rich country's problems, which the poor should only wish they had? What is the role that population growth plays in causing these problems? These questions form the basis for the general considerations raised in this section.

The "Running Out" Thesis

The concerns that give rise to these questions can be considered a new form of neo-Malthusianism, the thesis of which is that population and economic growth in the world are proceeding at such a pace that minerals, fuels, and the environmental carrying capacity of the earth are being exhausted at rates far in excess of the ability of science and technology to find solutions for these problems. Indeed, one recent book asserts that global catastrophe in the form of dramatically increased death rates is likely within the next 100 years unless both population and material economic growth in the world cease within the next few decades.[1] If this view is correct, it would be irresponsible for policy-makers in both developed and developing countries to continue giving high priority to the goal of improving material living standards and low priority to population control and family planning.

Many doubts can be raised about this prophecy. If raw materials are becoming more scarce, their relative price should be rising; but, on the average, this has not been the case during the last 50 to 100 years, although recent trends will bear watching. Moreover, a recent, item-by-item assessment of the likely availability of worldwide minerals and fuel supplies during the next 50 years raises no serious causes for alarm: some prices will probably rise significantly, but it should be possible to find substitutes in production and consumption, at least within this time-frame, so that material welfare does not suffer, and indeed, may even continue improving for at least some portions of mankind.[2]

Then too, it is sometimes argued that this global "running out" thesis is a generalization of concerns that may be valid in older industrial nations but not in developing countries, where the process of mineral search and exploitation is still in its infancy.

More fundamental is the very definition of "resource." And, upon reflection, it seems clear that no definition is possible that does not assume some technological basis. Some of today's waste products may be important resources tomorrow. To truly "run out" of resources means running out of our ability to transform one resource into another—the very technological basis for modern society.

But, in truth, we must admit that there is virtually no basis on which to judge the validity of this prophecy. Beyond the next few decades there is no way to know how much or little technological development is likely. Nor do we know much about the seriousness of the global environmental problems being discussed today. No one knows how much pesticides, nitrates, and heavy metals can be dumped into the oceans or how many oil spills can occur before serious, persistent damages are observed. Equally uncertain are the effects of growing levels of carbon dioxide and heat emitted into the earth's atmosphere as a consequence of combustion, the risks of large-scale crop failure as a consequence of loss of genetic diversity in the germ stock of feed grains, or the risks of global viral epidemics due to intercontinental travel and congestion.[3]

Undoubtedly, when such a thesis is applied to specific countries, especially to poor, densely-populated countries, we can easily imagine it having some validity. If a country is too poor to purchase needed resources from abroad or to use them to build up a material and human capital base as a substitute for an inadequate endowment of resources, continued population expansion may place it in a Malthusian trap, despite the availability of resources elsewhere on earth.

On the other hand, many developing nations are themselves primary producers. To the extent that the developed world "runs out" of its own resources or finds nonbiodegradable synthetics no longer acceptable, the primary producing nations will find their own economic positions strengthened, their export prices rising, and their ability to import growing. As noted in Chapter Nine, the negative external balance caused partly by their rapid population growth would be offset by the excessive per capita requirements of the developed nations.

It is sometimes thought that scientific knowledge is an important exception to the generalization that some countries may encounter specific resource scarcities, even though the resources may be abundant worldwide: scientific knowledge is often assumed to become globally available soon after its creation, virtually free of cost to all but the producer. But is this really the case? An expensive infrastructure of educational and research institutions must be maintained in order to understand, adapt, and apply new knowledge. Moreover, much of it may not be applicable even with adaptations. More than 90 percent of all research and development expenditures are made in the developed countries and quite naturally focus on the problems of these countries. Some developments, like nuclear power production, may be directly applicable, but many problem areas, such as those associated with tropical agriculture and medicine, get relatively short shrift.

Accordingly, while the more extreme versions of the "running out" thesis may have no basis in fact, our general ignorance of the long-term effects of man's actions on the globe, plus the special situation in which many poor countries find themselves, leaves little room for complacency. Poor countries have no choice but to continue pursuing the goal of economic development; but in the process it would be prudent to give higher priority than is typically the case to controlling population growth, to basic research on problems of special concern to them that research efforts in developed countries are likely to overlook, and to natural resource exploration and development.

Sources of Pressure

Resource requirements and environmental pressures are related to five sets of determinants. First is the *population size and rate of growth*. The larger the population, the larger the flow of materials necessary to sustain the population at any given level of living and the more congestion of all kinds one must be prepared to tolerate. The more rapid the rate of population growth, the more difficult it is to resolve these problems, to build schools and train teachers fast enough to provide a decent education for all children, to keep the unemployment rate from rising—let alone lower it—to build the mass transit systems necessary to offset traffic congestion, and so on. These points have been developed at length earlier in this volume.

The second main determinant is *per capita income or GNP*. It is generally assumed that the higher the per capita income, the larger the through-put of resources needed to run the economy and ultimately to be disposed of. Hence the resource and environmental problems and concerns of the rich countries. But there are serious environmental problems associated with poverty as well. These arise largely from the inability to afford adequate health and sanitation facilities, flood and pest control, safety devices, and the like. As a country becomes richer, investments in resolving these problems make them diminish, but in the process others come to the fore.

Third, the *composition of the material goods produced and consumed* plays an important, independent role in determining both the character and the severity of the resource and environmental problems. A copper producing country will have some environmental problems that a copper importing country will not have; the problems of an agricultural country will be different from those of an industrial country; a country whose population has a taste for throw-away bottles and high-speed cars will have more environmental problems than will a country where education and art consume a larger fraction of incomes. Although the composition of output tends to change with the level of per capita income, we stress this as an independent factor since government can use taxes, subsidies, and even direct controls to change the composition in the interest of improving environmental quality without seriously affecting the level of income.

The fourth factor, *spatial distribution of both population and economic activities,* also plays a role somewhat independent of the other factors. Even countries with low incomes and low population densities will have urban environmental problems if most people and economic activities are located in a few centers.

Finally, the *technology* in use is an important determinant. High compression, internal-combustion engines produce more air pollutants than do other types of engines; chemical fertilizers are potentially more damaging than are organic manures; and some mining processes use far greater quantities of water than do others.

The degree to which technology is flexible in regard to its demands on the environment tends to be underestimated, particularly in receiving technological transfers; often the recipient does not know of the options that are available when particular packages of technology are transferred. To give just one example, from the pulp and paper industry, for the same level of output three important categories of water pollutants—suspended solids, dissolved solids, and biochemical oxygen demand—are some 30 percent lower when using the sulfate (kraft) process than when using the sulfite process (although some other problems such as odors are greater).

These five factors are the principal determinants of resource and environmental problems at one level of analysis. Underlying them are the institutions, tastes, and policies of a country, all of which can strongly influence these five factors. Examples are institutions and regulations governing the use, control, and ownership of land and minerals, import policies with respect to fuels and minerals, decisions made about location of public investments, and the way in which markets operate. The last example, the operation of the price system, is particularly important so far as environmental resources are concerned. Typically, it does not properly charge for the use of common property resources like air and water, with the consequence that there is insufficient incentive to limit the consumption of products that are heavy users of the environment or to use and develop technologies that will conserve on these increasingly scarce environmental resources.

It is of some interest to consider the role of population relative to that of per capita GNP, assuming for the moment that all other determinants of resource and environmental pressures are constant. As a crude first approximation, we can say that to support an economy twice its current size will require—very roughly—twice the resources currently used; and since matter is neither created nor destroyed, all the material inputs into production and consumption ultimately end up as waste products. Accordingly, we might also expect that pollution emitted into the air and water, plus solid wastes, would more or less double if resource use doubles. Since total GNP can be rewritten to equal population times per capita GNP, we can observe a relatively direct linkage between population increase on the one side and resource requirements and environmental pressures on the other. This formulation suggests that the importance of population and per capita GNP in determining such pressures depends on their relative size and rates of increase. If each is increasing at 2 percent per annum, each is equally important in causing increasing needs for resources and waste loads.

This picture, however, is clearly too simple. First, the relationships between environmental pressures and GNP are not proportional for all levels of development and all rates of growth. As a poor country develops, fuel use and combustion probably increase more rapidly than GNP; at a later stage in the development process when service sectors become more important, materials requirements will increase less rapidly. Moreover, economies and diseconomies of scale and threshold effects in environmental damage functions may at times add to the disproportionalities. Far too little is known about such relationships, however, to suggest how much different from strict proportionality they may be in any given situation.

Second, this picture suggests that population and per capita economic growth have completely symmetrical effects on resource and environmental problems, that is, that an increment of one would require the same increase in resource requirements as would an increment in the other. This is an oversimplification on two important counts. For one thing, an increase in population, holding per capita GNP constant, requires replication of existing facilities and resource requirements, whereas an increase in per capita GNP would mean a change in the composition of output. To put the matter more dramatically, consider two countries with the same land area and GNP, one having a small population and a high per capita GNP and the other having a large, poor population. The poor country will need more land and other agricultural inputs but less of the kinds of minerals and fuels used in manufacturing. Similarly, the environmental problems of the small, rich country will center around industrial pollutants, while those of the poor, heavily populated country may well involve land erosion and silting.

But the most critical difference between an increment of population growth and an increment of growth in per capita GNP is that the latter provides additional means by which the problems generated by either kind of growth can be dealt with. An increment of population growth offers no such offsetting advantage. The situation is clearest with environmental threats. Apart from reductions in population or economic growth, there are two general ways to cope with such threats: either one can attempt to make greater use of the absorptive power of the environment—for example, by locating polluting industries downstream and downwind from population centers—or one can utilize capital equipment to supplement these natural forces—for example, by treating industrial wastes before they are emitted into the water or air. Population growth makes the use of natural forces more difficult, slowly closing off this option. Economic growth, on the other hand, by making it easier to afford the capital equipment, opens up additional options for solving the problem. In this sense, at least, growth in these two components of GNP has asymmetrical effects.

Finally, of course, tastes, institutions, technology, the composition of output, and the geographic distribution of population and output cannot in fact be held constant as population and economic growth proceeds. Changes in such factors will affect the relationships between population growth and environmental problems. Unfortunately, however, there are few if any generalizations that can be made about the way in which they will change. To say anything concrete requires specific studies in specific countries.

Resource and Environmental Policy Planning

It should be clear from the above discussion that there are a number of points at which policy-makers can intervene to resolve or head off impending resource or environmental problems. Any one of the causes of these problems can be attacked, from population or economic growth to preferences and tastes for goods that are heavy users of resources and the environment. While the choice of areas on which to concentrate and of means to use in doing so must be made within specific contexts, a few general points can be usefully raised here.

First, the choice should be made on the basis of a much longer term assessment of the problems than is typically the case. We are dealing with an area where lead times must be estimated in decades. The time between the geological exploration of new resources and the commercial availability of those resources can easily be a decade. It may take two or three decades before all the ecological effects of a dam are felt. It may take more than a generation for new attitudes toward family size to become the norm. And the urban design laid down today may set the pattern for the next century. In this situation, the consequence of an assessment based on the typical five-year planning period may well lead to policies that are exactly the opposite of what is appropriate for the nation over a longer period. Just how far into the future one should plan, given all the uncertainties involved, is a difficult question; but surely present use of high discount rates and five-year plans leads to a neglect of longer run resource effects.

Such a long-term assessment is likely to suggest that no single attack on the causes of resource and environmental problems is adequate. Sooner or later problems of congestion will make population control inevitable; and because of lengthy lead times, the sooner a serious population control policy is introduced the better. But given the momentum involved in demographic variables, as well as current resource and environmental problems, such a policy will certainly not be sufficient. New urban centers must be planned; technological alternatives for increasingly scarce resources must be developed; environmental threats must be understood well enough to be treated. With one possible exception, all of the sources of resource and environmental problems sooner or later will have to be faced and attacked.

The possible exception, especially in a poor country, is per capita income. While it is true that the through-put of materials increases with economic development, resource and pollution problems may not if growth is wisely managed and controlled.

To illustrate from a recent study of the United States, it was found that with adequate treatment of pollutants before emission, pollution levels in the United States in the year 2000 could be substantially lower than they are today, despite the population and economic growth that is expected to occur in the interim, and that the cost of such treatment would reduce annual growth in output by less than one-tenth of one percent.[4] That one-tenth percentage point may be more than many developing countries feel they can afford. But the standards aimed for need not be as rigorous as were assumed for the United States. For example, instead of requiring stack cleaners, factories can be located downwind; indeed, this is easier for a developing country that is going to build a new plant than it is for a developed country that already has the plant in place.

Many of the environmental problems associated with development, therefore, arise as a consequence of poor or inadequate planning. Traditional investment projects are decided upon without taking into account all the benefits and costs, including the environmental spillover effects as well as the more direct, private implications of the project. Investment projects are decided upon either without any benefit-cost analysis—often the case in the public health field, where decisions are determined by the bargaining power of different ministries—or without including the environmental consequences of the project within the benefit-cost calculations. Such inadequate planning generally occurs because of ignorance of the spillover effects and long-term consequences of many actions and because of the absence of institutional mechanisms to force investors, often both public as well as private, to bear the full costs to society of their actions. To overcome these difficulties will take persistent efforts on the part of planners. Studies must be initiated to determine the environmental consequences of various actions, and means must be found to force utilization of this knowledge in project evaluation.

It is difficult to predict the results of a planning process that takes full account of environmental problems. Obviously, some traditional investment projects would not get funded, while other projects aimed at correcting environmental ills would. To this extent, economic development might be slowed down. But it could easily go the other way, a careful analysis showing, for example, that all things considered, incremental dollars invested in increasing food production might save more lives than an equal investment in the eradication of schistosomiasis or some other disease. In many areas, it will be possible to find means of reducing the negative environmental consequences of development through minor modifications in project design, for example, relocation or process changes. In any event, we see no justification for deliberately slowing down the rate of economic growth in order to alleviate environmental problems; if it occurs, it should occur as a consequence of appropriate benefit-cost analysis of individual development projects, not on the basis of general principles.

With some justification, it can be protested that this advice is easier to give than heed: quite apart from the technical and administrative problems involved in expanding project analysis to include environmental considerations, there is simply a lack of information on the broader consequences of investment and production activities. But there are three and possibly four levels of sophistication possible in such extensions of benefit-cost analysis. First, one can attempt to include those environmental consequences that sooner or later can affect the project. The effect on the quality of groundwater resulting from long-term use of fertilizers is an example. Second, one can attempt to include those environmental consequences that spill over to other sectors, affecting their output levels. While more difficult than the first case, these effects still fit within the general GNP accounting framework. The third category of impacts involves consequences that do not fit in this framework as easily, for example, effects on human health, deterioration of natural monuments, and effects on noncommercial animal and plant life.

The final category involves international spillover effects, that is, the environmental and other consequences for neighboring areas of local decisions, and, conversely, the effects on one's own economic future resulting from the economic and technological decisions made by others. Atomic power generation, for example, is likely to be viewed as a regional, if not world-wide, concern for some time to come. A full-blown cost-benefit computation should attempt to weigh these effects, also.

At a minimum, routine project analysis can be extended to include the first category; once this is properly included, and as research results on the other three levels become available, the analysis can be extended. It is not necessary to do everything in order to move in the proper direction.

These general considerations can be made somewhat more concrete by discussing specific problem areas, as is done in the next two sections. The discussion is limited to two particularly important areas in most developing countries: agriculture and urban development. Agriculture is by far the largest single economic sector in most developing countries, and its future development is bound to have significant resource and environmental implications. The urban sector, on the other hand, is where an increasingly large portion of the total population will have to be located; its environmental problems determine many important aspects of the quality of life experienced by the people of the country. In both cases we will discuss general trends for developing countries as a group rather than the problems of any one country.

AGRICULTURE IN DEVELOPING COUNTRIES

In a comprehensive study of agricultural development among developing countries, the Food and Agricultural Organization (FAO) projected the growth in demand for food at 3.9 percent annually from 1962, the base year of the study, to 1985.[5] This assumes population growth of 2.6 percent annually, per capita income growth of about 3.0 percent, and income elasticity of demand of 0.40–0.45. The projection allows for some improvement in diet, both in per capita caloric intake and in higher consumption of vegetable and animal proteins. Beyond 1985 we project some slowdown in the rate of growth of demand, but a slowdown that only becomes marked after the turn of the century.[1] Table 10.1 summarizes these projections.

Table 10.1 *Projections of Growth in Demand for Food in Developing Countries*

Year	Percentage increases attributable to		Average annual percentage increase in demand
	Population growth	*Income growth*	
1970–1985	43	24	3.9
1985–2000	38	23	3.6
2000–2020	37	22	2.6

SOURCE: See reference 5 and 6 and footnote 1.

Because of balance of payments problems, the difficulty of expanding exports, and the size and importance of the agricultural sector—among other things, as a principal source of employment—most of these projected increases in demand must be satisfied by domestic production rather than by imports. In fact, since production lagged behind demand during the 1962–1967 period, it will have to grow more rapidly than demand during subsequent periods to make up the shortfall. The FAO estimates that production will have to grow by 4.3 percent between 1967 and 1985 to overcome this problem. Combined with our estimates of future demand, this implies an average annual growth rate of 3.9 percent between 1970 and 2000. Considering the fact that between 1955/57 and 1965/67 food production in developing countries increased by only 2.7 percent annually, serious questions can be raised about the ability to achieve these production targets.[7] This is not our purpose here, however. Rather, we want to consider the measures that must be adopted to generate the increases in produc-

---

[1] For the period after 1985, population projections are based on those made by Tomas Frejka.[6] Per capita income is assumed to grow at 3.5 percent annually, the implicit rate in the United Nations 6 percent target growth rate for GNP in the developing countries in the 1970s.

tion that appear necessary if the development efforts of these countries are not to flounder.

It is reasonably clear that most of the needed increase in food production in the developing countries must come from rising output per hectare.[2] This is the only pattern likely to yield the desired increases in production and in farm per capita income. Moreover, it is the pattern that makes most economic sense. In many areas, particularly in Latin America and Africa, extension of the cultivated area involves the use of primitive "slash-and-burn" techniques, which contribute nothing to increased per capita production and may cause serious environmental deterioration. This is particularly true in the humid tropics, where removal of the forest cover exposes the soil to rapid leaching, heavy erosion, and in some areas laterization. The resulting loss of fertility may for practical purposes be irreversible. Of course the runoff of topsoil to rivers can cause the silting of reservoirs as well as other undesirable downstream effects.

Large-scale extension of the land frontier, as is occurring piecemeal in some Latin American countries, usually requires substantial new investments in transportation and infrastructure. Presently cultivated areas, however, are already served by existing infrastructures, the capacity of which can usually be expanded at small cost relative to the expense of building new facilities. Moreover, the most rapid increase in demand for food will be in existing urban areas, primarily because population in these areas will grow three to four times as fast as the rural population. Considerations of transport costs, therefore, would suggest the advisability of expanding production most rapidly in agricultural zones already serving existing urban areas.

For these sorts of reasons we assume that if food production is to increase by 3.9 percent annually over the balance of the century, yields must rise at an annual rate of about 3.4 percent.[3] From the mid-1950s to the mid-1960s, yields increased by an average of about 1.5 percent annually.[8] Hence the projections imply that the rate of increase over the balance of the century must more than double relative to the earlier trend. To achieve this, agriculture in the developing countries must undergo a rapid and profound transformation, the central feature of which must be the substitution on a vast scale of modern for traditional technology. The principal characteristics of the new technology are now well known: improved seeds, fertilizer, pesticides, mechanization in many but not all situations, and water control, all blended by a high level of managerial skill and encouraged by remunerative prices and adequate marketing facilities.

---

[2] In the distant future, "harvesting" the oceans and "hothouse" agriculture may contribute importantly to the world's food supply. Over the period of interest here, however, extension of the cultivated area and increased yields, particularly the latter, will be responsible for almost all the increment in food production.

[3] The FAO *Provisional Indicative World Plan for Agricultural Development* assumes that higher yields will contribute about 80 percent of the increase in production from 1962 to 1985 (see ref. 5). We assume that in the period after 1985, yield increases will account for virtually all of the growth in production.

For the period 1962 to 1985, the FAO projects 2.9 percent annual growth in the area harvested on irrigated land. Much of this represents the spread of multiple cropping. By 1985 irrigated land would constitute 16.3 percent of total arable land in the developing countries compared with 13 percent in 1962.[9] No doubt the share of irrigated land in total harvested area would be greater than 16.3 percent because multiple cropping is more common on irrigated land.

The increase in irrigated area would be accompanied by an enormous expansion of other nonlabor inputs, particularly fertilizers and pesticides. Fertilizer consumption would rise from 2.6 million nutrient tons in 1962 to 31.2 million nutrient tons in 1985, an increase of 11 percent compounded annually. Consumption per hectare of arable land would rise from 4.6 kilos to 47 kilos over this period. The volume of pesticide consumption, in total and per hectare of land, would increase by almost the same percentage amounts.[10]

The projected rates of increase in consumption of these inputs are extraordinary. With respect to fertilizer, however, the 1985 levels of consumption per hectare are low in comparison with recent consumption in the countries of Western Europe, Japan, and Taiwan, as Table 10.2 indicates.

Table 10.2   Fertilizer Consumption in Selected Countries, Mid-1960s

Country or area	Kg. of nutrient per hectare
Netherlands	557
Belgium	501
West Germany	328
Japan	304
Taiwan	237
United Kingdom	154
Developing countries (1985 projection)	47

SOURCES: Individual countries from Economic Research Service, US Department of Agriculture, *Taiwan's Agricultural Development* (Washington, D.C.: Government Printing Office, 1968), p. 71. Developing countries from FAO, *Provisional Indicative World Plan for Agricultural Development: Summary and Main Conclusions* (Rome: FAO, 1970), p. 24.

Comparative data for pesticide consumption are not readily available, but in the developing countries as a whole the average apparently was well under one kilo per hectare in 1962–1964.[4] In the United States in 1962, sales of syn-

---

[4] The FAO *Indicative World Plan* shows that consumption per hectare of arable land averaged about US 30 cents in 1962–1964. Scattered evidence indicates that in that period the average price per kilo of pesticides was well above 30 cents in the developing countries (see ref. 8, vol. 1, p. 210).

thetic organic pesticides were about 1.5 kilos per hectare of arable land, and the figure is probably higher yet in Western Europe, Japan, and Taiwan, where agriculture is much more intensive in use of the land than in the United States.[11] Consequently, it is probable that pesticide consumption per hectare in the developing countries generally lags well behind the levels in the developed countries and in Taiwan. In this event, consumption in the developing countries probably could increase by, for example, a factor of seven or eight between 1962 and 1985 and still not be high in relation to present consumption levels in the developed countries.

While projections of fertilizer and pesticide consumption are not available for the period after 1985, it is obvious that continued increases will be necessary. Annual increases in yields may slow somewhat in comparison with the pre-1985 period, suggesting slower rates of growth in fertilizer and pesticide consumption. However, because the absolute quantities of these inputs will then be substantially above pre-1985 levels, their marginal products are likely to be lower, indicating that larger increments of these inputs will be needed to obtain given increments of production.

But even if per hectare consumption of fertilizers and pesticides continues to increase rapidly beyond 1985, these levels of consumption will still be modest by comparison with the developed countries. For example, fertilizer consumption per hectare in the developing countries is projected to increase by a factor of ten from 1962 to 1985, an exceptionally high annual increase of 11 percent. Yet maintenance of this rate after 1985 would yield a consumption per hectare figure of only 214 kilos by the year 2000; even then, fertilizer consumption per hectare in the developing countries generally would be less than the level achieved in Taiwan in the mid-1960s, and well under half the levels in the Netherlands and Belgium. (See Table 10.2.)

The tentative conclusion that emerges is that the levels of fertilizer and pesticide consumption needed to achieve the high growth rates in food production needed by the developing countries over the next 30 to 50 years probably would not generate unmanageable environmental threats in those countries. This conclusion should be tempered with certain caveats, however. First, it assumes that the consumption per hectare rates existing in developed countries and in Taiwan are not now causing environmental damage. This may not be the case, particularly when one considers the amounts of persistent pesticides that will accumulate in the environment over time.[12]

Second, the very rapid rates of increase anticipated in pesticide and fertilizer use might pose environmental threats even if the absolute amounts employed were relatively modest. This is because knowledge of possible side effects of using these substances is essential to avoid unwanted environmental damage, and this knowledge may be inadequate or may come too late in areas where their use is growing rapidly. The experience with the use of pesticides in the Cañete Valley of Peru in the 1950s illustrates this point. In the early 1950s cotton farmers in the valley applied rapidly increasing amounts of DDT and other insecticides to their fields, using airplanes, cutting down trees to give them freer scope, and covering the entire valley indiscriminantly. Cotton yields nearly doubled. But then side effects began to appear. Birds that formerly nested in neighboring trees disappeared, as did insect predators and parasites. Insect resistance to the new chemicals developed. By the mid-1950s these pests were rampant and the farmers were faced with economic disaster. Eventually, with the help of the local experiment station and the ministry of agriculture, pest control was restored and yields rose to new high levels.[13] The point here, however, is that rapidly expanding use of pesticides without knowledge of or concern about environmental side effects can quickly convert a highly promising situation into a disastrous one.

This emphasis on the importance of knowledge of environmental side effects suggests still a third caveat to the conclusion that projected amounts of fertilizer and pesticide use in the developing countries do not appear high relative to present rates of use in developed countries and Taiwan. Unlike many developing countries, the developed countries and Taiwan are not in tropical areas. In such areas, the flora and fauna are different and biological processes operate much faster than in temperate zones. Consequently the environmental responses to fertilizer and pesticides in temperate zones may prove poor guides both to the kinds of responses likely in tropical areas and to the speed and scale of these responses.

In the humid tropics, particularly where forest cover has been removed, soil erosion is a more serious threat than in temperate zones because rainfall is much heavier. The runoff that carries topsoil into neighboring streams will also carry fertilizers and pesticides that have been applied to the fields. Hence, given amounts of pesticides and fertilizers per hectare are likely to contribute more to stream pollution in tropical areas than in temperate zones unless special measures are taken to prevent it.

This suggests another way in which the consumption per hectare measure of environmental pressure may be misleading for tropical areas. The projections of fertilizer and pesticide use are for the developing countries as a whole. If the runoff of fertilizers and pesticides is greater in humid tropical areas than in temperate zones, then consumption of these products per hectare would have to be greater in the humid tropics than in temperate zones to achieve a given production response. Moreover, soils in the humid tropics are generally of lower natural fertility than in other areas; they also respond less well to fertilizer because they lack the structural compounds necessary to hold the fertilizer nutrients and make them available to plant life.[14] For these reasons the consumption of fertilizer per hectare needed to achieve the 1985 production targets in tropical areas may be substantially greater than the average of 47 kilos projected for all developing countries. This figure, may, therefore, understate the potential environmental threat posed by prospective fertilizer consumption in tropical areas.

As noted earlier, a key ingredient in the new agricultural technology is water control. In recognition of this, the FAO *Indicative World Plan* calls for an expansion of 35 million hectares of irrigated land in the developing countries between 1962 and 1985, an increase of just under 50 percent. Because of more multiple cropping, the increase in harvested irrigated land would be 67 million hectares or almost 95 percent over the 1962 level. While no projections are available beyond 1985, it is not difficult to believe that the increment of irrigated area in the developing countries in the last one-third of this century could be as large as the entire area under irrigation at the beginning of the century. The expansion of the cultivated irrigated area no doubt would be substantially greater, reflecting the continued spread of double cropping.

Experience indicates that this massive expansion of irrigation in the developing countries could pose serious environmental threats in the affected areas. Soil erosion, laterization, alkalinization, silting of canals and reservoirs, endemic diseases, the disruption of aquatic ecosystems, and the destruction of certain species and the proliferation of others have all been suggested as possible consequences, particularly if the irrigation projects are not planned well.[15] The public health problems, illustrated by the rapid spread of bilharzia, which have emerged as consequences of the Aswan Dam are among the most dramatic and well known of these unanticipated side effects of irrigation projects. Other instances could be cited. Some of these consequences can be prevented or ameliorated with proper advance planning, but many, especially those associated with large-scale irrigation projects, are irreversible. The area flooded by large reservoirs will never again be the same. Not only will the habitats of aquatic and other wildlife be drastically altered, but local climates might also be affected.

In summary, the swift and large-scale incorporation of the new agricultural technology that must occur if the developing countries are to achieve satisfactory growth in food production carries the potential for serious environmental damage. The threat from large-scale expansion of irrigation works probably is more severe than that posed by increased consumption of fertilizers and pesticides. The greatest problems with the latter may arise in the humid tropics because experience with the use of these substances and their environmental consequences is much more limited in those areas than in temperate zones. The threat from increased irrigation may be more general and more serious because mistakes once made may be more difficult to correct.

None of this is to say that the developing countries are faced with a stark choice between inadequate agricultural performance and environmental disaster. The threats posed by the new agricultural technology are real and our present knowledge of them is far from perfect. Hence there is no room for complacency. But neither is there reason for despair. The essential condition for effective counteraction is that government leaders in these countries be aware of the existence and nature of these threats and that they be prepared to assign the resources necessary for dealing with them.

THE URBAN ENVIRONMENT

The pattern of agricultural development consistent with overall development objectives in the developing countries is certain to have profound consequences for urban growth in those areas. If farm per capita income is to grow at satisfactory rates—say, not less than 2.5 percent annually—then the projected increase in farm production implies that farm population cannot grow by more than 1.0–1.5 percent annually. Since the prospective natural increase in rural population is on the order of 2.5 percent, the conclusion is inexorable: about half the people born in rural areas will have to find employment in urban areas if development objectives are to be achieved. The implied increase in urban populations poses perhaps the most worrisome environmental threat likely to confront the developing countries during the next half century or more. If population growth of 2.5–3.0 percent annually constitutes an explosion, then what will happen in urban areas of these countries is a mega-explosion. Since about 1950 these areas[5] have been growing at annual rates of 5–6 percent. Preliminary estimates by the United Nations indicate continued growth at 4–5 percent annually throughout the balance of the century.[16] If per capita income grows at 3.5 percent annually, as assumed above, then in urban areas the rate should be more than this, probably no less than 4.5 percent.[6] Total income and demand for goods and services in urban areas therefore would grow at an annual rate of about 9 percent. Over the 30 years from 1970 to the end of this century, this would constitute a 13-fold increase in the through-put of materials and services.

This rate of increase is hard to comprehend. It means, for example, that the metropolitan area of Mexico City, which in 1970 generated about $8 billion in total income (assuming that per capita income was $1,000 and population 8 million), would have a total income of $104 billion in the year 2000. This figure is greater than the total income today of any country in the world with the exception of the United States, the Soviet Union, West Germany, Japan, France, and the United Kingdom. The very thought is staggering in its implications for the already over-burdened environment of metropolitan Mexico City. Indeed, to cite these figures is virtually to conclude that growth of such magnitude could not occur because the environment could not tolerate it. This is *not*, therefore, a projection of expected growth in metropolitan Mexico City, but it does illustrate the scale of the problem many urban areas in the developing countries will confront over the next several decades, given virtually unavoidable increases in population and desired increases in income.

---

[5] Urban areas here means places with 20,000 or more inhabitants.

[6] If, as assumed above, 2.5 percent is taken as a minimum target for per capita income growth in rural areas and the country-wide target is 3.5 percent, then given the present rural-urban distribution of population, urban per capita income would have to increase by about 4.5 percent annually.

As indicated earlier, environmental pressure is not only a function of population and income growth. A materials-services mix that is high in thermal electricity, steel mills, pulp and paper plants, food processing activities, and automobiles will generate more environmental pressure than a mix that is high in electronics manufacture, scientific research and development, opera singers, and bicycles. But it is hard to believe that major urban areas like Sao Paulo, Calcutta, and Djakarta, in addition to Mexico City, could accommodate anything like a four-fold increase in population and a 13-fold increase in the through-put of materials and services over the next 30 years without serious environmental damage, no matter how light the pollutants in the materials-services mix. More likely, the future will see the development of many more cities of the size and character of these, with all their attendant problems.

There is little that can be done to ameliorate this trend without disrupting the growth process itself. As noted above, about one-half of the natural increase in rural population must migrate to the cities if farm income targets are to be achieved. Even so, population pressure on the already narrow arable land base of the developing countries will increase. The OECD has estimated that the developing countries (excluding those "centrally planned") had one hectare of arable land per head of agricultural population in 1965. This is projected to fall by some 40 percent by 2000.[17] This pattern is consistent with the projections of food production and yields made above. Those projections assume that the adoption of modern agricultural technology in the developing countries can be labor-absorbing in the sense that the man/land ratio rises even though the capital/land and capital/man ratios rise even faster. The greater absorption of labor would be possible primarily because of the spread of irrigation and increased multiple cropping.

The prospective 4–5 percent annual increase in urban population ought to be taken as a fact of life by planners in the developing countries since they are not likely to be able to do much about it. It may be possible, however, to affect the regional distribution of the urban population, reducing growth in the already very large centers by directing it toward medium and small ones. (See Chapter Seven in this volume.) But it is not possible to rely upon private decisions to accomplish this, for private decision-makers will not take into account the environmental and other social costs (or externalities) they impose on others in deciding to move to a large urban center. How effective such an urban location policy might be would, of course, vary from place to place, depending on the policy instruments available to the governments and the skill with which they could be used. Instruments might range from flat prohibitions of additional growth, to tax, subsidy, and other economic incentives, to moral suasion. For countries in which governmental structures and philosophies reflect the Western tradition, policies based on economic incentives probably would appear particularly attractive. There is evidence that such policies, by altering the interurban structure of rates of return to labor and other resources, can affect interurban rates of growth in population.[18] While the evidence is thin, it is consistent with the behavior expected in areas where resources are free to move in response to prospects of economic gain. The key to much of this is employment policy; that is, creating jobs at attractive wages in nonagricultural industries and in small and medium-sized cities. (See Chapter Three.)

But our purpose in this essay is not to discuss the pros and cons of such policies. Rather, we wish to emphasize the urgency of considering the problem of optimum population distribution, given the inevitability of high rates of urban population growth in the developing countries. Failure to address this question today could lead within a decade or two to such deterioration in some urban environments as to make the present situation appear a Golden Age.

CONCLUSION

This chapter has discussed and illustrated some general relationships between resource and environmental concerns on the one side and population and the imperatives of economic growth on the other. Given the diversity of problems and situations in which countries find themselves, plus our lack of detailed quantitative knowledge about resource availabilities, environmental effects of man's activities, and technological changes that may come along in the future, we cannot be very specific. But the following general conclusions seem warranted.

More work is needed to identify problems, consequences, and causes more clearly. To a considerable degree, this research work must be undertaken within the developing countries since the results of research by the developed nations may frequently prove to be irrelevant to the conditions in many developing countries.

Once such research results are available, decisions will have to be made about the weights or values to be applied to the environmental consequences described by the research. This is a topic we have not addressed, but it follows from much that has been said that the appropriate weights will not be the same for all countries and all consequences. In particular, a poor country is likely to place a higher value on material growth relative to environmental quality than is a rich country. This is particularly likely where the threat of growth is to environmental amenities, but it may occur also where the threat more directly affects welfare. For example, air pollution increases the risk of disease. A poor country may well give a higher weight to the pollutor's addition to national income and a lower weight to the consequences for human health than a rich country. Applying these different weights to benefit-cost analysis is likely to yield significantly different policy conclusions. Thus, poor countries are likely to find it appropriate to permit more environmental deterioration and to institute more stringent measures to control population growth than would be appropriate in rich countries.

There is a natural temptation to postpone action on many of these issues since the payoff is so far in the future. Since, for example, no rational policy can have much impact on population growth over the balance of the century, it may be concluded that formulation of such a policy might as well be deferred. Such a conclusion would be quite erroneous. Failure to act now would indeed be of little visible consequence a generation hence, but in two generations the consequences would be numbered in billions of additional people in the developing world. Other examples we have given are similar: the longer action is postponed, the more difficult it will be to correct the situation in the future. Recognition of the long lead times involved—in research on resource and environmental problems, population control programs, urban planning, and applications of broadly-based, benefit-cost analysis to project evaluation—should lead to more rather than less urgency to get on with these jobs at once.

REFERENCES

1. Donella H. Meadows, Dennis L. Meadows, Jorgen Randers, and William W. Behrens, III, *The Limits to Growth* (Washington, D.C.: Potomac Associates/Universe Books, 1972).

2. Leonard L. Fischman and Hans H. Landsberg, "Adequacy of nonfuel minerals and forest resources," in Commission on Population Growth and the American Future, *Research Reports of the Commission on Population Growth and the American Future*, vol. 3, *Population, Resources, and the Environment*, Ronald G. Ridker, ed. (Washington, D.C.: Government Printing Office, 1972), chap. 4.

3. Sterling Brubaker, *To Live on Earth* (Baltimore: Johns Hopkins Press for Resources for the Future, 1972).

4. Ronald G. Ridker, "The economy, resource requirements, and pollution levels," in Commission on Population Growth and the American Future, *Research Reports of the Commission on Population Growth and the American Future*, vol. 3, *Population, Resources, and the Environment*, Ronald G. Ridker, ed. (Washington, D.C.: Government Printing Office, 1972), chap. 2.

5. Food and Agricultural Organization, *Provisional Indicative World Plan for Agricultural Development* (Rome: FAO, 1970).

6. World Bank, *Population Planning*, Sector Working Paper (Washington, D.C.: World Bank, May 1972).

7. Food and Agricultural Organization, *Provisional Indicative World Plan for Agricultural Development: Summary and Main Conclusions* (Rome: FAO, 1972), p. 7.

8. Organization for Economic Cooperation and Development, *The Food Problem of Developing Countries* (Paris: OECD, n.d.), p. 20.

9. See ref. 7, p. 23.

10. See ref. 7, p. 24.

11. J. C. Headley and J. N. Lewis, *The Pesticide Problem: An Economic Approach to Public Policy* (Washington, D.C.: Resources for the Future, Inc., 1967), pp. 7, 10.

12. For a balanced treatment of the environmental hazards of pesticides, see ref. 3, pp. 78–88.

13. This account of the Canete Valley experience is from Ray I. Smith, "Integrated control of insects: A challenge for scientists," *Agricultural Science Review* 7, no. 1 (1969).

14. The second point is based on an unpublished manuscript of Raymond J. Dasmann, quoted by William Vogt, "Whatever happened to krilium," in W. Zelinsky, L. A. Kosinski, and R. M. Prothero, eds., *Geography and a Crowding World* (New York: Oxford University Press, 1960), p. 181.

15. Ignacy Sachs, "Environmental quality management and development planning: Some suggestions for action," in *Development and Environment*, Report of a Panel of Experts to Maurice Strong, Secretary-General of the United Nations Conference on the Human Environment, Geneva, 1971.

16. Reference to the United Nations estimates is in Frank W. Notestein, "Population growth and its control," in Clifford M. Hardin, ed., *Overcoming World Hunger* (Englewood Cliffs, N.J.: Prentice-Hall, 1969), p. 39.

17. See ref. 8, p. 70.

18. Pierre R. Crosson, "Rural-to-urban migration in Mexico" (Washington, D.C.: Resources for the Future, May 1972, unpublished).

ELEVEN

Toward Socioeconomic Population Planning

WARREN C. ROBINSON

In this final chapter we return to essentially macro policy and planning considerations in an effort to tie together the various sectors and problems treated in the other chapters.

Chapter One dealt at some length with the recent emergence of "population policy" and "population planning" as meaningful concepts. It was suggested that population policy consists of conscious, identifiable government actions aimed at affecting population size, growth, distribution, or composition. From the perspective of development planning, distribution and composition may be fully as important as growth. Population planning is, then, the deliberate, systematic use of such policies to achieve certain desired goals or objectives.

It can be argued that population planning has always existed implicitly in the way in which societies come to terms with their environment:

Three critical ratios emerge when we analyze even the simplest human societies. One is the composition of the group, notably the relation of consuming mouths to producing hands. A second is the relation of the group's demands to the resources of the area on which it is effectively free to draw. A third is the extent to which the group can enlarge its use of these resources or extend its access to them. This third element, the relation of its actual to its potential command of available resources, has proven to be the most elastic of all. It includes both the dimension of technology and the dimension of physical expansion, whether by colonization, rapine, or trade.[1]

Population is a social and economic process involving people. Because government has no stake in the matter separate from that of its people, population policy must reflect this social context and be implemented with social consensus. As Goldscheider puts it:

> The cumulative processes of population events and the resultant implications for the size, distribution, and composition of populations are fundamental to the structure and functioning of human societies. People are the stuff from which families, groups, societies and nations are constructed: the processes of population are the building blocks shaping the form and content of social units. In turn, the individual and personal aspects of population phenomena are conditioned and affected by the power of social forces: what appear on the surface to represent biological and idiosyncratic events are by their nature social as well.
> . . . The size, growth, density, concentration of population, birth and death rates, cityward and suburbanward migrations, have become social issues for many reasons and in various social contexts, but mainly because population processes affect and are affected by the organization and anatomy of society. The quantity of population shapes the quality of social life. The reverse is equally true; the quality and fabric of social life shape the quantity and character of population processes.[2]

Thus, it is society, not government, that shapes consensus and can exert pressure on individuals. But, unless a particular policy truly represents a need or a goal recognized by the social groupings concerned, it is unlikely to have any significant results. Indeed, many barriers to adoption and implementation of policy arise because a social consensus does not exist.

OBJECTIVES OF DEVELOPMENT

We will turn now to the specific objectives and goals of development planning and how population planning ought to enter into general development planning.

One basic objective of development is to raise living standards. This usually means increasing the availability and quality of health care, education, nutrition, housing, and employment. The most fundamental point that has emerged in our survey is that the future potential quantity, quality, nature, and location of these services is affected by the demographic processes, especially fertility and migration. Equally important, these demographic processes are themselves affected by the production and allocation of these public services. In framing policies and programs in the areas of health, education, housing, and employment, therefore, the demographic consequences must be constantly borne in mind. At the decision-making level, this requires that planners be aware not only of possible undesirable consequences of policies and programs, but also of ways in which government can *positively* influence demographic trends. Two other requirements of effective development planning are reasonably accurate, current demographic data and alternative population projections by standard age groups. These are necessary because planning decisions should be based on both assessments of short-term needs and on estimates of future requirements.

A second development planning goal, and one that is increasingly mentioned as a major objective, is a greater degree of equality in the distribution of income. Even accepting that absolute equality of income among all households or primary socioeconomic units is not possible, most developing countries aim at raising all above some social minimum and reducing the range of disparity between top and bottom. As we have seen, equity is a consideration that motivates many sector programs. However, if high fertility is associated in a specific country with extreme poverty, as is often the case, then it does not make sense to attempt to raise income levels without also attempting to lower fertility. Taiwan is frequently cited as an example of a land reform and income redistribution scheme preceding a rapid fertility decline.[3] In fact, a close examination of the facts reveals a more complex picture:

> It seems probable that land reform with its incentives to the individual farmer introduced him to the idea of economic calculation. This stress on rationality may have helped in the relatively rapid adoption of contraception in the rural sector, especially in the late 1960s. However, since the individual farmer still had incentives to have sons both to work on the farm and to inherit it, the traditional stress on having three or four children and one or two sons continued. Therefore, the fertility decline was mainly preventing unwanted births above this number, but the ideal number of children and sons fell very little. Therefore, it is likely that the very rapid adoption of contraception had less effect on fertility decline than would have occurred if the institutional factors had not continued to support the value of children and sons. This is a point of some importance, because it indicates that the very successful Taiwan land reform program in its initial stages had mainly beneficial effects: in its later stages, however, *the continuing stress on improving output by intensive cultivation had an undesirable restraint both on agricultural efficiency and on the potential fertility decline.*[4]

Some 60 years ago the distinguished American economist F. W. Taussig considered this question at some length and with great perception and subtlety. "High birth rates, high death rates, backward industrial conditions, low wages—these commonly go together. But, which is cause and which is effect?"[5] The conventional Malthusian reply, then and now, is that the birth rate is the cause and the others effects. Taussig was not so sure, however. He argues that low productivity and incomes mean poverty and near subsistence living for many families. These circumstances can so demoralize people that efforts at self-improvement are viewed as hopeless. Moreover, low productivity and wages raise the value of children to the family because of their potential earning power. Thus, low incomes may encourage high fertility.

Taussig says, "A limitation of numbers is not a cause of high wages but it is a condition of the maintenance of high wages." National productivity and income depend on technology, its useful application, and capital. When these are favorable, productivity and income will rise, and "restraint on multiplication, though not in itself a cause of gain, will enable the gain to be maintained."[6]

In short, Taussig denies that reducing numbers will automatically cause any change in economic conditions, but says it is necessary to sustain a change once begun.

The objective of removing families from the "culture of poverty" is neither pronatalist nor antinatalist in itself, but the process of economic upward mobility by lower socioeconomic groups is very likely to have an antinatalist effect. Thus, a government policy for "upward leveling" is antinatalist, at least in the long-run.

A third objective of development planning is to maintain a balance between the use of land and natural resources in the present and the preservation of such resources for the future. In theoretical terms, this "present versus future" trade-off is a part of the broader question of defining the optimum welfare-maximizing time-path of growth for the economy. Chapter Ten argues cogently that rapid population growth puts pressure on policy-makers for intensive present use of all resources. This pressure must be resisted; long-term options must be kept open. At the same time, agricultural and other resource programs must not, even accidentally, have pronatalist effects. If all land can be cultivated and population continues to grow, then all land *will* be cultivated. If, however, some land is protected by strict legal provisions and set aside, then pressure to reduce population growth will be felt earlier and more keenly.

A fourth objective of development planning is structural change. Most of the policies and programs that would be adopted in pursuit of this objective are more or less neutral with respect to affecting population growth. However, population distribution may well be affected. For, once the process of industrialization has taken hold, it will almost certainly be concentrated in a few large urban centers. Industrial concentrations tend to attract still more businesses and industries wanting to take advantage of economies or "spillovers" (such as a trained workforce) generated by the urban center. A policy of maximizing total output or growth in urban areas will encourage rural-to-urban migration, which may be judged undesirable. On the other hand, to the extent that rural fertility exceeds urban, urban migration might lower fertility. Thus, rural-to-urban movements should not be banned or prevented thoughtlessly. Urban migration should be weighed to judge its impact on all the objectives of development we have enumerated, plus its impact on fertility.

Last, development planning usually attempts to protect a nation's balance of payments position. Perhaps this is not so much an objective as a device by which economic development can be achieved. It seems clear that population growth, distribution, and composition affect both long- and short-run aspects of the balance of payments and, in turn, are affected by these factors.

Thus, all the major development objectives, sectors, and programs do have a population component. When even the most simple interrelationships between demographic processes and socioeconomic planning are taken into account, this becomes clear.

POLICY IMPLICATIONS

Perhaps the most obvious goal of development planning is to raise income levels of the people. Historically, high-income countries and groups have shown low fertility and low-income countries and groups high fertility. Therefore, many believed that policies aimed at increasing national income were also likely to reduce fertility. In fact, the relationship between income and fertility is an intricate one, far more so than was realized earlier. The recent surge of work on the "economic theory" of fertility has thus far raised many new questions without answering definitively any old ones.[7] The key elements in this conceptual approach are the familiar ones from consumer demand theory. Thus, at very low levels of income, the notion of choice is largely absent from the thinking of the households involved. Occupation, diet, housing, and family size appear to be determined by forces outside the individual's control. At slightly higher income levels, choice and alternative options begin to appear. Trade-offs arise and the notion of a "desired" family size becomes meaningful. Most commonly, realized family size exceeds desired size because of lack of the necessary knowledge, skills, and technology to efficiently contracept. At still higher income levels, as access to education and contraceptive technology become assured, the gap between actual and desired family size narrows. When "excess" fertility is eliminated, households are in some sort of equilibrium—they are planning and meeting their targets. However, the desired family size may still be such as to yield considerable population growth in the aggregate. A four-child family norm with a "modern" death rate can mean annual population growth approaching 2 percent.

Thus, the key theoretical question is, how are income and family size related once absolute income is reasonably high and relative income has become the major determinant of the composition of demand. There is some evidence that the income elasticity of demand for additional children is positive and that, in the absence of an income constraint, households would desire and plan for more children.[8] Many things enter into this picture and, as indicated, research has not yet yielded any definite conclusions.

Some policy implications do seem reasonably clear, however. First, efforts to raise the absolute income of the lowest income group are probably favorable to fertility reduction. Whether their relative position in the overall pattern of income distribution is improved or not, raising their absolute level increases their options and encourages planning. Provision of public transfers or services does not need to be tied to fertility reduction and, indeed, this is not desirable.

For upper-lower or middle-income groups, however, government provision of transfers or services does potentially have an effect on fertility. In the past, government policies in housing, health, and education have often had the effect of subsidizing high fertility; that is, of relieving the family units of some of the costs of educating and caring for their children and passing these costs on to society. The thrust of many present proposals (which, taken together, are sometimes called "beyond family planning") is that the terms and conditions for any social service or transfer to a household should be such as to fully "internalize" all the social costs, environmental as well as pecuniary. Note that this approach is still indirect and involves no real economic coercion: no one is taxed because of family size; they simply are not subsidized. This obviously means that a strong preference for children and a willingness and ability to pay the full social costs could still lead any given household to have a large number of children. Critics of such a voluntaristic, market-oriented policy could argue that it does not guarantee an ultimate zero growth situation.

Berelson and others have drawn up more exhaustive lists of all the policies government can employ.[9] These include, for example, more rigid controls on marriage, enforced sterilization after some nth birth, punitive taxes, and so on. Such measures would be beyond even the most rigorous effort to "internalize the externalities" and have a nearly ideological overtone. No example exists of how such policies could be implemented.

A PROPOSED POPULATION POLICY AND PLANNING UNIT

Given the complexity and multiplicity of the effects and interactions between demographic processes and socioeconomic development and the many ways in which population policy and planning can be used to influence development, it seems clear that present clinic-oriented family planning programs and the usual location of a "population research unit" in the ministry of health are not well-suited or sufficient to the task of monitoring and interpreting these complex effects and interactions and making policy recommendations. What is needed is a multi-faceted, interdisciplinary population policy and planning unit at the highest level of government. For most developing countries, the ministry of planning or the planning commission or board is the logical location, since only the planning agency is likely to have broad, interagency responsibilities and powers. It is also most likely to be close to the top executive and thus sensitive to the changing social consensus.

The purposes of such a unit would be:

1. To articulate in detail the desired population objectives and the specific requirements for reaching them. This function would be on-going since objectives change, as do the optimal ways of reaching them.

2. To screen all new program and project proposals to determine the likely demographic effects (in both directions) and to render a recommendation from this perspective. Thus, if a proposal is made to irrigate a large area with a new dam, the population planning unit's task would be to determine, insofar as possible: (a) the effect of the proposed project on fertility and growth in the area; (b) the effect on the settlement pattern of the population; and (c) the desirability of the proposal from the population perspective. The project may be approved even with a negative reading on population aspects, but presumably this would imply that other net benefits were very great indeed. The idea of routinely

screening projects for population effects has precedent in other areas—the foreign exchange implications of any project are always presented in the project appraisal, as are the employment-creation effects.

3. To insure that adequate statistical data and analytical materials are available so that population planning and targeting can be based on a sound factual basis. This does not mean operating a survey unit, but it does mean close coordination of the work plan of the statistical office or bureau, university research projects, and data collected by other government agencies.

As the essays in this book have revealed, our understanding of the links between demographic processes and many of the economic planning variables are based on intuition or logic. We simply do not have enough detailed empirical studies of these relationships to permit any generalizations. For the population policy and planning unit to function well, this base of understanding must be expanded. The unit should have a modest research capacity of its own, but, more importantly, it should serve as coordinator and sponsor of such research in universities and other institutions at home and abroad. Preference obviously should be given to research institutions within the country, but foreign institutes or groups may prove useful so long as the planning unit retains complete control over all data.

The exact organization of such a population policy and planning unit obviously cannot be described here because it will necessarily vary from country to country. What is important is that it be headed by a senior official so that it has status within the government structure and that its staff, while mainly economists by training, also include people with interests and training in sociology, agriculture, geography, public health, and demography. The narrow skills of the economist will be less useful in accomplishing the evaluative function than will experience and detailed understanding of the area under consideration, but the decisions of the unit will not be taken seriously by other economic planning units unless economists are on the staff.

Southeast Asia currently seems to lead the way in the degree to which population planning has been incorporated into overall economic planning. In Indonesia, Malaysia, the Philippines, and Thailand, population planning units exist within the central planning agency. Representatives from these countries and others have met at least once as an informal working group to discuss common problems.[10]

Drawing upon their own experience, the participants at this workshop addressed themselves to several questions, including:

Is a unit specifically and exclusively concerned with population needed? If so, (a) what professional staff is it likely to require? (b) where should it be located in the planning structure? (c) what relation, if any, should it have to the department or bureau of statistics? to the national family planning program? to national research resources such as universities or institutes? What should its responsibilities and functions be?

The participants unanimously agreed that a unit concerning itself primarily with population and staffed with an adequate number of competent professionals is needed in their countries. They noted the remarkable progress made by the Republic of Singapore in the absence of a formal, independent, and distinct government population unit in any of its ministries or departments, but felt that Singapore may represent a special case because of its size. Given the difficulties inherent in the administration and management of a more complex governmental organizational structure in the larger developing countries in the region, there is need for a population unit that will bring about the maximum utilization of available national resources for the development needs of the country.

The participants concluded that for such a unit to be effective, a well-coordinated, active, and continuing participation of all the different sectors involved in development planning is essential. The important role of research (an activity that should be built into the work program of universities and institutes) in development planning was emphasized. The participants felt that relevant research findings should be used in the planning process and in the implementation of such development plans.

It was agreed that the prime minister's office may be the best place in which to locate a population planning unit. Such a unit should be capable of drawing all the major sectors concerned with socioeconomic development into the total planning process in the country. The unit should also direct and coordinate such activities and formulate population policy proposals that are responsive and sensitive to the priority needs of the country.

CONCLUSION

We have demonstrated the historical reasons for the relative neglect of the population factor in development planning, and the useful but also quite limited role of macro models in articulating the full range of population-development interactions in the various sectors of the economy. The complexity and richness of those interactions has been examined in a series of sector and topic studies, some of which are admittedly exploratory and even speculative. This final chapter has attempted to pull together these specific interactions, summing up how demographic processes affect and are affected by development in all its aspects. We feel we have made a strong case for the greater inclusion of population in development planning and believe that a population policy and planning unit, acting with top political and administrative support, with inter-ministerial status and having considerable interdisciplinary technical expertise, is a necessary step toward sound population-development planning.

REFERENCES

1. Geoffrey Vickers, "Population policy—its scope and limits" (Address delivered at the Plenary Session, 1974 Annual Meeting of the Population Association of America, 18–20 April 1974, New York.

2. Calvin Goldscheider, *Population Modernization and Social Structure* (Boston: Little, Brown & Co., 1971), pp. 3–4.

3. James E. Kocher, *Rural Development, Income Distribution, and Fertility Decline* (New York: The Population Council, 1973).

4. Paul Ke Chih Liu, *Interactions Between Population Growth and Economic Development in Taiwan,* Monograph Series no. 7 (Taipei: Academia Sinica, Institute of Economics, 1973), pp. 195–196. Italics added.

5. F. W. Taussig, *Principles of Economics* (New York: Macmillan Co., 1918), vol. 2, p. 212.

6. See ref. 5.

7. See, for example, T. W. Schultz, "New economic approaches to fertility," *Journal of Political Economy* 81, no. 2, pt. 2 (March–April 1973).

8. See Dennis J. O'Donnell, "The micro-economics of completed family size: A simultaneous equations approach" (Ph.D. diss., Pennsylvania State University, August 1974).

9. Bernard Berelson, "Population policy: Personal notes," *Population Studies* 25 (July 1971): 173–182; Ozzie G. Simmons and Lyle Saunders, "The present and prospective state of policy approaches to fertility" (Paper presented at the Ford Foundation Population Meeting, Cali, Colombia, October 1974.

10. A full report on the workshop, *Population and Development Planning,* Report on an IGCC Regional Workshop, Penang, Malaysia, 27–29 September 1973, has been published by The Inter-Governmental Coordinating Committee, Southeast Asian Regional Cooperation in Family and Population Planning, and is available from the IGCC Secretariat, P. O. Box 550, Kuala Lumpur, Malaysia. A summary of the Report has also been published; see L. S. Sodhy and Rafael A. Esmundo, "Population and development planning in Southeast Asia," *Studies in Family Planning* 5, no. 11 (November 1974): 342–343.

Appendix ONE

Demographic Measurement and Data Collection

USES OF DEMOGRAPHIC DATA

Three basic reasons for collecting or using demographic data can be listed.

First, demographic data guide government agencies in setting policy and in planning. Macro-level data on population growth and distribution and at least key economic characteristics—labor force status, literacy, income, and so on—are certain to be required. Any five-year plan needs current data, at the least, and probably trends also. Future projections are likely to be required as well.

Second, monitoring and evaluating specific sector programs and projects require population or population-based data. For example, detailed fertility data are needed to evaluate an on-going family planning program. Detailed data on changes in settlement patterns are necessary to plan land reclamation or development schemes for the rural sector. These data are likely to be regional or subregional in scope, with the primary focus on selected characteristics or attributes.

Third, demographic data are required for the scientific study of interrelationships between demographic processes and social and economic processes at either the micro or macro level. This objective is never paramount in data collection except perhaps for some university-based survey supported by outside funds. However, the purely scientific study of today may provide valuable planning and policy data for tomorrow. To the extent possible, such research should be encouraged.

Generally speaking, these needs are not inconsistent or contradictory, but they may place different requirements on the demographic statistics collection system. In our view, the planning and policy function should take priority, with program evaluation a close second.

This appendix draws very heavily on an earlier paper by William Seltzer, *Demographic Data Collection: A Summary of Experience* (New York: The Population Council, 1973).

CONCEPTUAL PROBLEMS

Most experienced statisticians agree that, compared to other behavioral fields—economics, psychology, or sociology—demography presents the least problem for quantitative measurement. The concepts themselves are based on clearly identifiable events—birth, death, change of residence—or characteristics that are readily understood—sex, age, occupation, marital status, literacy, and so on. This is not to say that there is no ambiguity connected with what these events or attributes mean in statistical terms, for there certainly is. For example, in many cultures a child is not named or given full family status for several weeks after birth. If an infant dies during this period, in the minds of the parents (and even the official registrar or enumerator), it is as if the child had been lost during pregnancy or at birth. To a demographer, the events are considered a live birth and an infant death but probably will not be so recorded in many cultures. Again, if a young man leaves his family, moves to the city, finds work there, and stays for several years, he has clearly migrated. However, his unmarried status, his continued loyalty to his family, and his sentimental attachments may lead him to think of his village as home, and he (and his family) may still record him as a "member" of the village household.

Thus, although the basic demographic events and processes can be defined in scientific terms that are internationally agreed upon and understood by demographers and statisticians, they must be translated for the survey respondent at the national level with care and in full awareness of local circumstances and practices.

The same is even truer of attributes or characteristics. There is no ambiguity about sex, but there certainly is about age. To the respondent (or even the interviewer), age can mean: age at last birthday; age at next birthday; age at closest birthday; age rounded off to nearest number ending in 0 or 5; or other possibilities. Age may also be reported according to several different calendars, which may be lunar or solar in basis. Ambiguity may also surround the concepts "usual occupation," "marital status," "income," and "social status."

These conceptual ambiguities are compounded by ignorance and recall lapse where the processes or attributes being investigated occurred at some earlier point in time. Thus, a person may simply not know his true date of birth. Women are sometimes very vague about their husband's current employment, particularly if he is a marginal worker. A woman may be able to report how many children she has now, but counting "children ever born" may involve remembering a baby who died a few weeks after birth ten years ago. Such data are likely to be unreliable.

All in all, despite such conceptual and measurement problems, the fact remains that demographic data are probably easier to collect and more reliable than almost any other socioeconomic information. Demographic processes and events are important, universal, and relatively well-defined. Many of the inaccuracies that do creep in are to be blamed on the collection techniques, not the events themselves or the respondents.

SOURCES OF DEMOGRAPHIC DATA

The sources of demographic data include: (a) registration systems under which births, deaths, and other vital events are recorded as they occur; (b) periodic censuses in which population size and characteristics are recorded as of a point in time; (c) sample surveys and pilot registration areas, which produce estimates of what a national census or registration system would reveal, or which at least permit some inferences to be drawn; (d) so-called "model" populations, which summarize the experience of many populations for which historical evidence is available and from which estimates of the growth rate or the vital rates of the unknown population can be made, given one or two of its parameters; (e) fragmentary demographic information collected by an essentially nondemographic inquiry—households reported by a malaria program, labor force reported by a survey of manufacturing establishments, births or deaths recorded by hospitals.

The developed countries typically can draw upon both registration systems and regular, reliable censuses and, indeed, both sources are needed if the flow of annual births and deaths and the stock of the base population are to be known accurately. In developing nations, demographic data are not so readily available, and special surveys, model population estimates, or even scattered fragmentary data have been used in place of proper census or registration data.

Registration

Registration systems aim at the routine recording of vital events—births, deaths, and perhaps change of residence or marital status—as they occur. The motivation for such systems originally was not to collect demographic data but rather because important civil or political consequences were attached to these events. Death must be established in order to probate a will; a child must have proof of birth date to enter school; marriage often involves a property settlement; and so on. Registration constitutes, then, legal evidence that the event has occurred. Where such evidence is useful, motivation to register events is strong. However, in many developing nations, such civil or legal implications are slight and the need for proof of events very rare. In these circumstances, there is no positive motivation to register events.

In developing countries, the official responsible for registration is usually a local person—the village headman, the watchman, the police constable, the priest, the midwife, the undertaker—who acts as registrar in addition to quite separate normal duties. The registrar may also be without training or facilities for filling out complicated forms and maintaining elaborate records. These factors all militate against complete, timely, accurate registration.

The figures and rates reported by such registration systems should not be accepted as meaningful demographic estimates without careful scrutiny. For example, if the registered death rate is 5 per thousand and the registered birth rate is 25 per thousand, one might be tempted to use the difference of 20 per thousand, or 2 percent, as the growth rate. Both rates are clearly too low but perhaps, one may surmise, they are too low by the same proportion so that the indicated growth rate is correct. In fact, such reasoning is erroneous. The inaccuracy of birth and death data arises from different problems. Deaths are usually more poorly registered than births, but sometimes the reverse is true. In our example, the true death rate may be 15 and the true birth rate 45, yielding a growth rate of 3 percent. Or the true death rate might be 25 and the true birth rate 35, for a growth rate of only 1.0 percent.

The moral for policy-makers is clear: Make every effort to provide the right combination of incentives and penalties to the public and registration officials to improve the accuracy of registration. But, until accuracy is on the order of 90–95 percent and until a good deal about the sources of remaining inaccuracies is known, one must be very careful about using the registration data as a basis for planning or programs.

Sample registration schemes have also been used on occasion. Seltzer has summarized these very well:

> The difficulties encountered in utilizing the civil registration system as a reliable measurement device have prompted the development of special registration systems in some countries. A major advantage of these special registration efforts is that they can be designed and administered exclusively as statistical reporting systems; that is, the requirements imposed on a civil registration system because of its legal purpose need no longer be operative. Special registration systems usually employ full- or part-time personnel to canvass actively for births and deaths, and they overcome many of the administrative problems of a national registration system by confining registration activities to a probability sample of the country. The success of any special registration system is closely related to the nature of the canvassing operation carried out by the special registrar. This can range from an informal, multi-round survey of vital events conducted at approximately monthly intervals, to a sensitive surveillance system utilizing neighborhood contacts, midwives, and others as intermediary informants. Because special registration systems are usually based on samples, they cannot provide local area data for large parts of the country as can a civil registration system. On the other hand, extensive data on the socioeconomic characteristics of events can be obtained.
>
> The Indian Sample Registration Scheme, which is currently operational throughout India, is an example of a massive special registration effort designed to meet the urgent statistical needs of a developing nation (India, 1972; Mehta and Shah, 1966). Other special registration systems that have been reported on include those established in connection with dual record systems in Pakistan (Population Growth Estimation, 1971) and in Morocco (Krotki and Rachidi, 1972), and at the Cholera Research Laboratory in Bangladesh (Mosley et al., 1970). In addition, Linder (1970) has urged that developed coun-

tries establish similar sample-based vital events surveillance systems which, unlike traditional civil registration systems, could be fully dedicated to the methods and needs of demographic measurement.[1]

Except for the countries of Europe, the United States, and the British commonwealth, registration systems are rare. Full-scale registration systems are operative in areas covering only about 29 percent of the population of the world. The following is a 1965 estimate, by region, of the percent of the population covered by vital registration:

Region	Percent
Africa	3
Asia	9
Latin America	44
Oceania	78
Europe	100
North America	100

SOURCE: N. Keyfitz and W. Flieger, *World Population: An Analysis of Vital Data* (Chicago: University of Chicago Press, 1968), p. 4.

Population Censuses

A census is a total enumeration of the population. Usually selected characteristics are recorded in addition to number. Sex, age, marital status, place of birth, place of residence, source of livelihood, religion, and literacy are characteristics commonly collected for each member of the population.

Historically, census counts were often motivated by civil or political concerns: the desire to establish current tax rolls, to determine the base population for military service, or to make possible fair apportionment for electoral purposes. For some years past, however, the typical national population census has been an important source of demographic, economic, and social data, and the collection of these data has probably become its main purpose.

Censuses are large, expensive operations requiring a good deal of preparation and planning. Experience shows that the accuracy and usefulness of the final data are directly related to the adequacy of the planning. Proper selection, training, and motivation of the field enumerators and the middle-level supervisory personnel are particularly crucial. A census is normally taken only once every five or ten years but it is wise to retain the key staff people in the census office during the inter-censal period. As in anything else, experience is invaluable, and trained, experienced personnel produce better data.

The processing of the data—editing, coding, tabulating, and printing—is a massive job. Simple processing procedures are usually the best. Labor-intensive methods for the main counts still have much to recommend them. Efforts to fully computerize census data-processing have sometimes proved premature in developing countries due to lack of experienced programmers, mechanical breakdowns, and competing demands on limited computer time. For any type of planning, current data are better than old data, so that every effort must be made to get at least preliminary results and main characteristics reported promptly.

Because of the size of the tabulation job involved, most analytical cross-tabulations of the questions (educational attainment by occupation, for example) are not attempted using 100 percent of the data. Increasingly, such analysis is done using a randomly drawn sample of the census schedules. This is to be recommended because it reduces considerably the tabulation cost and time.

In recent years, sampling has also been used even in the basic census count. For the few important questions, such as age and sex, a full 100 percent enumeration may still be used. But this can be a relatively short schedule that is self-coding and easy to tabulate. A longer schedule asking detailed socioeconomic as well as demographic characteristics can then be used on, say, every fifth or tenth household. This still results in a very large number of completed schedules, more than enough to permit sub-samples for tabulation if so desired, but it reduces greatly the volume of data to be processed and stored. The 1970 census of the United States used this approach quite successfully.

Sample Surveys

In addition to the use of sampling techniques in connection with census enumerations, sample surveys are often undertaken in and of themselves to collect demographic data. Sample surveys are subject to the same errors and inaccuracies arising out of conceptual misunderstandings between respondents and interviewers, as well as the usual errors of editing, coding, and tabulating. But there is another potential problem in connection with sample surveys that does not come up in using census data. This is sampling error. Let us again quote Seltzer on this point:

> The advantages of sampling in terms of costs and the quality of field work are now well recognized in demographic research. Sometimes, however, the responsibilities imposed on those using sampling in data collection are forgotten. First, an effective probability sampling design must be employed to avoid biases in the selection of units to be included in the sample and to permit the estimation of sampling errors.[1] Second, a sampling expert should be consulted to ensure that the sample has been properly designed and selected.

---

[1] "As used here, the term "probability sample" means any sample where all members of the population have some nonzero probability of being included in the sample and where the probability of selection for each unit included in the sample is known." (Footnote in original.)

Third, estimates of sampling error need to be considered in both designing the sample and interpreting the survey results.[2]

Today, few would question the value, in principle, of employing the methods of probability sampling. Almost always the failure to use probability sampling either occurs by mistake or is excused on the grounds that operational constraints, such as costs, prevent its use. However, such excuses have little justification, at least in the area of demographic measurement. Unless a probability design is employed, it is very difficult to ensure that major selection biases will not occur, and such biases can result in serious distortions in the estimated levels and patterns of fertility and mortality. Seen from this perspective, the issue becomes whether one can afford to use any design that fails to employ probability sampling at every stage of selection, unless the study is designed solely as a training exercise.

.... Large sampling errors can be as harmful to the user as large measurement errors, and all surveys must be designed with an eye to both types of error. Unfortunately, the requirements of low sampling error and low measurement error are often in conflict. The control and elimination of most of the major sources of measurement error can be achieved most readily when the size of the sample is small. That is, for a given effort, one can come closer to the ideal of controlled observation in small samples than in large samples. On the other hand, large samples, and particularly samples with many first-stage sampling units, are necessary to achieve estimates with small sampling errors.

Let us consider an illustrative example of the effect of sample size on the uncertainty introduced into sample estimates of fertility. Estimates of the crude birth rate based on samples of from 1,000 to 100,000 persons selected from a population with a birth rate of 40 per 1,000 will usually (in about 19 out of 20 samples) fall within the intervals shown in the [right-hand] column of Table 12.[3]

These intervals reflect only the variability due to sampling and thus ignore the possible impact of measurement errors although, as already indicated, measurement error tends to be smallest where sampling error is largest. In addition, because of cost factors, any sample used in practice would involve some clustering of observations. Clustering would tend to widen these intervals, most noticeably where the sample of a given size is based on a relatively small number of large clusters.[4] It should be clear from this discussion that the

---

[2] "Sampling error may be understood as the variability associated with a sample estimate because it is based on information obtained from only a portion of the units in the population being investigated. Only if probability sampling methods are used is it possible to determine the size of sample error that pertains to a given sample estimate." (Footnote in original.)

[3] "Assuming a simple random sample of persons from a very large population in which births are assumed to follow a binomial distribution." (Footnote in original.)

[4] "This occurs because persons living in the same local areas tend to have similar fertility so that a sample consisting of a small number of clusters (even if each is relatively large in size) may not adequately reflect the fertility of the total population. On the other hand, stratification or certain methods of estimation could be employed to reduce these intervals somewhat." (Footnote in original.)

Table 12   Illustrative examples of the sampling errors associated with estimates of the crude birth rate and the age-specific fertility rate, by size of sample

(Sampling errors shown as the two-sigma (2σ) confidence intervals around an assumed crude birth rate [CBR] of 40 per 1,000 population.)

Size of sample (persons) [a]	CBR $\pm 2\sigma$ [b]
1,000	28–52
3,000	33–47
5,000	35–45
10,000	36–44
50,000	38–42
100,000	39–41

[a] Assuming a simple random sample of persons from a very large population in which births are considered to follow a binomial distribution.
[b] Interval expressed in terms of a rate per 1,000 population.

impact of sampling error must be considered during both the planning and analysis phases of any demographic study employing sampling. More specifically, even moderate-sized samples can provide only very approximate estimates of the level of the crude birth (or death) rate using data obtained for a 12-month period.[2]

Nevertheless, a sample of 100,000 households is still a manageable survey from which to obtain a quick intercensal reading on fertility and growth. Sampling error can be guarded against in a more precise and systematic way than can respondent errors or processing errors.

Model Populations

The logic of "model populations" is that there are similarities among groups of populations with respect to their underlying demographic structures.

For example, a series of "model populations" were prepared by Coale and Demeny having a range of values for birth rates, death rates, growth rates, and age distribution. These range from very high fertility, low mortality, rapid growth to low fertility, low mortality, low growth. Each of these patterns of vital rates also implies a particular age distribution, assuming the rates have prevailed for some time. If for any given population we know only the age distribution and have also an estimate of mortality, we can then find the "model" that best matches these values and read an estimate of fertility and the growth rate. This is the procedure followed in the Coale-Demeny models, the most elaborate and most widely-used set of "model populations."[3] Model mortality tables have been especially widespread.

The great advantage of such model estimates is that for only a very small amount of real information (and even this can be estimated), one can obtain estimates of the key elements determining a population's growth pattern. In the absence of two censuses or vital registration data, these model estimates can be very useful.

Their drawback is that they do not provide any data on characteristics or any sub-national rates or patterns. The models present the minimum data required for macro planning but are not a real substitute for detailed data from some other source.

Fragmentary and Partial Data

Very little need be said about these sort of data. Quantitative data are always generated by various legal or other requirements. Thus, a department of industries may register all firms of a certain size and collect, thereby, some labor force data; hospitals collect fertility and mortality data; and so on.

Such data are useful for the clues and insights they provide. They should not be overlooked since they are already collected and can sometimes be used for only a small additional input of cost and time. However, they are not likely to be substitutes for the other sources we have listed. Even "model population" data are to be preferred for macro planning since scattered, non-random fragmentary data may be seriously biased. On the other hand, for some given micro problem, fragmentary, non-random data may still be very useful.

CONCLUSION

We will conclude our brief discussion of demographic measurement and data collection with Seltzer's useful list of eight basic propositions that should be followed in designing and conducting demographic surveys:

> *First,* treat the measurement of demographic phenomena as seriously as the measurement of any other topic, foregoing the intuitive impression that demographic measurement is easy measurement.
>
> *Second,* be clear about the objectives, and formulate the content and design of the survey accordingly.
>
> *Third,* standardize concepts for the purpose of international comparability, but incorporate these concepts in the study questionnaires in ways that are meaningful to the interviewer and the respondent in each country.
>
> *Fourth,* good interviewing is a prerequisite for reliable survey estimates; therefore, pay, train, and supervise the field staff adequately so as to establish a data-gathering process that does not depart greatly from the ideal of statistical control.
>
> *Fifth,* increasing the number of unrelated subject-matter areas covered by the survey, other things being equal, will increase the *nonsampling* errors of the survey estimates.

Sixth, increasing the number of primary sampling units in the sample, other things being equal, will both reduce the *sampling* errors of the survey estimates and increase the *nonsampling* errors of these estimates; the sample design and study procedures must take account of both types of errors.

Seventh, make the detection and the evaluation of sampling and nonsampling errors in the basic estimates an integral part of the study design.

Eighth, publish the basic estimates and the results of evaluative studies, and publish them as they become available.

Most of these propositions are obvious enough to be truisms of applied statistics. My only justification for listing them is that in practice they are too commonly forgotten. Ultimately, the value of any demographic survey will depend upon how consistently we manage to implement them.[4]

REFERENCES

1. William Seltzer, *Demographic Data Collection: A Summary of Experience* (New York: The Population Council, 1973), p. 36. The following sources are referred to in the excerpt from Seltzer: Government of India, Office of the Registrar General, *Sample Registration of Births and Deaths in India, 1969–1970* (New Delhi: Government of India Press, 1972); D. C. Mehta and B. V. Shah, *Report on Sample Registration Scheme (Pilot), Rural Gujarat* (Gujarat, Ahmedabad: Directorate of Health and Medical Services, 1966); Pakistan Institute of Development Economics, *Final Report of the Population Growth Estimation Experiment, 1962–1965* (Dacca: Pakistan Institute of Development Economics, 1971); K. J. Krotki and M. Rachidi, "Program and first experiences (PGE/ERAD) of the Moroccan Demographic Center" (Paper presented at the 1972 meeting of the Population Association of America, Toronto, 1972); W. Mosely, A. K. M. Chowdhury, and K. M. A. Aziz, *Demographic Characteristics of a Population Laboratory in Rural East Pakistan* (Bethesda, Md.: U.S. National Institute of Child Health and Human Development, Center for Population Research, 1970); and F. Linder, "A proposed new vital event numeration unitary system for developed countries," *The Milbank Memorial Fund Quarterly* 48, no. 4, part 2 (October): 77–87.
2. See ref. 1, pp. 40–42.
3. Ansley Coale and Paul Demeny, *Regional Model Life Tables and Stable Populations* (Princeton, N.J.: Princeton University Press, 1964). See also United Nations, Department of Economic and Social Affairs, *Age and Sex Patterns of Mortality: Model Life-Tables for Under-Developed Countries,* Population Studies no. 22 (New York: United Nations, 1955).
4. See ref. 1, pp. 45–46.

Appendix T W O

Population Projections for Development Planning

As has been made clear repeatedly in this volume, population projections are an integral part of national demographic and economic planning. The more detailed these projections can be, the better for specific sector, project, and regional planning. The making of population projections is a laborious procedure unless one has resort to a computer. A manual is now available that explains how to make population projections on the computer for development planning, teaching, and research purposes. The manual, *Computational Methods for Population Projections: With Particular Reference to Development Planning,* by Frederic C. Shorter and David Pasta, and the accompanying computer package program are available from the Population Council, 245 Park Avenue, New York, New York 10017.

In order to use the manual, the special computer package program must be installed locally where it will be accessible. The first step, however, if one is interested, is to order the book and, with the book in hand, to determine in consultation with a local computer center whether the package can be installed. Appendix two of the manual contains detailed information about installation. Any computer having less than about 40 K bytes of core memory will not be able to accept the package. The Population Council will supply the computer package on magnetic tape or cards to any institution that completes and mails to the Council an order form found at the back of the manual.

If the local computer is suitable, the package is easy to install. Usually a programmer can do the work in a few hours. After installation, persons with no previous computer experience can learn to give instructions on cards to the computer. Thus, anyone can produce population projections rapidly and according to his own needs without depending thereafter upon a programmer.

The manual is introduced by a discussion of the uses of population projections in development planning. The relationship of demographic (projection) models to economic models is explained. The exogenous variables of the demographic model are the initial age-sex-location structure of the population and the components of change through time: fertility, mortality, and migration. The outputs of the model are the age-sex-location structure of the population at future dates and flows through time of births, deaths, and balances of migrations. The demographic model corresponds with a cohort-component projection of the population.

Subsequent chapters describe in detail how to prepare assumptions and make projections on the computer. Chapter one, "Projections by Modified Cohort-Component Method," is a self-contained step-by-step explanation of how to use the package program to make projections. All that is necessary is for the user to submit to the computer a small deck of cards such as the one illustrated below. In this example, the cards are sufficient to produce a simple 35-year projection. More complex requests may be made to the computer by invoking special options described in subsequent chapters of the book.

```
0          1          2          3          4          5          6          7          8
1234567890123456789012345678901234567890123456789012345678901234567890123456789012345678901234567890

YEAR.TITLE
YR.1984.ALTERNATIVE 7: CONSTANT FERTILITY DECLINING MORTALITY (POP IN THOUSANDS)
INIT.POP
INIT.F.A    2237.7     1884.8     1656.7     1430.8     1101.2      976.3      856.8
INIT.F.B     854.9      740.3      593.2      490.2      410.9      403.3      320.1
INIT.F.C     220.5      120.8
INIT.M.A    2257.7     1899.7     1700.8     1440.6     1090.3      970.2      846.8
INIT.M.B     844.9      735.2      595.2      483.1      405.8      400.1      315.9
INIT.M.C     219.5      118.7
MORTALITY
MORT.EZ.F     56.6       58.        60.        62.        64.        66.        68.
MORT.EZ.M     54.8       56.        58.        60.        62.        64.        66.
FERTILITY
TOTAL.PERT     6.1
FERDIST1.7    .015       .051       .049       .039       .028       .012       .006
FEND
END PROJECTION

1234567890123456789012345678901234567890123456789012345678901234567890123456789012345678901234567890
```

Chapter two, "National Projections," is a complete illustration of the projection procedure applied to a national population. Since population projections are models that can simulate stationary, stable, and destabilizing populations, they have many uses in analysis. Chapter three, "Model Distributions of the Population by Age and Sex," shows how to generate models that are of practical value for such purposes as adjusting inaccurate age distributions or investigating the demographic sources of changes in crude birth, death, and growth rates.

For planning purposes, a large amount of detail concerning age and sex structure is usually required. Chapter four, "Annual Detail and Special Age Groups," explains how to obtain practical estimates of population stocks (age, sex, and location) and flows (births, deaths, and balances of migration) on an annual basis.

Projections for "Urban Population and Migration" are explained in chapter five. Methods of adjusting for age misreporting in urban populations are included. Urban projections may be made independently of other projections or as part of a strategy for subdividing national or other "parent" projections. The application of a cohort-component technique for subdividing populations is recommended in chapter six, "Subdividing Populations." Application on the computer of the classical ratio method is also explained.

The concluding chapter, "Social and Economic Projections," shows how the age-sex-location projections may be translated into projections of labor force, households, school eligibles, and other variables by the application of age-sex-specific rates. The computations are all done by the package program. Complete linkage of the demographic model to a general planning model can be accomplished by using outputs of the projection as inputs for the planning model, and specifying outputs of the planning model that can serve as variable inputs for the demographic model. A short-cut way of doing this "on the table" by several iterations rather than by resort to special computer programming is proposed.

At the end of the manual there are appendices that give the mathematical basis for computations, a directory of the words and card formats by which the user communicates with the computer, and a list of error messages that are printed by the computer for the user.

Index